APPLIED MACROECONOMICS FOR PUBLIC POLICY

APPLIED MACROECONOMICS FOR PUBLIC POLICY

RAFAEL YANUSHEVSKY
r.yanushevsky@randtc.com

CAMILLA YANUSHEVSKY
cyanushe@gmail.com

Research and Technology Consulting
5106 Danbury Rd.
Bethesda, MD 20814
United States

ACADEMIC PRESS

An imprint of Elsevier

Academic Press is an imprint of Elsevier
125 London Wall, London EC2Y 5AS, United Kingdom
525 B Street, Suite 1650, San Diego, CA 92101-4495, United States
50 Hampshire Street, 5th Floor, Cambridge, MA 02139, United States
The Boulevard, Langford Lane, Kidlington, Oxford OX5 1GB, United Kingdom

Notices
Knowledge and best practice in this field are constantly changing. As new research and experience broaden our understanding, changes in research methods, professional practices, or medical treatment may become necessary.

Practitioners and researchers must always rely on their own experience and knowledge in evaluating and using any information, methods, compounds, or experiments described herein. In using such information or methods they should be mindful of their own safety and the safety of others, including parties for whom they have a professional responsibility.

To the fullest extent of the law, neither the Publisher nor the authors, contributors, or editors, assume any liability for any injury and/or damage to persons or property as a matter of products liability, negligence or otherwise, or from any use or operation of any methods, products, instructions, or ideas contained in the material herein.

Library of Congress Cataloging-in-Publication Data
A catalog record for this book is available from the Library of Congress

British Library Cataloguing-in-Publication Data
A catalogue record for this book is available from the British Library

ISBN: 978-0-12-815632-2

For information on all Academic Press publications visit our website at
https://www.elsevier.com/books-and-journals

Working together
to grow libraries in
developing countries

www.elsevier.com • www.bookaid.org

Publisher: Candice Janco
Acquisition Editor: Scott Bentley
Editorial Project Manager: Hilary Carr
Production Project Manager: Mohana Natarajan
Cover Designer: Vicky Pearson

Typeset by TNQ Technologies

CONTENTS

ABOUT THE AUTHORS

Rafael Yanushevsky was born in Kiev, Ukraine. He received an MS in mathematics and in electromechanical engineering (with honors) from the Kiev University and the Kiev Polytechnic Institute, respectively, and a PhD in optimization of multivariable systems from the Institute of Control Sciences of the USSR Academy of Sciences, Moscow, Russia.

He worked at the Institute of Control Sciences of the USSR Academy of Sciences. His research interests were in optimal theory and its applications: optimal control of differential-difference systems, signal processing, game theory, and operations research. He had published over 40 papers in these areas and two books *Theory of linear optimal multivariable control systems* and *Control systems with time-lag.* He was an editor of 14 books of the publishing house "Nauka." After immigrating to the United States in December 1987, he started teaching at the University of Maryland, first in the Department of Electrical Engineering, then in the Department of Mechanical Engineering, and at the University of the District of Columbia in the Department of Mathematics. Since 1999 he has been involved in projects related to the aerospace industry. In 2002 he received a Letter of Appreciation from the Department of the Navy, the Navy Area Theater Ballistic Missile Program. He wrote the books *Modern Missile Guidance*, 2007, which was translated in Europe and China, and *Guidance of Unmanned Aerial Vehicles* (2011). The author was invited to teach the short courses based on his books in the United States, Europe, and Australia.

Starting in 2010, his company Research and Technology Consulting focuses on economic problems related to the 2008 economic crisis. He published with coauthors eight papers concerning the government fiscal policy in the period of high unemployment and debt, as well as effective decision-making in the stock market. The book is based on the abovementioned publications.

Dr. Yanushevsky has published over 90 papers, was the chair of the Lyapunov Session of the Second and Fourth World Congress of Nonlinear Analysts and a member of the Organizing Committee of the Fourth Congress and is a reviewer of several journals (e.g., Journal of Asset Management, IEEE journals, etc.). He is included in "Who's Who in America," "Who's Who in Science and Engineering," and "Who's Who in American Education," as well as "International Professional of the Year 2008," and "2000 Outstanding Intellectuals of the 21st Century" (International Biographical Centre, Cambridge, England).

Camilla Yanushevsky was born in Maryland, USA. She received her education at the University of Maryland, College Park—Robert H. Smith School of Business and Bocconi School of Economics and Management (Milan, Italy). Starting in 2012, she was involved in the macroeconomic analysis of the results of the 2008 economic crises. She developed models allowing economists to evaluate government stimulus policy for countries with a high debt to GDP ratio and analyzed whether the economic plans proposed by American politicians are political or practical. Currently she works as a Markets and Deals, Subject Matter Expert for S&P Global Market Intelligence.

PREFACE

The field of macroeconomics can be divided roughly into two branches: a theoretical branch, which considers how the aggregate economy behaves (the national economic system as a whole: its total production, total consumption, total savings, and total investment), and an applied branch, which deals with actual policy questions such as: fiscal and monetary policies and their influence on output; should monetary policy be used to offset recessions? are investment in infrastructure and/or tax cuts efficient approaches to fight recession? should the government fight recessions with spending hikes rather than tax cuts? etc. The applied branch, applied macroeconomics, should provide mathematical tools that governments can use to develop/justify their fiscal and monetary policies. The reliability of the answers to these questions depends on the accuracy of the developed related models.

The recent financial crisis, which took economists by surprise, demonstrated that there were glitches in existing macroeconomic models that economists were unable to foresee. The 2008 crisis has renewed interest in investigating the effects of the sources of uncertainty on the macroeconomy that rise sharply during recessions. Macroeconomic uncertainty is an integral part of many macroeconomic models. It relates to our limited or inexact knowledge to predict outcomes.

The main source of uncertainty is the human factor in macroeconomic models presented by the so-called utility functions. In his *Manuale d'economia politica* (1906) Vilfredo Pareto, Italian economist and sociologist, indicated that men act nonlogically, "but they make believe they are acting logically." The Old and New Keynesian models use different utility functions containing several parameters by which values should be determined. The economy is populated by a representative household, and the household's problem is to maximize the utility function.

In his Nobel Prize lecture, Robert Solow gave the following eloquent characterization of macroeconomic models: "...the economy is populated by a single immortal consumer, or a number of identical immortal consumers. The immortality itself is not a problem: each consumer could be replaced by a dynasty, each member of which treats her successors as extensions of herself. But no short-sightedness can be allowed. This consumer does not obey any simple short-run saving function, nor even a stylized Modigliani life-cycle rule of thumb. Instead she, or the dynasty, is supposed to solve an infinite-time utility-maximization problem." Economists want people to act rationally, maximizing a certain criterion.

Daniel Kahneman, who was awarded the Nobel Prize in economics "for having integrated insights from psychological research into economic science, especially concerning human judgment and decision-making under uncertainty," challenges the assumption of human rationality prevailing in modern economic theory. The abovementioned means that the utility functions in macroeconomic models contain uncertain parameters that influence the model's outcome. Economic uncertainty is difficult to quantify. In contrast with such variables as, for example, growth or inflation, uncertainty cannot be directly observed because it relates to individuals' subjective beliefs about the economy.

Some scientists explain the inability of economists to predict the 2008 economic crisis by the excessive mathematization of economics and even corrupt politicians. Although such accusations are too strong, they contain a kernel of truth. A group of American politicians irresponsibly insisted on the relaxation of existing mortgage standards, motivating this by the desire to get all Americans into homes—even low- and moderate-income people with poor credit histories. As a result, household debt increased significantly, and the so-called subprime lending, which is lending to low-income borrowers, rose quickly.

Governments and central banks have the responsibility of upholding financial stability through proper supervision and regulation of the financial markets and its institutions. Many politicians supporting this dangerous economic policy forgot about the mentioned responsibility and acted in their own interests: the new rules attracted new voters—happy buyers of houses, persons who acted irrationally because they had no resources to pay back their debt. It is obvious that macroeconomic models with the rational households are unable to explain the 2008 economic crisis and indicate a way out of the crisis.

The two camps of economists have different views concerning how to improve the economy in times of economic downturn. Representatives of the first camp do not believe that a large national debt will inevitably undermine economic growth and can even throw the economy into recession (comparing current debt levels with that of a number of advanced countries, the United States included, have had in the past and been dealt with). They consider government spending on infrastructure as an efficient strategy and support the approach based on additional government borrowing. Another group of economists that concerns with high government debt, which, as they believe, can inevitably undermine economic growth, supports austerity measures. Economists belonging to this camp consider the solution of the huge national debt problem as an urgent task. They believe that the approach based on additional government borrowing with a hope that this will help decrease the debt in the future has less probability of success than immediate austerity measures.

The reputation of economists as being unable to agree on anything can be explained by the specificity of macroeconomics as science.

Rigorous science includes many principles that are considered to be laws of nature. Many of them were obtained in the analytical form after multiple experiments proving their universal character (for example, Newton's laws of motion). Economic theory is not supported by such laws. One of the most basic economic laws, the law of supply and demand that ties into almost all economic principles, is not considered by some scientists, who deny its universal nature, as a law. They believe that even the term *economic law* is misleading because most economic laws are *observed regularities* in phenomena and human behavior. But *regularities* are not necessarily universal. As a counterexample, they consider speculative bubbles (the rising prices become a causal factor for the increased demand).

Irrational human behavior cannot be described satisfactory in an analytic form. As a result, the absence of rigorous laws presented in analytic form enables researchers to test various hypotheses and build various models to establish the relationship between the output and control variables based on historic data. The errors for each model can be estimated. The developed models are applied to evaluate the dynamics of certain macroeconomic variables in the future. In this case, the errors' estimate presents a difficult problem. Among existing models, it is important to choose such ones that would produce the estimate with a minimal error. In some cases, the models that evaluate a low limit of the considering variables are very efficient because this case excludes the necessity of error analysis.

The gross domestic product (GDP), the most salient characteristic of a country's wealth, demonstrates the efficiency of government policies so that in the corresponding dynamic model the GDP is its output and the government spending and revenues (the result of fiscal policy) and the interest rate (the result of monetary policy) are controls. There exists several models describing the GDP (output) dynamics. One class of such models presents a detailed description of its components (consumption, investment, etc.) and contains more than 100 equations. Other models curb the number of variables (about 20 equations or even less). In many cases, the GDP forecast can be obtained directly from its time series. The comparison of the mentioned models shows that the models with less variables can describe the GDP dynamics more accurately. The Cobb—Douglas function presents the GDP model from the supply side (the aggregate relationship between GDP and its inputs—capital and labor) with a small number of variables. It is preferable to develop models that do not require the precise values of a parameter for a certain period; they produce the same or very close results for the time at the end of the period for an average value of this parameter. The reliability of a model is affected by the level of uncertainty in the model. Less uncertainty makes the model more reliable.

Similar to the balance sheet (a summary categorizing all of a company's resources, its assets and liabilities) and income statement (also called a profit and loss statement) used by businesses, which characterize the financial position of a company, the government budget and related statements (spending, revenue, deficit/surplus, debt, etc.) characterize a country's state of economy. The mentioned economic variables are the main parameters of applied macroeconomics models. The most reliable models are those whose creators try to take the human element out of the analysis and deal solely with the data to avoid the fickleness of the people underlying the numbers.

The authors use the control theory approach to macroeconomic problems. Spending and revenues, the elements of fiscal policy, and interest rates, the element of monetary policy, are considered as controls that influence a country's economy, which is characterized by three main variables: GDP, debt, and unemployment. Financial multipliers are interpreted as the control gains. Methods of control theory are used to analyze the developed models, including (directly or indirectly) these variables. Formally, the goals of government economic policy should be maximization of GDP and minimization of debt and unemployment. However, for such a global optimization problem, the optimal solution does not exist. A compromised solution (a representative set *of* Pareto optimal solutions) is a result of a decision-making process.

Experts dealing with complex dynamic systems know that simple models with well-identified parameters work and produce better results than complex multicriteria models with many uncertain parameters. Such models are more reliable for decision-making. They are built and discussed in this book.

Politicians look seldom beyond the next election. That is why their long-term proposals are usually too rosy and not realistic. To prove this economists need simple and efficient tools. The considered models provide economists with such tools. Human factor in the developed models is embedded in multiplier values so that a chosen multiplier value influences the model's accuracy. Monetary policy that is not highly affected by politicians as fiscal policy is presented in the considered models by interest rates. Fiscal policy is presented by two variables—expenditures and revenues. Instead of formulating a multicriteria problem, which would require a compromised criterion, we consider the expected values of the GDP growth as one of the government policy goals. The GDP growth rate and interest rate values, as well as the fiscal multiplier values characterize a set of scenarios based on which the final decision concerning fiscal and monetary policies should be made. Forecasting of the growth and interest rates presents separate problems that have been discussed in the literature. There exist various models that determine multiplier values (the authors offer a new approach to evaluate the multiplier value).

Among problems of applied macroeconomics, the authors pay the most attention to the debt problem that became toxic for many countries. They hope that their book will add insight to the debate concerning how to improve the economy in times of economic downturn. The important issue is discussed: whether it is better to let debt increase in the hope of stimulating economic growth to get out of the slump or cut spending to get national debt under control? The developed debt to GDP ratio dynamics model is used to analyze whether government stimuli can improve the economic situation and whether this government fiscal policy is an effective tool in boosting the economy. Some aspects of the debt reduction problem are considered.

Basic facts about stimulus and austerity policies are given in Chapter 1. The control theory and system approaches are used to analyze these policies. The existing macroeconomic models are analyzed. Their specific features, main goals, and related macroeconomic parameters are discussed. Special attention is paid to the debt to GDP ratio, which is considered as a compromised criterion to evaluate stimulus and austerity policies. Chapter 2 contains the debt to GDP ratio dynamics models developed to forecast the evolution of debt to GDP ratio over a 10-year horizon and evaluate the efficiency of government stimulus policy. The offered approach enables the authors to build relatively simple models to determine the lower limit of the debt to GDP ratio. The developed models enable one to analyze the effect of stimulus spending and tax cuts implemented separately or simultaneously. The generalized debt to GDP ratio dynamic model with time-varying parameters, which estimates more precisely the debt to GDP ratio than the indicated earlier models, is also considered. It reflects reality—a real effect of stimuli becomes visible at least about a year later; as a rule, stimulus is injected into the economy by steps; its implementation is distributed in time. The effect of monetary policy is examined. For all developed models, simulation results using the current data of the US economy are discussed. Austerity policy is discussed in Chapter 3. The results of optimal theory are used to obtain optimal yearly debt levels that should be realized by an appropriate fiscal policy of the government. A more moderate policy of balancing the budget by a specific year is also discussed. In Chapter 4 the theoretical results of Chapters 2 and 3 are used to evaluate the economic proposals of the US 2016 presidential candidates, which were tested initially by using the Taxes and Growth Model developed by the Tax Foundation, the tax policy research organization. Unwillingness of politicians to offer radical and efficient measures to improve the economy is discussed. Specifics of decision-making related to macroeconomic problems is considered (economic policies during the 1929, 1981, and 2008 economic crises were analyzed). Comparative analysis of the obtained results, based on the developed models, with the recommendations used by the US government during the 2008 financial crisis and expectations, which were not well founded, is presented. It is shown how the developed models can improve the decision-making process. Although detailed research based on historical data shows that in countries with debt to GDP ratios above the threshold of 90% the GDP growth is very small, it is shown that for such countries as the United States economic growth can be 3% and above. Several approaches that can improve the economy are considered. Based on the material of Chapter 3, the US government proposal to balance the budget over the decade is evaluated. Chapter 5 contains software developed to solve multiple examples presented earlier. It can be useful for researchers who would test the considered models to use them in practice. Appendix A contains the material that enables one to determine the parameters of the Cobb—Douglas function without the assumption of being homogeneous of degree 1 (constant returns to scale). The material of Appendix B shows how to determine the multiplier value for a stimulus package based on information about the multiplier values of its components. The multiplier values problem is also considered as an identification problem. Appendix C contains the results of optimal theory related to minimization of the quadratic functionals for linear continuous and discrete models. Its results are used in Chapter 3. Appendix D explains how to choose proper data to solve the discussed problems.

Bernard Shaw (1856—1950), an Irish playwright and cofounder of the London School of Economics, was right in saying "If all the economists were laid end to end, they would not reach a conclusion." Unfortunately, this is also true today. The authors hope that this book will supply economists with new ideas that, when crystallized, will allow them to obtain interesting and useful results.

CHAPTER ONE

Problems and Tools of Applied Macroeconomics

Contents

A theory can be proved by experiment; but no path leads from experiment to the birth of a theory.

Albert Einstein

1.1 INTRODUCTION

The 2008 global financial crisis has resulted in large deficits and national debt burdens across many countries. According to IMF (2009) estimates, the level of national debt for advanced countries would reach over 100% of gross domestic product (GDP) by 2014, a level unseen since the World War II. The United States has a huge national debt (over 20 trillion dollars in 2017); in 2012, it has surpassed 100% of GDP. The European Union (EU) average debt was about 85% of GDP in 2012; it was 158% in Greece, 115.6% in Portugal, 110.2% in Ireland, 127% in Italy, 75.7% in Spain, 90% in the United Kingdom, 87% in France, 69.5% in Germany, 91.4% in Belgium, and 75.9% in Hungary. In the second quarter (Q2) of 2013, government debt of Greece jumped to 169.1% of GDP; Italy's debt grew to 133.3%. Spain's debt to GDP ratio became about 92.3%. Spain's borrowing rate rose to 7.5%, a level that economists consider as unsustainable. The ratio of Portugal's debt to its GDP was 107% when it received the bailout. However, the ratio has grown since then and reached 131.3%. It lies above the European Union-agreed ceiling of 60% of GDP.

Applied Macroeconomics for Public Policy
ISBN: 978-0-12-815632-2
https://doi.org/10.1016/B978-0-12-815632-2.00001-8

1

The $840 billion stimulus package enacted by the US Congress (the American Recovery and Reinvestment Act of 2009) intended to boost the economy. The 2008 European Economic Recovery Plan containing €200 billion stimulus perused the same goal. As a result of stimulus policies, during the 2008—09 period in many of the mentioned countries, government spending rose and taxation fell. However, such policies resulted in increased government deficits (for the majority of EU Member States, deficits were above the 3% of GDP reference value, the level required according to Article 126 of the Treaty on the Functioning of the European Union (TFEU)). The reverse occurred in 2010—12. Many EU countries have undertaken austerity measures, which tightened their deficits to bring their finances under control. Most countries drew down their temporary spending increases, many raised taxes, and some cut spending below prerecession levels. In the United States, Republicans succeeded in blocking further stimulus packages and cutting government spending. Some economists believe that this stalled the economic recovery, which began in June of 2009.

Of course, the range of actions related to a concrete economic policy depends on a country's economic power. What is admissible, for example, for the United States, the world's largest national economy, is not admissible for countries with a weak economy. The United States can allow itself even erroneous economic decisions, which would only delay the economic recovery. Countries with a weak economy cannot allow themselves such a luxury. The crises in Greece demonstrated that. In contrast to Greece, Latvia showed how an efficient economic policy can restore economic health in a short period of time. In 2008 and 2009, the financial crisis actually looked far worse in Latvia than in Greece. Its GDP declined 24% for 2 years. Greece's GDP decreased by almost 18% in 2009. However, the countries chose opposite policies: Latvia strict austerity and Greece late and limited austerity. In 2009, Latvia carried out a fiscal adjustment of 9.5% of GDP, whereas Greece tried to stimulate its economy. Latvia decreased government expenditures from a high of 44% of GDP to a moderate level of 36% of GDP and kept a flat personal income tax at 21% and a low corporate profit tax at 15%. In 2011 and 2012, Latvia's economy grew by more than 5.3%, the highest growth in Europe, with a budget deficit of only 1.5% of GDP. In 2010, Latvia's debt to GDP ratio reached 44.5%. In 2013, it dropped to 38.1%. Estonia, a country with the debt to GDP ratio not more than 10%, aggressively fought the recession (its GDP rate was 0.8% in 2008 and −14.9% in 2009) by cutting government spending and tax rates, and the economy started booming (after 2010 the GDP growth rate is above 6%).

Disappointment with a slow economic recovery and inefficiency of the stimulus—austerity measures taken to boost the economy (the EU expected GDP in the 18-country Eurozone to expand only 0.8% in 2014, significantly below earlier forecasts) moves many European countries back to the initially tested stimulus policy. (Only healthier economies such as Germany and England do not see any reasons to change their fiscal policy.) This reverse course is influenced partially by the encouraging growth of the US economy although American stimulus supporters believe that the government should have done more while its austerity advocates believe that it is time for significant government spending cuts.

Multiple discussions about *austerity versus stimulus* in the public media look groundless. It is of importance not only which policy is used but also how it is executed. The considered policies are recommended by economists and "corrected" by politicians, and only after that they are executed. Quality of execution and specifics of a country's economy are important as well. Results of the implemented policy are a function of all parameters characterizing the whole process rather than the policy itself.

The recent economic crisis showed that economists were better prepared than in 1930. However, its duration and the subsequent slow economic recovery demonstrate that the existing economic tools are still unable to be trusted as undisputed decision-making means. Macroeconomic models suffer serious disconnection from reality. Instead of a unique macroeconomic theory, there are several competing theories and applied economists try to choose among them appropriate tools to use.

The main object of applied macroeconomics should be economic illness and how to cure it. In the Preface, we indicated that the applied branch of macroeconomics dealt with actual public policy problems and pointed out some of them. As Blanchard et al. (2010) indicated, "The great moderation lulled macroeconomists and policymakers alike in the belief that we knew how to conduct macroeconomic policy. The crisis clearly forces us to question that assessment... it clear that there is a lot we do not know about the effects of fiscal policy, about the optimal composition of fiscal packages, about the use of spending increases versus tax decreases, and the factors that underlie the sustainability of public debts, topics that had been less active areas of research before the crisis."

Below we pay main attention to the macroeconomic analysis of the stimulus and austerity policies during and after economic crises, the periods when the guidance from economists and politicians is needed most of all. These times test a country's leadership team, its fiscal and monetary policy, as well as its ability to work efficiently with economists to restore the country's economy.

Although control and system theories provide tools to deal with complex systems such as macroeconomic systems, most of them only are marginally used in macroeconomics. System and control theory approaches allow us to make this analysis more rigorous and to formulate two important policy analysis problems, which, in our opinion, should accompany any decision-making process related to the implementation of the considered policies.

1.2 BASIC GOALS AND PARAMETERS OF MACROECONOMIC SYSTEMS

Decision-making to ensure full employment and growth is carried out by fiscal and monetary policies. Governments carry out mainly fiscal policy, whereas monetary policy is mostly in hands of the central banks. All decisions are based on the macroeconomic analysis that refers to the process of using macroeconomic factors and principles in the analysis of the economy. Main macroeconomic factors include GDP, debt, unemployment, inflation, government policies, and interest rates. Such factors enable economists and financial analysts to make an informed assessment of the state of the economy of a nation. This analysis allows the economists to evaluate the state of a country's economy and to forecast its future.

Because the main macroeconomic goal is to create stable economic growth, which would get and keep people's living standards high, the GDP is considered as an important parameter of macroeconomic models; it is used as a key economic indicator characterizing the state of the economy. Another important macroeconomic goal is full employment (or low unemployment). Labor is the most important resource that is necessary to produce goods and services to satisfy our needs. Labor earns wages and salaries, which fuel consumer spending. Conventional economic theory considers economic output as a function of labor and capital. In other words, labor and capital are the two ingredients that determine economic performance (e.g., see Filipe and Adams, 2005). The unemployment rate indicator is tied to other indicators; for example, a high unemployment rate implies low consumer confidence and a decrease in GDP growth.

The macroeconomic analysis includes a study of government policies that have a bearing on the economy. When the government has too many unfriendly economic policies (e.g., excessive taxes), it discourages economic growth. The important parameters characterizing government policy and the related state of a country's economy are government expenditures, taxes, and debt.

Fiscal policy can be defined as the use of taxation and government spending for the purposes of macroeconomic goals. In the past, government spending increased during wars and then typically took some time to fall back to its previous level. However, in the 20th century, government spending began a rapid and steady increase. Although economists and political scientists have offered various theories about what determines the level of government spending, no one of them gives a satisfactory answer. Governments have grown in recent decades, and economists do not really know why. There is a variety of approaches to fiscal policy, and it is not necessary to assume that governments follow strictly to recommendations of a certain theory: that a country raises taxes and also cuts spending, as well as a country increases spending, is accompanied with tax cuts. This happens because there exists no macroeconomic theory accepted by the majority of economists that could be recommended as a reliable practical tool.

When the government borrows more money to spend, the result is an increase in the national debt. The consequences of a high debt can be dangerous. Unfortunately, the debt problem has not received a proper attention in macroeconomic theory. Only in the past years, the empirical results were published, establishing a negative correlation between national debt and economic growth (Reinhart and Rogoff, 2009; Kumar and Woo, 2010). According to Reinhart and Rogoff (2010), this correlation becomes particularly strong when national debt approaches 100% of GDP. An adamant proponent of fiscal stimulus economic policy Krugman (2010) believes that debt does not have a causal effect on growth but low economic growth leads to high levels of national debt. Former Federal Reserve (Fed) Chairman Ben Bernanke (2010) stated that "Neither experience nor economic theory clearly indicates the threshold at which government debt begins to endanger prosperity and economic stability. But given the significant costs and risks associated with a rapidly rising federal debt, our nation should soon put in place a credible plan for reducing deficits to sustainable levels over time." Panizza and Presbitero (2012) take a conciliatory position. Although they did not find a negative effect of debt on growth, they believe that it does not mean that countries can sustain any level of debt and that there exists a level of debt beyond which debt becomes unsustainable.

We will use the GDP growth rate, debt, and the debt to GDP ratio in the considered below models.

1.3 MACROECONOMIC TIME SERIES

The state of a country's economy is characterized by macroeconomic variables such as GDP, rate of growth of GDP, unemployment rate, price level, inflation rate, debt, government revenues and spending, and interest rates. The past values of these variables help to estimate their future values. Without the reliable future estimates, it is impossible to make responsible decisions concerning fiscal and monetary policies.

The past macroeconomic data presented by the time series concerning the most important macroeconomic variables are used mostly for forecasting. Forecasting models are built to explain the past with a hope to make the future more understandable. The analysis of the past data can be used to develop mathematical models describing dynamics of macroeconomic variables.

Based on the analysis of the related time series, relationship between certain factors can be established. The model accuracy depends on the number of properly chosen factors. On the one hand, ignoring of some factors can make the model meaningful. On the other hand, including too many factors can contribute to extensive errors undermining its reliability.

A single or several macroeconomic variables presented by the time series serve as parameters in a class of models built based on the known basic macroeconomic equations. A certain property of time series (if it is valid) enables one to build a class of dynamic models concerning the variables presented by the time series. The developed macroeconomic models help also examine the dynamics of macroeconomic variables and control them.

In contrast to the models of objects of nonlive nature, the presence of human factor in macroeconomic models makes the process of their identification (the process of constructing models from experimental data) extremely difficult. Objects of nonlive nature allow one to test them applying inputs with known properties. Unfortunately, such a situation is impossible in macroeconomics. Presence of the human factor makes researchers slaves of the past data that they should decipher properly. Estimated on the macroeconomic level, a country's economic activity is a result of actions of separate individuals guided by main life instincts. As mentioned earlier, their behavior depends on various factors, many of which do not obey any rigorously formulated laws. In contrast to the models of the physical sciences and engineering, testing the accuracy of forecasting models is restricted by the available historic data. Several years old economic data are not sufficient to build a reliable model. However, usually the extension of the time interval for the used data only makes the examined process blur because in different years different factors are dominant and they may be interconnected.

Random and mostly unpredictable consumer behavior reflected in various economic time series attracted attention of statisticians. Macroeconomic data present a delicious food for them. However, the existing mathematical methods applied to build mathematical macroeconomic models and use them for forecasting and control cannot be considered as reliable ones. Mathematical tools of statistics and stochastic equations are limited. The assumptions that accompanied the statistical approaches cannot be justified for many macroeconomic models. That is why, as we indicated earlier, macroeconomic models suffer serious disconnection from reality.

Any series of observations ordered along a single dimension, such as time, may be thought of as a time series. The emphasis in time series analysis is on studying the dependence among observations at different points in time. What distinguishes time series analysis from general multivariate analysis is precisely the temporal order imposed on the observations. Many economic variables, such as GDP and its components, price indices, sales, and stock returns, are observed over time. In addition to being interested in the contemporaneous relationships among such variables, we are often concerned with relationships between their current and past values, i.e., relationships over time.

Most statistical methods are aimed to be applied to independent experiments or sample survey results: observation ordering has no special meaning (as occurs typically, e.g., in biology, agronomy, sociology, etc.). In economics, data often take the form of sequences (series) of observations on one or several variables taken at different dates: These observations cannot typically be assumed to be independent; that is, usually, in macroeconomic time series, successive observations are dependent.

Widely spread mathematical analysis of time series, a sequence of discrete-time data related to certain economic parameters is used to analyze the process to forecast the series future values based on the previously observed values and ability to control the process. Based on a limited amount of information to build a mathematical model (using finite-length time series), statisticians make inference about the mechanism that produces the series. In statistics, prediction is a part of statistical inference. Models for time series data can have many forms and represent different stochastic processes. Predictions derived from nonlinear models should work better than those derived from linear models, but only if the nonlinear structure is chosen properly, which is the main obstacle of using nonlinear models.

There is a set of conditions under which much of the theory is built. Among them there is assumption that the process is stationary/seasonally stationary.

A stochastic model based on a time series reflects the fact that the observations close in time are more closely related than observations further apart. A common assumption in many time series techniques is that the data are stationary. A stationary process has the property that its mean, variance, and autocorrelation structure do not change over time; that is, the series are without trend, with constant variance and autocorrelation structure over time and without periodic (seasonality) fluctuations.

If the time series is not stationary, it is often possible to transform it to stationary with one of the following techniques.

Sometimes observations meet better the assumption if the observation scale is changed (for example, logarithms of the considered variables are used). For nonconstant variance, taking the logarithm of square root of the series may stabilize the variance. For negative data, one can add a suitable constant to make all the data positive before applying the transformation. This constant can then be subtracted from the model to obtain predicted values and forecasts for the future process.

Some linear combinations of values of the considered variable can be less correlated compared with values of this variable. If coefficients of such a linear combination are known (for example, difference), it can be used in the developed model. Given the series z_i, we create the new series $y_i = z_i - z_{i-1}$.

Time series techniques are divided into parametric and nonparametric methods. The parametric approaches, focused on the estimation of parameters of models describing stochastic processes, assume that the underlying stationary stochastic process has a certain structure that can be presented by a small number of parameters (for example, using an autoregressive or moving average model). By contrast, nonparametric approaches explicitly estimate the covariance of the process without assuming that the process has any particular structure.

The series methods take into account possible structure in the data. They account for the fact that data points taken over time may have an internal structure (such as autocorrelation, trend, or seasonal variation) that should be accounted for.

In many cases, time series are considered as a result of independent random deviations from a function representing a trend. If the data contain a trend, we can fit some type of curve to the data and then model the residuals from that fit. When observations represent a sequence of dependent random variables, the process (its random part) is assumed to be stationary. However, validity of this assumption requires a rigorous analysis and usually is inapplicable to macroeconomic time series.

In some cases, the examined trend is a known function of time and other observable variables. If this function is linear, then linear regression models can be built. However, in reality, curves of growth are described by nonlinear functions.

Relatively simple models that describe time series, the so-called "error" models, consider observations as independent random deviations from some functions representing a trend. More complicated models describe sequences of dependent random variables. As mentioned earlier, usually stationary stochastic processes are considered; that is, the models, in which there is a trend and the random terms, constitute a stationary stochastic process.

When the trend has a specific structure and depends on a finite number of parameters, problem of inference concerning these parameters is considered. When the trend is not specified so exactly, nonparametric methods (for example, smoothing) can be used to estimate the trend.

When the stochastic process is specified in terms of a finite number of parameters, such as an autoregressive process, the estimate of the coefficients, testing hypothesis about them, is the main concern. A null hypothesis of particular interest is the independence of random terms; this hypothesis may be tested by using the serial correlation coefficients. When the process is stationary, but specified more loosely, we may estimate the covariance or the spectral density. Such procedures are rather nonparametric.

Methods of prediction act when the structure of the process is known. The procedures of testing hypotheses and setting up confidence regions have been based on the assumption that the observations are normally distributed. As mentioned above, the error models treat time series as a sum of systematic parts or trend and random parts or errors; the random parts are assumed to have equal variances at all time points and to be uncorrelated. This assumption does not correspond to macroeconomic reality. Sometimes the assumptions of equal variances and of the additive nature of the trend and error are approximated well by measuring logarithms.

The polynomial trend summarizes the overall characteristics of the series. Usually, it is a substitute for a more complicated (but unknown) function of time. The fitted polynomial can be used for interpolation but must be used cautiously for extrapolation because there is a question of how good an approximation polynomial is to the underlying trend outside the range of the given data.

Smoothing a time series means representing the trend at a given point in time by a weighted average of the observed values near the point. The observed value is considered to be a sum of the trend and a random error. The weighted average of the trend is roughly the same as the trend at that point, and the weighted average of the random terms will tend to be numerically small (the random terms being independent and having expected values 0). Hence the weighted average of the observed values will estimate the trend.

The variate difference method has been proposed for estimating the variance of the error term when the trend is smooth. It is based on successive differences of elements in a time series.

The difference between various time series methodologies is in fine details, related to data processing, like giving more recent data more weight or discounting certain outlier points. By tracking what happened in the past with a hope to be able to give a prediction about the future, it is important to remember that the data are always going to be old and there is no guarantee that the conditions in the past will continue to exist in the future. Prediction errors by using forecasting models are inevitable; the longer the forecast period, the larger the probability and value of the forecast errors.

Many economists believe that modern macroeconomic models have become highly technical, theoretical, and statistically sophisticated to be used in practice. Some of them even proclaim that the dynamic stochastic optimal models are the future of macroeconomic theory. However, the reality proves opposite. A real theory is inseparable from practice. Most of the existing macroeconomic modeling approaches produce qualitative rather than quantitative results. Overloaded by unrealistic statistical assumptions and the desire to justify the prescribed consumer behavior, these models were unable to help solve efficiently problems caused by the 2008 financial crisis. Moreover, unfortunately, there exists no a rigorous macroeconomic theory accepted by all economists. Passion for statistics ignores the fact that the economic policy is the result of deliberate actions, the policies based on experience and science. They are strictly deterministic rather than random. That is why it is reasonable, especially in the applied branch of macroeconomics, to build the macroeconomic dynamic deterministic models with several parameters that should be estimated from time series analysis. Their future estimates allow one to consider several possible future scenarios. Such an approach is very practical, and the below developed models demonstrate its efficiency.

1.4 THEORETICAL ASPECTS OF STIMULUS AND AUSTERITY POLICIES

A major unresolved issue among economists is whether government spending increase programs or tax cut programs, designed to stimulate the economy, actually work. The short-run impact of government spending to stimulate the economy is a topic of intense academic and political debate.

As indicated earlier, the two camps of economists have different views concerning how to improve the economy in times of economic downturn. Those who support a Keynesian view of the economy argue that government spending can provide a powerful boost to economic growth. In contrast to those who consider government stimulus policy as an efficient strategy and support the approach based on additional government borrowing, another group of economists, concerned with dangerous consequences of high accumulated government debts, argues that government spending has a relatively weak stimulative effect and supports austerity measures.

These views are based on theoretical results that each of the mentioned groups considers as valid and applicable to a crisis situation. Advocates of stimulus strategy use Keynesian arguments: in a period when the economy is below full employment fiscal stimulus, either in the form of direct government spending, transfer payments, or tax cuts, can create additional demand and grow the economy from the bottom up (see Keynes, 1998). They suggest that increasing government spending and decreasing tax rates are the best ways to stimulate aggregate demand and produce strong economic growth and full employment even though this entails government deficits and debts. Usually, the Keynesian prescription is for government to borrow money and to run deficits during an economic downturn rather than to decrease taxes. Austerity measures are inadmissible in this period because they make a recession worse by further reducing aggregate demand. Keynesians also believe that fiscal stimulus should be reinforced by monetary stimulus. However, monetary stimulus is considered only as a complement to fiscal stimulus because they doubt that monetary stimulus alone has the power to cure a severe recession. The magnitude of the combined fiscal stimulus and monetary stimulus should be set large enough to increase employment and raise aggregate demand for goods and services back to normal. As to the resulting deficits, it is assumed that they would be paid by an expanded economy during the boom that would follow.

However, it is questionable whether this time will come. No such theorem has been proved. That is why austerity measures are discussed to decrease government spending and mounting national debt. Moreover, some economists believe that the government stimulus is inefficient because of the "crowding out," the term used to refer to the contraction in economic activity associated with deficit-financed spending (Heim, 2008): Government spending yields less economic growth than Keynesians would expect.

There exists no rigorous theory supporting austerity policy. Austerity measures generally refer to government policies to reduce expenditures in an attempt to shrink their growing budget deficits. These policies include spending cuts and/or tax increases. It is almost obvious that removing spending from the economy, as well as increased taxes, will reduce levels of aggregate demand and contract the economy more. Such a strategy is inadmissible in the period of a struggling economy.

A reasonable question is: why a compromised strategy—decreased taxes (stimulus) and government spending (austerity)—cannot be applied? Such a policy has been tested partly in the 1980s during Reagan's presidency. Although Reagan increased defense spending (this was the period of the Cold War), he supported a reduction in the growth of government spending and a reduction in the federal income taxes and capital gains taxes, as well as government regulations. These policies, commonly associated with *supply-side economics* (promoting lower marginal tax rates and less regulation), were criticized by many economists (see Atkinson, 2006), as well as Reagan's political opponents, and, as the result, were not realized completely.

An empirical analysis of the dynamic effects of changes in government spending and taxes (Blanchard and Perotti, 2002) shows that influence of tax cuts on economic growth can be as effective as increased government spending. This explains positive results of the above mentioned policy.

Using terminology of system and control theories, the goal of stimulus policy can be formulated as maximization of GDP. The policy itself is control actions focused to realize this goal. The goal of austerity policy can be formulated as minimization of debt, and the policy itself is control actions to realize this goal. The formulated problems are interconnected, and formally the whole problem is a multicriteria problem. Building a multicriteria dynamic optimization model is not realistic based on the current level of existing economic models. Many uncertain parameters in such a model would make a related Pareto analysis unreliable. Below we offer a compromised criterion—the debt to GDP ratio—to analyze the discussed policies.

1.5 FISCAL MULTIPLIERS

Fiscal multipliers play a central role in macroeconomic theory. They measure the short-term impact of discretionary fiscal policy on output; and a classic question in macroeconomics about the size of the government spending multiplier was extensively discussed in economics literature. The spending multiplier is the ratio of a change in national income to the change in spending that causes it. The mechanism that produces a spending multiplier effect (the ratio exceeds one) is that an initial incremental amount of spending leads to increased consumption spending, which, in turn, increases further income and hence consumption, etc., resulting in an overall increase in national income greater than the initial incremental amount of spending.

The more general definition of the fiscal multiplier is the change in GDP or other measure of output caused by a one-unit increase in a fiscal variable. For example, the tax multiplier presents the ratio of change in GDP to an autonomous change in taxes. Better estimation and use of multipliers can play a key role in ensuring macroeconomic forecast accuracy.

Real GDP is the production of goods and services measured at constant prices, whereas nominal GDP is the production of goods and services measured at current prices. There exist three approaches to view GDP. The *production approach* (also called the *output approach* or the *"net product"* or *"value-added"* approach) adds the value of final products sold; the *expenditure approach* adds up the value of purchases made by final users; and the *income approach* sums the incomes generated by production and obtained by all producers in the country. In contrast to the expenditure approach that begins with the money spent on goods and services, the income approach starts with the income earned (wages, rents, interest, profits) from the production of goods and services. In this case, GDP is considered as a measure of aggregate income. The production approach is used in the production function models (see, e.g., Filipe and Adams (2005) and Simon and Levy (1963)). It considers GDP from the output side.

The three methods of measuring GDP should result in the same number, with some possible difference caused by statistical and rounding differences. The credibility of the data is always a significant concern in any form of research. The expenditure approach is the most widely used way to estimate GDP. An advantage of using the expenditure method is data integrity. The US Bureau of Economic Analysis considers the source data for expenditure components to be more reliable than for either income or production components. The production approach is used in some EU countries. Their choice is explained by the presence of a reliable information base.

The basic equation of the GDP Y used in the expenditure approach has the following form:

$$Y = C + I + G + (X - M) \tag{1.1}$$

where C (consumption) is the consumer spending or total private consumption; G is the government spending, I (investment) is the sum of all the country's investment, including businesses capital expenditures; X represents the gross exports; and M represents the total imports. Exports can be considered as a loan to the rest of the world, and imports are equivalent to borrowing from the rest of the world.

The right part of Eq. (1.1) is interpreted as the aggregate expenditure. The above equation is presented also as

$$Y = C + I + G + X_N \tag{1.2}$$

where $X_N = X - M$ is net exports.

Consumption refers to total consumption spending by households on final goods and services. Investment is the purchase of new goods that increases the capital stock, allowing one to produce more output in the future. Investment is divided into three categories: business fixed investment (purchases of physical capital for the production of goods and services), new residential construction (the building of new homes), and inventory investment (change in inventories of final goods). Government spending includes all purchases of goods and services by the government.

The components of the right part of Eq. (1.1) can be considered as controls that can change GDP and can be used as tools of government economic policy. The use of government policy to improve functioning of the economy was advocated by economists in the wake of the Great Depression.

Usually, the term *stabilization policy* refers to the fiscal (changes in taxation and the level of government purchases) and monetary (changes in interest rates and other tools that are under the control of the monetary authority of a country) policies focused to prevent large fluctuations of real GDP.

In the United States, the Federal Reserve Bank controls monetary policy, whereas fiscal policy is controlled by the president, the Congress, and state governments. In the countries of the European Union, monetary policy is controlled by the European Central Bank, and fiscal policies are controlled by the individual governments of the member countries.

There are two reasons explaining a decrease in real GDP: (1) firms decided to produce less output, and, as a result, the level of the consumer spending decreased; (2) households started spending less, and, as a result, firms reduced their production.

Following Keynes (1936), if many households decide at the same time to increase their saving and reduce their spending, they may make themselves worse off by causing aggregate expenditure to fall, thereby pushing the economy into a recession; the lower incomes in the recession might mean that total saving does not increase, despite the attempts by many individuals to increase their own saving. The idea to stimulate consumption during the Great Depression by pumping government spending into the economy (for example, by investing in infrastructure) belongs to Keynes (1998). Keynes focused on consumption spending as the principal determinant of income growth, arguing that consumption releases purchasing power to producers and thereby validates their investment plans.

Consumption C is the largest and most important component of GDP. In the long run, C and GDP changes are approximately the same. But in the short run, consumer expenditures fluctuate less than GDP because they depend on *disposable income* (DPI), income after taxes—the amount of money that households have available for spending and saving after income taxes (DPI = total personal income − personal income taxes). Consumer spending is a function of *disposable income*. Assuming the linear relationship between the indicated variables, consumption C in Eq. (1.1) can be presented as

$$C = C_0 + \rho_C(Y - T) \qquad (1.3)$$

where C_0 is a basic level of consumption people will undertake regardless of income, T is taxes, and $0 < \rho_C = dC/dY < 1$ is the *marginal propensity to consume* (MPC) showing the level of the consumer spending, the level of additional income that households consume.

The importance of people's disposable income in determining their spending is a pivot of the Keynesian theory of consumption: Consumers will increase their planned expenditures if the disposable income increases. Substitution Eq. (1.3) into Eq. (1.1) gives

$$Y = \left(\frac{1}{1 - \rho_C}\right)(C_0 - \rho_C T + I + G + X_N) \qquad (1.4)$$

It follows from Eq. (1.4) that tax changes are negatively related to GDP with a multiplier effect $\rho_C/(1 - \rho_C)$, whereas changes in government spending G and net exports X_N are positively related to GDP with a multiplier effect $1/(1 - \rho_C)$. The multipliers $1/(1 - \rho_C)$ and $\rho_C/(1 - \rho_C)$ are called the *spending multiplier* and the *tax multiplier*, respectively. As it follows from the model Eq. (1.4), the tax multiplier is smaller than the spending multiplier. Some economists explain this from the fact that any new expenditure requires money; additional government spending means injecting new money into economy, while lower taxes are not accompanied with injecting new money. However, if in Eq. (1.3) we consider the taxable income $T = \tau Y$, where τ denotes the tax rate, the term ρ_C in Eq. (1.3) should be changed to $(1 - \tau)\rho_C$. That is why the above indicated tax multiplier can relate only to the autonomous tax revenues T_0 that do not depend on the current income Y (for simplicity, here we ignored the autonomous tax component because it is significantly less than the tax component).

The basic Eq. (1.1) shows only that the output Y is a function of variables C, G, I, X, and M. The Keynesian theory uses the relationship Eq. (1.3) to explain the multiplier effects of increased government spending. In the basic Keynesian model, government expenditures G are assumed to be independent of income. However, government spending influences income indirectly (see Eq. (1.3)). As to investment I, Keynes, at least in the short run, viewed it as an independent of income expenditure, that is, the level of investment expenditure is constant with respect to current income. Exports in the Keynesian model are considered dependent on spending choices and income levels abroad, so that they are unaffected by changes in a nation's domestic output level and spending. In contrast, increases in domestic income will induce consumers to purchase more foreign as well as domestic goods. So the level of imports increases as income rises. Because exports remain constant but imports increase as aggregate income expands, a nation's net exports X_N will decline as income rises, so that according to Keynesian theory, there is a negative relationship between a nation's net exports and its aggregate income.

The above model (Eq. 1.4) can be modified if we use $T = T_0 + T_1$ and the tax rate $\tau = T_1/Y$ (T is the total taxes; T_0 and T_1 are the taxes independent and dependent of Y, respectively) and present the investment and net exports terms as

$$I = I_0 + \rho_I Y \tag{1.5}$$

$$X_N = X_{N0} - \rho_X Y \tag{1.6}$$

where $\rho_I = dI/dY$ is the *marginal propensity to invest* (MPI) showing the level of income used for investment purposes (the greater ρ_I, the more likely that additional income is invested rather than consumed) and $\rho_X = dM/dY$ is the *marginal propensity to import* (MPM) showing the change in imports induced by a change in income (an economy with a positive MPC is likely to have a positive marginal propensity to import); X_{N0} is the autonomous net exports.

Substituting Eq. (1.5) and Eq. (1.6) in Eq. (1.4), we have

$$Y = \frac{1}{1 - (1 - \tau)\rho_C - \rho_I + \rho_X}(C_0 + I_0 - \rho_C T_0 + G + X_{N0}) \tag{1.7}$$

where the spending multiplier equals to $1/(1 - (1 - \tau)\rho_C - \rho_I + \rho_X)$.

Some economists believe (see, e.g., Carlson and Spencer, 1975; Heim, 2008, 2012) the growth of government deficits (T-G) influences consumer and investment spending. The government deficit "crowds out" private investment because government deficits are financed by borrowing. This can be caused by increased interest rates—an intuitive natural reaction to increased borrowing. Krugman (2011) is right when he argues the mentioned crowd out effect pointing out that, after the beginning of the recession in 2008, the federal government borrowing increased by hundreds of billions of dollars, but interest rates actually fell. This fact shows that a proper government monetary policy can keep interest rates under control. The crowd out effect may happen when governments raise taxes to fund new welfare programs or to expand existing ones. With higher taxes, individuals and businesses are left with less discretionary income to spend. In addition, it can be explained by consumers' behavior—purchasing power of consumers decreases during recessions.

The crowd out effect on consumption can be presented as $\sigma_D(T - G)$, where $\sigma_D > 0$ represents the marginal crowd out effect of the government deficit on consumer spending, and combined with Eq. (1.3) (Heim, 2008)

$$C = C_0 + \rho_C(Y - T) + \sigma_D(T - G) \tag{1.8}$$

so that instead of Eqs. (1.4) and (1.7) we have, respectively,

$$Y = \left(\frac{1}{1 - \rho_C}\right)(C_0 - (\rho_C - \sigma_D)T + I + (1 - \sigma_D)G + X_N) \qquad (1.9)$$

$$Y = \frac{1}{(1 - (1 - \tau)\rho_C + \sigma_D\tau - \rho_I + \rho_X)}(C_0 - (\rho_C - \sigma_D)T_0 + I_0$$
$$+ (1 - \sigma_D)G + X_{N0})$$

$$\qquad (1.10)$$

As seen from Eq. (1.9), the tax multiplier, showing the marginal impact of a change in taxes, is now $(\rho_C - \sigma_D)/(1 - \rho_C)$. The spending multiplier, showing the marginal impact of a change in government spending, is now $(1 - \sigma_D)/(1 - \rho_C)$. If the crowd out effect is greater than zero, both T and G net marginal stimulus effects will be smaller (in absolute terms) than they would have been without the crowd out effect (see Eq. (1.9)), and as it follows also from Eq. (1.4), for $\sigma_D < \rho_C$ the tax multiplier is less than the spending multiplier.

The crowd out effect on investment can be presented as (Heim, 2008)

$$I = \sigma_I(T - G) - \theta r \qquad (1.11)$$

where σ_I characterizes the marginal effect of crowd out on investment spending; θ represents the marginal effect of interest rates r.

Under the assumptions (1.3), (1.9), and (1.11), the basic Eqs. (1.1) and (1.2) transform in

$$Y = \left(\frac{1}{1 - \rho_C}\right)(C_0 - (\rho_C - \sigma_D - \sigma_I)T - \theta r + (1 - \sigma_D - \sigma_I)G + X_{N0})$$

$$\qquad (1.12)$$

In this case, the tax multiplier, showing the marginal impact of a change in taxes, is $(\rho_C - \sigma_D - \sigma_I)/(1 - \rho_C)$; that is, the normal stimulating impact of tax cuts $(-\rho_C)$ on the GDP is offset in part by the effects of deficit—induced changes in credit availability $(\sigma_D + \sigma_I)$. The spending multiplier, showing the marginal impact of a change in government spending, is now $(1 - \sigma_D - \sigma_I)/(1 - \rho_C)$; that is, it is reduced per dollar of expenditure $1 - \sigma_D - \sigma_I$ times.

The model (1.12) contains T as an independent variable, so that the tax multiplier value relates only to the autonomous part of T. As seen from Eq. (1.10), tax rates influence the spending multiplier; lower rates increase its value. The crowd out effect on investment presented by Eq. (1.11) does not contain the autonomous part I_0 that can be substantial for some countries. Moreover, the crowd out influence on the value of the spending multiplier, the most important parameter used by economists making recommendations concerning the government fiscal policy, is seen from Eqs. (1.5), (1.8), and (1.10). Below we modify the model (1.12) by considering, instead of Eq. (1.11),

$$I = I_0 + \rho_I Y - \theta\, r \tag{1.13}$$

which reflects the influence of interest rates r on investment; the crowd out effect on investment is reflected in Y indirectly (see (Eq. 1.8)).

The modified model has the form

$$Y = \frac{1}{(1 - (1 - \tau)\rho_C + \sigma_D \tau - \rho_I + \rho_X)}(C_0 + (1 - \sigma_D)G + I_0 - \theta r + X_{N0}) \tag{1.14}$$

The modification of Eq. (1.10) gives

$$Y = \frac{1}{(1 - (1 - \tau)\rho_C + \sigma_D \tau - \rho_I + \rho_X)}(C_0 + (1 - \sigma_D)G - (\rho_C - \sigma_D)T_0 + I_0 - \theta\, r + X_{N0}) \tag{1.15}$$

These equations enable one to understand deeply the dependence of the spending multiplier on many factors and the reasons of its changeableness, as well as why the multiplier values recommended by economists are so different. Multiple regression models built by Heim (2008, 2012) examine the crowd out effects and determine coefficients of Eqs. (1.3), (1.8), and (1.11) and of more complicated relationships. Using these coefficients, Heim (2008, 2012) obtains the values of the spending and tax multipliers influenced by the crowd out effect. In his efforts to show that government tax cut programs or spending increase programs, designed to stimulate the economy, do not work, he disregards the influence of monetary policy on the multiplier value. It is not obvious that such an approach enables one to obtain reliable values of the spending and tax multipliers. An appropriate monetary policy during recessions can influence the crowd out effect.

Because taxation and spending are the parts of fiscal policy, the desire to properly evaluate them is understandable. However, as indicated earlier, for the tax multiplier, different models should be used, which would take into account the dependence of tax revenues from the income and vice versa.

The presence of interest rates in Eq. (1.14) demonstrates the attempt of some authors to insert an element of monetary policy in the basic model (1.1). Formally, the aggregate expenditure model does not contain any link with monetary policy, the impact of the price level on aggregate expenditure (increases in the price level cause aggregate expenditure to fall, and decreases in the price level cause aggregate expenditure to rise), so that the approach based on Eq. (1.13) cannot be considered as too persuasive because it relates only to investment. Special models should be developed (see, e.g., Christiano et al., 2011).

The expression (1.14) shows how many parameters influence the value of the spending multiplier. The parameters are interconnected through the output Y. Moreover, it is difficult to indicate agreeable values of the constant terms in Eqs. (1.3), (1.5), (1.6), (1.8), and (1.13). The simple spending multiplier $1/(1 - \rho_C)$ is the simplest variation of G and includes only induced consumption. Every other component—investment, expenditures, government purchases, taxes, exports, and imports—are assumed to be autonomous. Testing under such an assumption for various components presents certain difficulties. They are explained by reverse causation— spending reacting to economy.

The spending multiplier determined by Eq. (1.14) based on the values of the parameters obtained separately from Eq. (1.3) or Eqs. (1.8), (1.5), (1.6) or Eqs. (1.11) and (1.13) would accumulate errors of the separate steps, and it is possible to expect unreliable multiplier values. That is why some scientists call the fiscal multipliers obtained based on the above equations the static "textbook multipliers."

Any changes are described by a dynamic process, so that the multiplier effect is considered in time. The above multipliers are called *impact multipliers*, in contrast to the *cumulative multiplier* defined as the cumulative change in output over the cumulative change in fiscal expenditure at some time horizon. One of the possible approaches is to consider directly the input— output relationship (e.g., stimulus—GDP) excluding all intermediate parameters. Vector autoregressive (VAR) models (see, e.g., Mountford and Uhlig, 2005; Auerbach and Gorodnichenko, 2012a,b; Blanchard and Perotti, 2002; Ilzetzki et al., 2013), describing the input—output relationship between GDP (output) and expenditures and G and taxes T (inputs), are used to determine the dynamics of spending and tax multipliers obtained as the impulse response of the corresponding linear system. However, as mentioned by Gechert and Will (2012), divergent results of the various identification strategies in VAR models seem to be partly due to multiplier calculation methods and horizons of measurement that reflect different shapes of impulse response functions. Fiscal multipliers are usually calculated either as the peak response of GDP at some horizon after some initial change in a specific fiscal instrument (impact multipliers) or as the cumulated response of GDP divided by the cumulated policy changes over a specified horizon (the cumulative multiplier).

It is not necessary to consider separately the effects of stimulus and crowd out because the stimulus actions are control actions and the crowd out is an internal part of a certain model describing the considering process.

More complex models containing utility functions describing households' behavior, based on confidence in their economic future, are also used to determine the fiscal multipliers. Various behavior assumptions result in different models with different results. Some models do not include the so-called utility maximizing households but estimate macroeconomic consumption and investment functions similar to Eqs. (1.3), (1.5), (1.8), (1.11), and (1.13).

The discussion concerning fiscal multipliers has lasted for decades, and still economists struggle on the value of the multiplier. The discussion was about crowding in versus crowding out effects in private consumption, investment, and net exports, whether the multiplier effect is below or above 1. Despite the plurality of identification strategies, specifications, and models, unsurprisingly the results are far off consensus (see Gechert and Will, 2012; Batini et al., 2014; and literature surveys related to fiscal multipliers). It seems now economists agree only that multiplier effects are highest, when central banks accommodate fiscal policy at a close to zero bound on interest rates, that is, when monetary and fiscal policies work in perfect harmony.

The issue of fiscal multipliers attracted increased attention during the 2008 financial crisis. Both the tax multiplier and spending multiplier link to government fiscal policy and economic output. The 2008 financial crisis tested the US government's ability to use properly its spending and taxation policies to speed up the economic growth and improve the country's economic situation. According to the Congressional Budget Office, during the first 20 months, starting September 2008, stimulus spending was $343 billion, whereas tax deduction was only $183 billion. In 2010 and 2011, the stimulus falls to roughly half its peak level, and effects in the following years were insignificant. The biggest part of the tax reduction program was a conventional tax rebate. Because it was refundable (that is, it resulted in a taxpayer receiving money back rather than paying less tax), it can be considered partly as government spending (the refunds) and partly as reduced taxes. The study of fiscal stimulus (Romer and Bernstein, 2009) shows that when the government increases its purchases of output, say concrete for new bridge, GDP rises immediately by about the amount of the purchase (1.05 in the first quarter) and then rises to about 1.6 times the amount of the purchases. For tax cuts or other programs that give families more purchasing power, the immediate response is more likely half the amount the government spends; the other half goes into savings. In both cases, the multipliers rise as time passes because of follow-on effects—increased spending by those influenced by the immediate effects. However, according to Hall and Woodward (2009), the measurement of these multiplier effects is intensely controversial. They believe that the stimulus effect in the mentioned study is overstated, especially in the case of tax cuts. According to their estimate, the spending multiplier is around 1—1.5 and the tax cut multiplier is quite a bit lower. However, this refers to tax cuts that hand families more purchasing power, such as the refunds; the effect of tax changes that give focused incentives for immediate spending (tax rebate) can be much larger. However, the 2008—09 experience shows that consumers do not hurry to spend rebate money when they receive it. Instead consumers smooth the spending increase, reserving most of it for future consumption, by saving it or using it to pay down debt. As a result, it makes an income tax rebate ineffective as a stimulus concentrated at the time most needed (Hall and Woodward, 2008). According to Woodford (2011), in a fairly broad class of simple models, the spending multiplier is 1 in the case that the monetary authority maintains a constant path for real interest rates. "The multiplier can be considerably smaller, however, if the monetary authority raises real interest rates in response to increases in inflation or real activity resulting from the fiscal stimulus. A large multiplier is especially plausible when monetary policy is constrained by the zero lower bound on nominal interest rates."

In contrast to the conventional Keynesian model, where spending multipliers necessarily exceed tax multipliers, the empirical results of Christina Romer and David Romer (2010) show that the tax multiplier is about 3. This result can be explained by the fact that the tax cut stimulates demand not only by increasing disposable income and consumption spending (according to Keynes) but also by incentivizing more investment spending. These results look consistent with the empirical findings of Blanchard and Perotti (2002), Mountford and Uhlig (2005), and Alesina et al. (2002). The results of all these authors suggest that the short-run effects of fiscal policy cannot be explained properly by the standard Keynesian model. As to tax increase, Barro and Redlick (2011) indicate that increases in average marginal income tax rates have significantly negative effects on GDP.

Perotti (1999) and Ilzetzki et al. (2013) who studied fiscal multipliers across different country groupings show that the effect of government expenditure on aggregate consumption may depend on initial conditions such as public indebtedness. They find strong evidence that government expenditure increases public consumption at low levels of debt or deficit and decreases it under the opposite circumstances. Romer and Romer (2010) offered an approach and estimated the impact of tax changes on output. The latest experimental results (e.g., see Blanchard and Perotti, 2002; Mankiw, 2008; Romer and Romer, 2010) indicate that tax multipliers are stronger than spending multipliers, and tax multipliers generally grow stronger over time, whereas spending multipliers generally weaken.

The magnitude of the fiscal multiplier, in theory and in the data, depends on the characteristics of the economy. The dependence of the stimulus impact of government spending on the economic environment was examined for different situations—fixed/floating exchange rates and high/low existing government debt. The following determinants of the size of fiscal multipliers were established: the degree of exchange rate flexibility, openness to trade, and the debt to GDP ratio. Ilzetzki et al. (2013) show that the stimulus impact of a government spending shocks varies with the economic environment: small open economies have smaller multipliers than large open economies (openness is measured in the context of trade of goods and services), and fiscal multipliers in open economies are lower than those in closed economies; the fiscal multiplier is relatively large in economies operating under predetermined exchange rate but zero in economies operating under flexible exchange rates; fiscal multipliers in high-debt countries are zero.

One important determinant is the level of government indebtedness—particularly when the nation's fiscal sustainability may be in doubt. If the fiscal situation is viewed as unsustainable, a bigger fiscal deficit may dampen private consumption by boosting precautionary savings. As debt levels rise, the latter will dominate the overall effect, so additional government spending tends to be inefficient. According to research of Nickel and Vansteenkiste (2008), once economies exceed a certain level of indebtedness, fiscal multipliers go to zero as additional deficit-financed spending generates offsetting declines in private spending. An increase in deficits today reduces private spending by increasing the magnitude of future fiscal adjustment costs. Nickel and Tudyka (2013) examined how the effects of fiscal stimuli interacted with national debt to GDP ratios. Based on the analysis of the data on GDP, private investment, and the trade balance, they suggest that the cumulative effect of fiscal stimuli on GDP is positive at moderate debt to GDP ratios (30%—40%) but turns negative as the ratio increases. In their experiments, above the 60% threshold fiscal stimulus appears ineffective. Eventually, at debt to GDP ratios beyond 90%, the overall effect on real GDP becomes significantly negative. They also found that the fiscal multiplier is lower when debt burdens are high, particularly in the long run. The mentioned results are similar to Ilzetzki et al. (2013) who indicated that "the 60% of GDP threshold, used, for example, by the Eurozone as part of the Maastricht criteria, is indeed a critical value above which fiscal stimulus may have a negative, rather than a positive impact on output in the long run."

Numerical estimates of the value of the fiscal multiplier vary significantly across model classes. Moreover, even models of a particular class can deliver quite different multiplier values, depending on the assumptions regarding monetary policy reaction functions. Within each class of models, they vary a lot with the economic and policy environment. The state of the economy is as, or more, important than other factors, such as the state of the financial system and the conduct of monetary policy. The most important insight arising from the debates over fiscal policy during and after the great recession is that the multiplier depends critically on the conduct of monetary policy.

Using traditional macroeconomic models, Christiano et al. (2011) under rather rigorous assumptions show that the multiplier varies enormously depending on how monetary policy reacts to the economy. They found the long-run effect to be positive and the multiplier can be as high as about 4. However, in most of the related publications, the multiplier peak value does not exceed 2.5. Eggertsson and Krugman (2010) and Corsetti et al. (2012) show that fiscal multipliers are largest exactly at times when expansionary fiscal policy is most needed. The results of some researchers differ significantly because the theoretical models used to examine the impact of government spending on GDP contain many interconnected parameters, which cannot be determined precisely. According to Ramey's (2011) analysis, spending multipliers range from 0.8 to 1.5. Auerbach and Gorodnichenko (2012a,b) show that in recessions the long-run multiplier effect is as high as 2.5 but as low as −1 in expansions.

In parallel with the spending and tax multipliers, their components were also examined. The multipliers generally vary significantly across spending and tax categories. The tax multiplier is actually a family of multipliers (e.g., related to personal income tax, corporate income tax, property tax, and sales tax that play important role in economic growth). Different types of taxes have different effects on the economy. Usually, empirical studies find that corporate and personal income taxes are the most damaging to economic growth, followed by consumption taxes and property taxes. Corporate taxes mostly affect investment and capital formation, whereas income taxes affect saving by individuals as well as investment by small business owners. A sales tax as a stimulus was considered by Poterba et al. (1986). It was shown that its properly decreased dose can be helpful, whereas big increase can have the reverse effect (the British sales tax increase caused a severe recession). The spending amplifier is also a family of multipliers. Among the various types of spending multipliers, the multiplier for transfers tends to be negative (see, e.g., Broda and Parker, 2014); the defense spending multiplier is about 0.6 (see, e.g., Hall and Woodward, 2009).

A big hurdle in obtaining precise estimates of fiscal multipliers is data availability that limits the scope for estimating multipliers. Most studies have relied on annual data, which makes it difficult to obtain precise estimates. In addition, historical estimates of the fiscal multiplier also condition on data when the financial system is operating normally or is at least not highly impaired. However, the financial conditions during crises are arguably abnormal.

The situation with the numerical estimates of fiscal multipliers is explained also by the indicated earlier specifics of macroeconomic models— the presence of human factor. Some models consider constrained and unconstrained individuals (those who can and cannot borrow or lend). In addition, individuals have only the choice between consumption and savings. The models assume a certain behavior of consumers or producers (for example, infinite-lived optimizing consumers and monopolistic competition; consumers are assumed to be one of two types—patient and impatient; constrained households are assumed to be more pervasive during crises).

Underestimating multipliers may lead countries to set unachievable fiscal targets and, as a result, miscalculate the amount of adjustment necessary to generate economic health. Moreover, erroneous actions of authorities in their efforts to make fiscal variables (balance, debt) reach unachievable projected targets, which can only worsen the economic situation. Blanchard and Leigh (2013) indicated that the underestimation of fiscal multipliers early in the 2008 financial crisis contributed significantly to growth forecast errors.

A reasonable question is: why do researchers obtain different and even contradictory values of multipliers? On the one hand, as we indicated above, the spending and tax multipliers present families of submultipliers, and in any concrete situation, the considering multiplier contains a different combination of submultipliers, which does not coincide with the one used in the researchers' models. On the other hand, the multiplier effect depends on a government monetary policy that accompanies its fiscal policy and works faster, which influence can be significant (it can increase the size of multipliers by a factor of 2−3 or, on the contrary, decrease it to zero if monetary policy is firmly targeting inflation).

Although it is very difficult, maybe even impossible, to determine precisely the multiplier value for a concrete macroeconomic shock, the use of database of multipliers for various scenarios (a country's specifics, characteristics of its fiscal and monetary policies) is an important decision-making tool. Every result of academic research should be critically evaluated. Fiscal multipliers calculated for some countries should be carefully reexamined in light of the current events.

Implementation of any economic policy is a deterministic process. Too passion for statistics and long time series can produce wrong results because any step back can bring us to a different situation. In the periods of large macroeconomic shocks, we should not neglect a fast rough evaluation of multipliers based on current available information. As indicated earlier, consumption is the highest GDP component, and the expressions (1.3) and (1.8) reflect properly the consumption process. By evaluating roughly ρ_C and σ_D, it is possible to evaluate approximately the spending multiplier. This will help to find close multipliers from the mentioned database. Later, more accurate values can be obtained. It is difficult to agree that there exist the discussed pure multipliers. Usually, government spending is accompanied with tax cuts; this influences ρ_C and σ_D. Current measurements accumulate the effect of all components of economic policies, so that the spending multipliers calculated based on Eqs. (1.3) or (1.8) reflect the result of these policies. Using the US 2008−15 economic data, we obtained that the simple spending multiplier is equal to about 4.3 for $C_0 = 0.005C$. Taking $\tau = 0.14$ and using the proper components of Eq. (1.7), we get the spending multiplier value a 2.96. A least square solution for Eq. (1.8) decreases the above indicated values to 1.7. Decision-making should be based on considering several alternatives corresponding to several scenarios.

The above simple calculations (close estimates can be done even by using only 2008 and 2009 data) enable us to evaluate roughly the multiplier effect, compare it with the results of existing mathematical models, and choose a proper multiplier values for the developed models.

The developed model of the debt to GDP dynamics contains the spending and tax multipliers as one of its important parameters. The veracity of our findings depends on how close to reality is the chosen value of the spending/tax multiplier. In most examples, we use two multipliers to cover the effect of various government spending and taxation.

1.6 SPECIFICS OF MACROECONOMIC MODELS

It is well known that investigation of processes and phenomena is linked, first of all, with the construction of mathematical models describing these processes and phenomena using mathematical language. The model is characterized by some parameters. These parameters include input variables (which are called *control actions* or simply *controls* if a system can be intelligently manipulated), output variables or output coordinates (which are called *controlled variables* if they are objects of control), and finally *state* variables (which characterize internal properties of processes and phenomena).

In most cases, processes are not considered in isolation. The influence of other processes and phenomena on the process under investigation is characterized by the so-called *disturbing influences* or, simply, *disturbances*.

Economists use the terms *exogenous variables,* whose value is independent from the values of other variables of the economic model, and *endogenous variables,* whose value is determined or influenced by the values of other variables of the model. This terminology linked to time series analysis of causal processes and econometric models, which economists use to forecast future developments in the economy.

However, the mentioned economic terms are explained differently in the economic literature (for example, *exogenous variables* are determined outside *the system; endogenous variables* are determined inside *the system*), and they do not add too much compared with the well-established terms— *independent* and *dependent* variables.

An exogenous variable is by definition one whose value is wholly causally independent from other variables in the system. There is statistical interpretation of exogeneity. The statistical or econometric concept emphasizes noncorrelation between the exogenous variable and the other independent variables included in the model. Normal regression models assume that all the independent variables are exogenous.

Webster's dictionary defines *exogenous* as originating outside, derived externally, and *endogenous* as proceeding from within, derived internally. System theory—related terminology looks more thought-out than the above discussed terms, and it can be used successfully for analysis of economic systems.

Macroeconomic models by their nature are simplifications of a complex economic reality. They capture the essence of an economy's dynamics and include fundamental forces that drive the economy. Macroeconomic models present a formalized description of different economic processes. Any model is a simplified reflection of the reality. Most of the models used in economics are static econometric models. Some of the more sophisticated models in macroeconomics are dynamic models. Over the course of human history, people have developed many validated ideas about the physical, biological, psychological, and social worlds. Those ideas have enabled following generations to deepen their knowledge about the material world and its phenomena. The existing theories are the result of observation, thinking, experimenting, and validating. The laws of physics are the result of studies of nonliving systems. The corresponding models are reliable tools, which are widely used in everyday practice. Behavioral sciences, analyzing human behavior and animal behavior, established many interesting facts. For example, observations of behavior of predators pursuing their victims allowed scientists to formulate the parallel navigation rule and create theory of guidance (see, e.g., Yanushevsky, 2011). However, in contrast to the physical laws, some behavioral and social theories are still cannot be considered as universal, especially those that relate to human behavior. Although scientists succeeded in establishing certain behavioral patterns of many animals, human beings are too complicated objects to be described by a certain comprehensive model. It is almost impossible to find two persons thinking and acting identically.

Being children of Nature, people are empowered by innate instincts and inherited complex patterns of behavior to satisfy specific needs. Despite various definitions of the term "instinct" and related theories based on its interpretation, the life instincts that deal with basic survival (the need to defend oneself from danger, to have a place to live, food, and clothing) and pleasure (the need to explore everything they need to know about their urge to feel good) are used by overwhelming majority of psychologists and considered as the most important ones. Instincts and instinctive behaviors can be considered as embedded genetic goals and the realization of these goals. In contrast to biologically programmed instincts that serve as internal stimuli, the environmental influence serves as external stimulus. Internal and external stimuli influence the behavior of individuals. As a result, each human is unique and the human population is so diverse: it consists of many complex social groups with an extremely wide variety of values, social norms, and customs. All above mentioned makes doubtful any attempt to present the behavior of a group of individuals by a pragmatic representative (although many existing models still use such an approach). Only in extreme situations (e.g., a war, economic crisis, epidemic, etc.), the behavior of many individuals shows similar features; but even in such situations, usually there are groups that behave differently.

Aristotle (see Ross, 1957) called Man "a political animal" as if underlying difficulties in building such a model. The human factor is an integral part of economic models. It is present—directly or indirectly—in economic models. *Supply* and *demand* are the results of human activity. People make goods and provide services, and they are consumers of goods and services. Their behavior depends on too many factors and hence cannot be predicted accurately. These specifics of economic models and related economic theories make it difficult to use them for long-term forecasts.

If it is logical to consider the government actions (fiscal and monetary policies) as deterministic; the behavior of consumers and producers, the creators of supply and demand, does not follow strict deterministic laws and cannot be described by certain deterministic functions. The stochastic approach requires additional assumptions, which make it unreliable for many practical applications. One of the assumptions is that people's actions are the result of the optimization of a certain criterion that characterizes their behavior. In some models the behavior is simply presented by a certain (usually linear) function of the output Y and other factors (see, e.g., Eq. (1.3)). Some models use stochastic equations to describe the behavior of a group (such as consumers) in the economy. However, such models are built under very restrictive assumptions to be used in practice.

The most important part of building a model is to identify main factors describing the process because too complex models can work as unsatisfactory as too simple ones. An extensive passion for statistics can be a source of big errors because any step back in the past may bring the situation drastically different from the current one.

The dynamic processes that we observe in our everyday life are self-regulated processes. They are self-regulated by their very nature. They have built-in feedback characteristics that cause the process to tend toward its initial or new stable position. Considering macroeconomic processes from the position of control theory, we should distinguish *market forces* (the interaction of supply and demand in a market environment) that produce the stabilizing effect (self-regulation) and *government control actions* (the fiscal and monetary policies) that focus to keep the process at a certain level (e.g., concerning its parameters such as GDP, debt, and unemployment). Macroeconomic shocks refer to any disturbance in the economy to internal or external factors (for example, oil price hikes, sudden fall in demand or supply for any commodity, new tariff barriers, change in stock prices of large companies). Any macroeconomic shock, without government intervention, can significantly damage a country's economy. Classical economic theory relies on the mentioned self-regulation property as the only means of stabilizing the economy. In modern economic theories, government fiscal and monetary policies have a decisive role to improve the economy by counteracting the negative effect of macroeconomic shocks. Specific government actions (tax cuts, spending, etc.) are control components, and the efficiency of the economic policy depends on concrete values of these components (the same as a drug effect depends on doses of its ingredients).

Economic activity is future-oriented, and the related macroeconomic models should help to obtain reliable forecasts of the main macroeconomic parameters (GDP, debt, and employment) that characterize the state of a country's economy. The detailed study of dynamic objects starts from analyzing their static characteristics. Looking at the static characteristics enables us to determine the level of an object's potentials and limits. In the GDP expression (1.1), consumption $C(Y, T, r)$ depends on income, which is a function of the output Y, taxes T, and an interest rate r. Monetary policy has a direct effect on consumption through interest rates. Investment $I(Y, r)$ depends on the output Y and interest rates. Monetary policy has a direct effect on investment through interest rates r. The level of imports $M(Y, T, G, r, P_i)$ depends on consumption plus investment plus government spending G, on the domestic price level, and on the import price level P_i. The short-term interest rate $r(Y, \pi)$ depends on output Y and the rate of inflation π. The exchange rate depends on the short-term interest rate and the domestic price level. The export price level $X(P, P_w)$ in local currency depends on the domestic price level P and a world price level converted to local currency P_w.

The above mentioned correlation shows a complex functional relationship between the output (GDP) and the variables characterizing fiscal and monetary policies (controls G, T, and r). Moreover, as indicated earlier, the presence of the human factor does not enable us to describe this relationship in the analytical form, and researchers test various hypotheses and build various models to establish the relationship between the output and control variables based on the available past data.

The quality of the data is never as good as one would like, especially if a dynamic model is built. Nevertheless, the time series approach to develop models is widely used in practice.

In the 1960s, large Keynesian macroeconomic models are widely used for macroeconomic forecasts. Klein (1950) built an early prototype Keynesian econometric model with 16 equations. By the end of the 1960s, there were other econometric models with hundreds of equations. At the same time, one group of economists criticized these models and questioned their logical foundations, whereas the other group tried to improve the existing large macroeconomic models and develop the new ones. For example, Sims (1980) suggested using vector autoregressive (VAR) models for macroeconomic forecasting. He forecasted American GDP using linear VAR model, and then Litterman (1986) extended this work using the Bayesian VAR aiming on reducing VAR's parameters estimation. Many models estimate and forecast GDP based on selected important economic indicators (see, e.g., Diron, 2008).

Although many economists today use VAR models, many others continue to forecast with Keynesian macroeconomic models (called traditional macroeconomic models).

A simple version of an empirical Keynesian model is (see Eqs. (1.3) and (1.11))

$$C_t = \alpha_1 + \beta_1(Y_t - T_t) + \varepsilon_{1t} \tag{1.16}$$

$$I_t = \alpha_2 + \beta_2\left(i_t - \pi^e_{t+1}\right) + \varepsilon_{2t} \tag{1.17}$$

$$\pi_t = \alpha_3 + \frac{\beta_3 Y_t}{Y_t^p} + \varepsilon_{3t} \tag{1.18}$$

$$\pi^e_{t+1} = \alpha_4 \pi_t + \alpha_5 \pi_{t-1} \tag{1.19}$$

$$Y_t = C_t + I_t + G_t \tag{1.20}$$

where $t = 0, 1, 2, \ldots, N$; i is the nominal interest rate; π and π^e are the measured inflation and expected inflation, respectively; Y^p is the potential GDP, which represents the maximum sustainable level of output that the economy can produce; α_j ($j=1, 2, \ldots, 5$) and β_j ($j = 1, 2, 3$) are the regression coefficients; and ε_t are the regression errors.

Here the components of the simplified model (1.15) are used; the net exports term is not included in the model. The expression (1.18) is the consumption function, in which real consumer spending C depends on real disposable income $Y - T$ (see (Eq. 1.3)). In Eq. (1.17), business investment spending I is determined by the real interest rate $i - \pi^e$ (the expressions (1.1)–(1.15) present the basic theoretical aspect of the GDP calculation without considering the difference between real and nominal rates; some details are given in Appendix D). In Eq. (1.18), inflation is determined by the GDP Y relative to the potential GDP Y^p; in this simple model, this equation plays the role of the Phillips curve, representing the relationship between the rate of inflation and the unemployment rate—an indirect measure of slack in the economy. In Eq. (1.19), the expected inflation during the next period is presented by a weighted average (with the coefficients α_4 and α_5) of current inflation and the previous period inflation.

To use the above models for forecasting, one must first estimate the model coefficients, usually by ordinary least squares. In practice, forecasting by using this model would not produce satisfactory results. It can be determined based on low R^2 statistics for several equations. The problem with the R^2, as a measure of model validity, is that it can usually be increased by adding more variables into the model. The developed macroeconomic regression models with many parameters can satisfy a high R^2 criterion. Most macroeconomic data series related to the US economy are strongly serially correlated, so simply including one or more lags of the dependent variable in each equation will substantially boost the reported R^2 values (see Eqs. (1.17–1.19)). However, many other variables could serve equally well, and an additional criterion is needed to choose the proper model.

One more important requirement for accurate regression models is that the used data should follow a normal distribution or a Gaussian distribution; that is, it is assumed that the populations from which the samples are taken are normally distributed. Normality and other assumptions should be taken seriously, for when these assumptions do not hold, it is impossible to draw accurate and reliable conclusions about reality.

The main drawback of the Keynesian class of macroeconomic models is that they are linear and the future values of macroeconomic variables, in essence, are determined from static linear models. Within the finite time interval (e.g., a quarter or a year), usually a small samples size is available, which is insufficient to build an accurate regression model. However, enlarging the sample size by including data from several more time intervals, we deal with a stochastic process. Trying to predict its future behavior by considering the standard linear regression procedure does not look persuasive. Understanding this, statisticians who found in economics a new extensive field for the developed statistical approaches started testing dynamic regression models.

Some economists offered a different explanation of a low accuracy of traditional regression models. They indicated that once the model coefficients have been estimated, a forecaster would need future time paths for the model exogenous variables. For example, in the model (1.16)−(1.20), G, T, and the potential GDP are determined outside the model; the monetary policy actions immediately affect the federal funds rate that, in turn, influence short-term interest rates r, which then become an input in the forecasting process.

The linkage between nominal and real variables is an important component of econometric models with a large sample size, including many periods of the data collection process (typically most of economic data presented in time series form, that is, covering more than one time period— say the monthly unemployment rate for the past several years). Friedman (1968) criticized the simple Phillips curve, similar to Eq. (1.19). Lucas (1972) demonstrated that a Phillips curve could fit previously observed data well but would not be valid if the monetary policy process were to change, that is, the simple Phillips curve was not a stable, dependable relation.

The expressions (1.17)−(1.19) do not have a firm theoretical foundation. Moreover, Keynesian econometric models, even more complicated than considered above, are unable to predict the effects of government economic policy, especially its monetary policy. One of the key elements of traditional Keynesian models is that prices do not adjust promptly to equate supply and demand; usually, the reasons underlying sluggish price adjustment are not modeled. Thus the models cannot answer the question of to what extent, in response to a policy change, the sluggishness of price adjustment would change. The above mentioned drawback explains a fundamental change in the strategy of building macroeconomic models in the 1980s.

Formally, VAR models offer a very simple method of generating forecasts. The simplest reasonable forecast can be obtained by extrapolating the recent past. For example, the GDP growth rate can be presented as a weighted average of recent growth rates for the single period last observed. That weighted average would be an autoregressive forecast, and such forecasts are often used by economists, at least as benchmarks. The autoregressive model (AM) specifies that the output variable depends linearly on its own previous values and on a stochastic term (an error); thus the model has the form of a stochastic difference equation. This approach can be generalized by considering an autoregressive forecast of a vector of variables (see, e.g., Litterman, 1986). VARs are natural tools for forecasting and analysis.

The simplest possible vector autoregression model is given in Eqs. (1.21) and (1.22), with only two structural variables (Y and r—the GDP and interest rate, respectively) and only one time lag value used for each variable (it can be easily presented a model with more time lags and more variables):

$$Y_t = -a_{yr}r_t + b_{yr}r_{t-1} + b_{yy}Y_{t-1} + u_{yt} \tag{1.21}$$

$$r_t = -a_{ry}Y_t + b_{rr}r_{t-1} + b_{ry}Y_{t-1} + u_{rt} \tag{1.22}$$

The matrix form presentation of this system is

$$\left\| \begin{matrix} 1 & a_{yr} \\ a_{ry} & 1 \end{matrix} \right\| \left\| \begin{matrix} Y_t \\ r_t \end{matrix} \right\| = \left\| \begin{matrix} b_{yy} & b_{yr} \\ b_{ry} & b_{rr} \end{matrix} \right\| \left\| \begin{matrix} Y_{t-1} \\ r_{t-1} \end{matrix} \right\| + \left\| \begin{matrix} u_{yt} \\ u_{rt} \end{matrix} \right\| \tag{1.23}$$

where a_{ry}, a_{yr}, b_{yr}, b_{ry}, b_{rr}, and b_{yy} are the structural parameters; u_{rt} and u_{yt} are uncorrelated structural shocks with standard deviation σ_r and σ_y.

These equations cannot be estimated by ordinary least squares (OLS) because they violate the assumptions of the classical regression model: noncorrelation between the structural variable and the error term. Suppose in fact that we estimate Eq. (1.22) by OLS; the variable Y will be correlated with the error term u_r:

$$cov(Y_t, u_{rt}) = cov(-a_{yr}r_t + b_{yr}r_{t-1} + b_{yy}Y_{t-1} + u_{yt}, u_{rt})$$
$$= cov(-a_{yr}(-a_{ry}Y_t + b_{rr}r_{t-1} + b_{ry}Y_{t-1} + u_{rt})$$
$$+ b_{yr}r_{t-1} + b_{yy}Y_{t-1} + u_{yt}, u_{rt})$$
$$= a_{yr}a_{ry} \, cov(Y_t, u_{rt}) - a_{yr}\sigma_{ur}^2$$

so that

$$cov(Y_t, u_{rt}) = -\frac{a_{yr}\sigma_{ur}^2}{1 - a_{yr}a_{ry}}$$

OLS estimates of Eq. (1.22) will yield inconsistent estimates of the parameters of the model unless we assume that $a_{yr} = 0$; that is, the contemporaneous effect of interest rate shocks on output Y is zero.

However, if we present the model (1.23) in the form

$$\left\| \begin{matrix} Y_t \\ r_t \end{matrix} \right\| = \left\| \begin{matrix} 1 & a_{yr} \\ a_{ry} & 1 \end{matrix} \right\|^{-1} \left\| \begin{matrix} b_{yy} & b_{yr} \\ b_{ry} & b_{rr} \end{matrix} \right\| \left\| \begin{matrix} Y_{t-1} \\ r_{t-1} \end{matrix} \right\| + \left\| \begin{matrix} 1 & a_{yr} \\ a_{ry} & 1 \end{matrix} \right\|^{-1} \left\| \begin{matrix} u_{yt} \\ u_{rt} \end{matrix} \right\|$$

$$(1.24)$$

Y and r can be estimated by OLS, but the error terms of the two equations are now correlated across equations, which means that we cannot identify the structural parameters from the residuals of the two equations. The two residuals of Eq. (1.24) will be linked to the structural parameters by

$$\varepsilon_{1t} = \frac{1}{1 - a_{yr}a_{ry}} \left(u_{yt} - a_{yr}u_{rt} \right)$$

$$\varepsilon_{2t} = \frac{1}{1 - a_{yr}a_{ry}} \left(u_{rt} - a_{ry}u_{yt} \right)$$

For different forms of presenting the VAR models, there exist procedures of evaluating the parameters of the considered structures (see, e.g., Tsay, 2001; Stock and Watson, 2001).

An important VAR characteristic is the impulse response with respect to the error terms, that is, the reaction of the structural variables to a discrete-time impulse δ_t ($\delta_t = 1$, $t = 0$; $\delta_t = 0$, $t \neq 0$). The impulse response function is considered as a practical way of representing the behavior of economic variables in response to shocks to the vector δ_t.

According to estimates of many economists, VAR models have proven to be especially useful for describing the dynamic behavior of economic and financial time series and for forecasting. In addition to data description and forecasting, VAR models are also used for structural inference and policy analysis. In structural analysis, certain assumptions about the causal structure of the data under investigation are imposed. These causal impacts are usually summarized with impulse response functions and forecast error variance decompositions.

Structural VAR (SVAR) models allow one to examine the effect of deliberate policy actions or changes in the economy. In SVAR models, certain restrictions are imposed on their structure (e.g., on the matrices in Eq. (1.23)), so that the effect can be evaluated by considering the impulse response of the system. A major difficulty of the SVAR approach is that there exist no reliable empirical methods for testing a restriction. Moreover, if different models give different results, there are no accepted criteria that can be used to identify superior performance.

SVAR models to determine the spending multipliers were developed by Blanchard and Perotti (2002), Auerbach and Gorodnichenko (2012a,b), and Mountford and Uhlig (2009).

In the above equations, we considered only a purely stochastic process with zero mean. The expressions including also deterministic terms are more complicated (see, e.g., Tsay, 2001; Stock and Watson, 2001).

Traditionally, VAR models are developed for stationary variables without time trends. The basic stationary VAR model that contains constant deterministic terms may be too restrictive to represent sufficiently the main characteristics of the data. In particular, other deterministic terms such as a linear time trend or seasonal dummy variables may be required to represent the data properly; trends can be presented by deterministic polynomial terms (see Section 1.3). There exist VAR models with stochastic trends in economic variables (see, e.g., Johansen, 1995). In the case of trends in some of variables, it may be desirable to separate the long-run from the short-run dynamics. Vector error correction models offer a convenient framework for separating the long-run and short-run components of the data–generating process (see, e.g., Canova, 2007). Despite extensive VAR applications in economics, normality and other assumptions should be taken seriously, for when these assumptions do not hold, it is impossible to draw accurate and reliable conclusions. In addition, linear regression models, as well as linear dynamic models, work satisfactorily only in a small vicinity of a certain area. That is why enhancing models with too many details can decrease substantially their accuracy. It is questionable whether additional artificially generated data in VAR models by using Kalman filters (to disaggregate time series by related series, that is, from a quarterly to a monthly periodicity) can increase accuracy because it can only add errors in the model.

Sims (1980) and others economists criticized Keynesian models for not being based on intertemporal optimizing behavior of individuals. They argued that VARs held out the promise of providing a coherent and credible approach to data description, forecasting, structural inference, and policy analysis. The developed new models were based on new theoretical results and promised to analyze the effects of government policies. A new component of these models is the utility function, a function of the amounts of the various goods and services consumed.

Consumers are decision-makers. Each individual makes decisions to achieve a certain goal, which can be presented by a criterion: for example, some measure of the level of satisfaction from consumption decisions, which are limited by a consumer's budget. A utility function and a budget constraint emerge the choices that a consumer makes, and these terms are pivot elements of consumer theory. A utility function can have any number of arguments, each of which affects the consumer's overall satisfaction level.

Modern economic theory states that, in the face of uncertainty, consumers' decision-making is based on their subjective expected utility; that is, a utility function is a random variable. For example, Christiano et al. (2011) considering a simple New Keynesian model and analyzing its implications for the size of the government spending multiplier assume that the economy is populated by a representative household, whose lifetime utility U is given by

$$U = E_0 \sum_{t=0}^{\infty} \beta^t \left[\frac{\left(C_t^{\gamma}(1 - N_t)^{1-\gamma} \right)^{1-\sigma} - 1}{1 - \sigma} + v(G_t) \right] \tag{1.25}$$

where E_0 is the conditional expectation operator, and C_t, G_t, and N_t denote time (t) consumption, government consumption (spending focused to produce and provide services needed to the public—health, education, etc.), and hours worked, respectively; it is assumed that $\beta > 0$, $\sigma > 0$, $\gamma \in (0, 1)$ and that $v(.)$ is a concave function.

The household budget constraint is given by

$$P_t C_t + B_{t+1} = B_t(1 + R_t) + W_t N_t + T_t \tag{1.26}$$

where T_t denotes firms' profits net of lump-sum taxes paid to the government; B_{t+1} denotes the quantity of one-period bonds purchased by the household at time t; P_t denotes the price level and W_t denotes the nominal wage rate; and R_t denotes the one-period nominal rate of interest that pays off in period t.

The household's problem is to maximize the utility given by Eq. (1.25) subject to the budget constraint given by Eq. (1.26).

The above utility function is more complicated than the utility function

$$U = \frac{\left(C_t^{1-\varsigma} - 1 \right)}{(1 - \varsigma)} - \frac{\eta N_t^{1+\vartheta}}{(1 + \vartheta)} \tag{1.27}$$

used in the New Keynesian DSGE literature (dynamic stochastic general equilibrium model literature; see, e.g., Del Negro and Scorefheide, 2012) (η, ς, and ϑ are positive numbers). Complex stochastic models containing VAR models are increasingly being used by central banks around the world as tools for macroeconomic forecasting and policy analysis. Impulse responses obtained using a linear approximation of nonlinear equations diminish significantly the accuracy of analysis based on such models. As to the VARs used for forecasting, their accuracy is also problematic.

If Blanchard and Perotti (2002) and Auerbach and Gorodnichenko (2012a,b) calculate their multipliers by comparing the *peak* response of output with the *initial* government spending shock, Mountford and Uhlig (2009) compare the *cumulative* output response with the *cumulative* path of government spending. The authors obtained different multiplier values and argue which approach is correct. The more complicated model of Christiano et al. (2011) that includes the utility function (1.25) shows that the spending multiplier value can be significantly larger than that in the papers of the aforementioned authors.

Most of the aforementioned publications relate to the GDP forecasting models. The forecasts of interest rates, much as the stock market, are very difficult to predict, especially during periods of instability. They are often misguiding during crisis situations, the periods when a more accurate forecasting is needed. The reason for this inaccuracy is simple: interest rates reflect human behavior. Interest rates depend on the economic climate in individual countries and the world economy as a whole. Interest rates are functions of asset prices, so their dynamics can be studied using the apparatus of asset pricing theory. Finance theory provides some specific guidance when forming forecasts of future interest rates. Macroeconomic variables (such as output and inflation) can be added to a dynamic term structure (of interest rates) model to produce a macrofinance model (there exist models with more macro parameters). In this case the dynamics of interest rates link with the dynamics of the macro variables. However, some economists are skeptical that it can improve interest rates forecast. Neither their short-run movements nor the long-run trends are easily predicted using existing models. Some models forecast well over certain periods (see, e.g., Christensen et al., 2011). However, no forecast approach has been able to consistently improve upon the simple "random walk" model, which assumes that increases and decreases are equally likely and therefore always forecasts no change (Duffee, 2013). According to Bauer (2017), although a large variety of statistical and theoretical models have been developed to better understand the properties and determinants of interest rates, their forecast performance is typically disappointing (see also Elliott and Timmermann, 2013).

Many macroeconomic time series get revised multiple times by the statistical agencies that publish the series. In many cases the revisions reflect additional information that has been collected by the agencies; in other instances the revisions are caused by changes in definitions. For instance, the US Bureau of Economic Analysis publishes three releases of quarterly GDP in the first 3 months following the quarter. However, the data are deterministic, and it is not obvious why they should be interpreted as stochastic. Moreover, in some cases, time series can be interpreted as values of an unknown function, and its successful approximation (on a certain interval) would enable one to evaluate its future values, as well as generate data within the existing time intervals.

The choice of a class of approximating functions is a decisive factor for building the approximation model. When a practical problem is considered, it is important to take into account the available data and their accuracy (a kind of the noise signal characteristics of data). Formally, based on discrete data, a continuous function is constructed, which exactly fits the data. The problem of constructing such a continuous function is called data fitting. For example, the choice of Lagrange polynomials for estimates of future values of some economic parameters can be justified by the fact that this approach is based only on the available data time series.

The predicted value of the function $x(t)$ at moment t_{k+1} based on its values at moments t_k, t_{k-1}, ..., t_{k-n} can be presented in the form (see, e.g., Jeffreys and Jeffreys, 1988)

$$x(t_{k+1}) = \sum_{i=1}^{n} x(t_{k+1-i}) \prod_{j \neq i}^{n} \frac{t_{k+1} - t_{k+1-j}}{t_{k+1-i} - t_{k+1-j}} \qquad (1.28)$$

where the error of extrapolation

$$e(t_{k+1}) = \frac{x^{(n)}(\xi)\omega_n(t_{k+1})}{n!}. \quad \omega_n(t) = \prod_{i=1}^{n} (t - t_i),$$

$x^{(n)}(\xi)$ is the nth derivative of the function.

Under the assumption that the third derivative is small, the Lagrange method has the same order of accuracy as the second-order Taylor approximation. It requires only three consecutive data values and does not require information concerning the rate of change of data. The error estimate of the extrapolated values grows with the degree of the polynomial extrapolation. However, Mateescu (2008) demonstrates that polynomial interpolation and function approximation can be used for forecasting in some autoregression models (in the given example $k = 4$).

The structure of current models belonging to a theoretical branch of macroeconomics includes three blocks: households, firms, and government. The primary economic role of the household sector is consumption C (see Eqs. (1.1−1.3)). Lucas (1987) argued that it is vital to reflect in models how people form expectations and believed they are rational. The households block of the models contains a utility function (see, e.g., Eqs. (1.25−1.27)), characterizing consumers' preferences. Households are assumed to optimize their preferences (maximize the utility function), subject to constraints they face. Firms are assumed to maximize profits, subject to their production plans being technologically feasible (their output is presented by the aggregated production function Y). Government uses its political tools (spending G, taxes T, money supply, etc.) to provide its economic policy subject to budget constraints.

In general case, the models with two maximization criteria describe multiobjective problems that have no single solution. There exist a number of Pareto optimal solutions, and an additional criterion is needed to make decision concerning the chosen Pareto solution. Narrowing the separate criteria to get a unique solution can make the model less accurate. The indicated earlier recent results in behavioral economics challenging a rational behavior of people question the validity of complex utility function. Although during crises, patterns in human behavior are more probable than in our everyday life, there is no need to describe them as an optimization process.

Economic equilibrium, a condition in the economy in which the quantity of aggregate demand equals the quantity of aggregate supply, is indispensable part of macroeconomic theory and analysis of modern macroeconomic models. Usually, this condition is chosen to evaluate the economy (output, prices, unemployment, inflation, etc.). The concept of equilibrium relates mainly to the mathematical mode of analysis—static and dynamic. Static equilibrium is central in the classical economics, which assumes that market prices always tend toward a long-run natural price. In dynamic models, equilibrium relates mostly to an end-state process. The trajectory of the transient process (excluding its end point) does not correspond to equilibrium state. The state of the economy during the transient mode leading to equilibrium as an end state (which can be inadmissible) is of importance. However, this problem is absolutely ignored by scientists. Showing that equilibrium existence publications does not prove its uniqueness and/or robustness. Moreover, the so-called *disequilibrium analysis* (see Malinvaud, 1977) shows that a steady point of the dynamic process can exist when demand can differ from supply.

The equilibrium conditions and theorems related to equilibrium of many macroeconomic models have no relation to economic reality because they are based on highly unrealistic assumptions, so that they cannot serve as reliable practical tools. Additionally, Austrian economic school pays special attention to a market economy as a system for encouraging the search for profitable opportunities, in contrast to neoclassical fixation with equilibrium.

As mentioned, many existing models are used to predict future economic activity. However, forecasting using historical data is tricky business. Past performance is not necessarily a good indicator of future performance. The types of models discussed above can work satisfactorily for short-run forecasts during a nonturbulent economic environment. However, they are not reliable for public policy analysis. The 2008 financial crisis was also a crisis for economic forecasting. The sophisticated forecasting systems of the Federal Reserve Board and the International Monetary Fund failed to predict the crisis. The financial sector of economies, where level of risk is significantly greater than that of the physical sciences and engineering and where the human factor demonstrates its unpredictability, is the most difficult economic component to describe properly in the models.

During and after the 2008 financial crisis, there were many publications that blamed macroeconomic theory, its models, and scientists working in this area for being unable to predict the crisis. It looks like such accusations are unfair. There are several definitions of macroeconomics, and none contains the word "crisis." The most concise and precise definition defines macroeconomics as the branch of economics that studies the behavior and performance of an economy as a whole and focuses on the aggregate changes in the economy such as unemployment, growth rate, GDP, and inflation. Demand from macroeconomics to forecast crises is equivalent to demand from medicine to predict new unknown infectious diseases. Similar to developed methods to mitigate disease spreading and eradicate it, macroeconomics should develop reliable methods to curtail economic crises and restore the economy in a short period of time. One of the important objectives of macroeconomics is minimizing the occurrence and durations of recessions. A real macroeconomic theory should provide government with tools to fight crisis situations, to respond efficiently when depressions happen. Dealing with such threatening events is an important part of government public policy. Applied macroeconomics models should provide necessary tools to do that.

In contrast to pure theories that explain mechanisms of various processes and phenomena, applied theories answer questions of practical relevance. Efficient models should be concise and operate with minimal number of variables related to the problem under consideration. Such models should be convenient to use.

Any government economic policies are deterministic actions so that for the efficient analysis of such actions, deterministic models can be veryuseful. Deterministic macroeconomics models include certain economic endogenous parameters that characterize the results of human activity (e.g., GDP, debt, employment, growth rate) and parameters (e.g., government spending, taxes) that reflect actions directed to reach certain goals, adopted and pursued by a government, political party, or ruler, that is, to implement a certain economic policy (fiscal and/or monetary).

It looks logical to build different models for economic forecasting and policy analysis. It is not necessary that the same model be used for both. As to forecasts, we should rely not only on the model equations but also on our economic judgments, our intuitive insights. (Information is a mother of intuition.) The models for policy analysis that include parameters obtained from the forecasting models would be small-scale models convenient for scenario-based decision-making.

It is known that at the initial stages of resolving complex problems, more simple models give more reliable estimates than complex dynamic models that contain many uncertain parameters. Below we demonstrate how reliable forecasting results related to a certain government policy can be obtained by building a simplified model with respect to a lower estimate, rather than the precise value, of an economic parameter and how to obtain a more precise estimate based on additional information concerning the model parameters.

1.7 THE DEBT TO GROSS DOMESTIC PRODUCT RATIO AS A COMPROMISED EFFICIENCY CRITERION

In 1981, in his first inaugural address, Ronald Reagan said: "You and I, as individuals, can, by borrowing, live beyond our means, but for only a limited period of time. Why, then, should we think that collectively, as a nation, we are not bound by that same limitation?" As a counterargument, one can say that there is nothing wrong in government borrowing if it is making public investments at the same time—bridges and highways, medical research, education—anything that will pay off in the long run. The problem with this argument is that the payoff almost never comes back to the government. Usually, such investment spending accumulates debt. Total debt as a percentage of income—the bank debt ratio—is widely used to determine the level at which businesses can afford to owe. Similar to this ratio, the debt to GDP ratio was introduced.

Harvard economists Reinhart and Rogoff (2009, 2010) used the debt to GDP ratio to measure the impact of debt on the economy. According to Reinhart and Rogoff (2009), debt to GDP ratios below a threshold of 90% of GDP ratios have no significant impact on growth; above the threshold of 90%, median growth rates fall by 1%, and average growth falls considerably more.

Reinhart and Rogoff (2009) collected data on dozens of countries across hundreds of years to document the rise and fall of debt. They divided the data into four categories (debt that is between 0% and 30% of a country's GDP, that is between 30% and 60%, that is between 60% and 90%, and that exceeds 90%) and examined the average growth rate of all country/year observations in each of the four categories. For their entire sample and for the United States, there is no significant difference in the growth rates in any of the first three categories. However, for both the entire sample and the United States, average growth rates in years where debt exceeds 90% of GDP are significantly lower.

Critics indicate that Reinhart and Rogoff assume that causality runs from higher debt levels to slower contemporaneous economic growth, whereas there is considerable reason to believe that causality may run the exact opposite direction; that is, slow economic growth may lead to higher levels of debt as revenues fall and spending increases. However, conclusions, supported by fuzzy statistics, prove nothing. There is no direct relationship between debt and economic growth. Many intermediate factors influence the values of these variables, and the statistical methods ignoring these factors cannot bring any reliable results.

Recently, Herndon et al. (2013) found an error in calculation of the threshold; they indicate that the average real GDP growth rate for countries carrying a debt to GDP ratio of over 90% is actually 2.2%, and the relationship between national debt and GDP growth varied significantly by time period and country. The discovered error added critic that there exists a well-defined threshold of the debt to GDP ratio above which economic growth becomes very small.

Despite the mentioned error, the obtained results of Reinhart and Rogoff (2010) are qualitatively correct: higher government debt, as a percentage of GDP, usually leads to slower economic growth. The earlier quoted President Reagan words are the best confirmation of the usefulness of Reinhart and Rogoff results.

As mentioned above, there exists no functional relationship between the GDP growth rate and debt and it would be useless to try finding it. There is no a rigorous proof that a high current debt will necessarily harm future economic growth. Even the question *"Does high debt cause poor economic growth or does poor economic growth lead to higher debt?"* is not correctly formulated. Historical examples show that both cases are possible. Countries that pursue irresponsible economic policies experience economic fall down and even financial crises. In its turn, an economic downturn produces higher debt if economic policies remain unchanged and nothing is done to fight a recession. However, it is also true that misguided austerity focused to decrease debt can produce weaker economic growth and less deficit reduction than policymakers would expect.

All depends on a concrete situation: Circumstances and government economic policy matter. The analysis of the US government debt over the past 70 years shows its huge change from high levels at the end of World War II to large budget surpluses in 2001. After World War II the US government spending fell from 42% of GDP in 1945 to 15% in 1947, but the country's debt was high. During the next three decades, although the economy grew faster than the debt, the debt rose from $219 to $640 billion. Starting in the mid-1970s, debt began to grow faster than GDP. The Gramm—Rudman—Hollings Balanced Budget and Emergency Deficit Control Act of 1985 and the Balanced Budget and Emergency Deficit Control Reaffirmation Act of 1987 were the first binding spending constraints on the federal budget and were early serious efforts to control deficits. However, Gramm—Rudman—Hollings failed to prevent large budget deficits, which, as well as debt, rose in 1990—91.

An economic boom in the United States, a lucky period of economic prosperity, generated by the innovations in the information technology and Internet-related areas, during which GDP grew continuously by an average of 4% per year for almost 10 years (the longest recorded expansion in the US history; since 2001, it is never grown by as much as 4%, and since 2005 not even by 3% for a whole year), produced the remarkable turnaround that generated the Balanced Budget Act of 1997, designed to balance the federal budget by 2002, and projections that current economic policies would continue to produce budget surpluses and declining debt. However, the budgets quickly fell out of balance after 2000 (surpluses were only in 1998–2001) and have run consistent and substantial deficits since then, so that the country's debt reached such a dangerous level that it became a hot and incredibly polarizing political topic.

Debt "leader" Japan is over 230%, Greece is just under 177%, with Italy in the third place at 133% of GDP. The United States is in the 14th place (of 34) with debt equal to 77% of GDP if we count only public debt and is among five leaders, if consider the national debt (i.e., include governmental holdings). Government spenders demonstrate modesty and prefer to be considered in the middle rather than among the mentioned leaders. Economists criticizing Reinhart and Rogoff (2009) believe that the 90% threshold for government debt should not be used as a guide for US fiscal policy. It is possible to argue concerning the value of the threshold level but it is impossible not to react when the national debt is close or exceeds 100% of GDP.

There exists justifiable criticism of the debt to GDP ratio as the insufficiently informative and most overused economic index. The mentioned ratio as if ignores important parameters such as the interest rates associated with the debt and when the debt matures. Some economists state that the debt to GDP ratio is a very poor measure of the health of a nation or its economy; the best measures are real GDP per capita, real GDP growth rates, unemployment rate, and inflation rate. Nevertheless, many economists and leading economic organizations use GDP and debt to GDP ratio to evaluate the health of the country's economy and its ability to handle the increasing debt load and to predict the future economic environment. The European Union requires that member state's national debt not exceed 60% of GDP.

Despite criticism of the debt to GDP ratio, it can serve as a compromised criterion of economic efficiency because it includes GDP that the government tries to increase to maintain a strong economy and debt that any sober economic policy should try to decrease or, at least, limit. The developed models enable one to evaluate economic policies based on this criterion. Some parameters of these models can be obtained from forecasting models. The higher the accuracy of the forecasting parameters, the higher the accuracy of the analyzed economic policies. Remembering the phrase "a good forecaster is not smarter than everybody else, he merely has his ignorance better organized," it is worthwhile to test several values of these parameters. This would enable decision-makers to examine several scenarios. Comparing various scenarios and economic strategies is a part of the optimal decision-making process.

In the next chapter, the debt to GDP ratio dynamics model is used to consider the impact of expansionary fiscal policy intended to increase economic growth by using stimulus spending and tax cuts, implemented separately or simultaneously.

REFERENCES

Alesina, A., Ardagna, S., Perotti, R., Schiantarelli, F., 2002. Fiscal policy, profitability and investment. The American Economic Review 571−589.

Atkinson, R.D., 2006. Supply-side Follies: Why Conservative Economics Fails, Liberal Economics Falters, and Innovation Economics Is the Answer. Rowman and Littlefield, Lanham.

Auerbach, A.J., Gorodnichenko, Y., 2012a. Fiscal multipliers in recession and expansion. In: Alesina, A., F.Giavazzi (Eds.), Fiscal Policy after the Financial Crisis. University of Chicago Press, Chicago.

Auerbach, A.J., Gorodnichenko, Y., 2012b. Measuring the output responses to fiscal policy. American Economic Journal: Economic Policy 4, 1−27.

Barro, R.J., Redlick, C.J., 2011. Macroeconomic effects from government purchases and taxes. Quarterly Journal of Economics 126 (1), 51−102.

Batini, N., Eyraud, L., Forni, L., Weber, A., 2014. Fiscal Multipliers: Size, Determinants, and Use in Macroeconomic Projections, IMF. International Monetary Fund, Washington.

Bauer, M., July 31, 2017. Bridging the gap: forecasting interest rates with macro trends. Economic Letter 21.

Bernanke, B., April 27, 2010. Speech Before the National Commission on Fiscal Responsibility and Reform, 2011 Reform: Achieving Fiscal Sustainability. www. Federalreserve.gov.

Blanchard, O., Perotti, R., 2002. An empirical characterization of the dynamic effects of changes in government spending and taxes on output. Quarterly Journal of Economics 117 (4), 1344−1347.

Blanchard, O., Dell'Ariccia, G., Mauro, P., February 12, 2010. Rethinking Macroeconomic Policy. IMF Staff Position Note.

Blanchard, O., Leigh, D., 2013. Growth forecast errors and fiscal multipliers. The American Economic Review: Papers and Proceedings 103 (3), 117−120.

Broda, C., Parker, J., 2014. The economic stimulus payments of 2008 and the aggregate demand for consumption,. Journal of Monetary Economics 68, 20−36.

Canova, F., 2007. Methods for Applied Macroeconomic Research. Princeton University Press, Princeton.

Carlson, K., Spencer, R., 1975. Crowding Out and Its Critics, Federal Reserve Bank of St. Louis. www.utm.edu/staff/davidt/finance/ISLM/Crowding_Dec1975.pdf.

Christensen, J., Diebold, F., Rudebusch, G., 2011. The affine arbitrage-free class of Nelson-Siegel term structure models. Journal of Econometrics 164 (1), 4−20.

Christiano, L., Eichenbaum, M., Rebelo, S., 2011. When is the government spending multiplier large. Journal of Political Economy 119 (1), 78−121.

Corsetti, G., Meier, A., Muller, G., 2012. What determines government spending multipliers? Economic Policy 521–565.

Del Negro, M., Scorefheide, F., 2012. DSGE Model-based Forecasting. Federal Reserve Bank of New York, Staff Report No. 554.

Diron, M., 2008. Short-term forecasts of Euro area real GDP growth: an assessment of real-time performance based on vintage data. Journal of Forecasting 27, 371–390.

Duffee, G., 2013. Forecasting interest rates chapter 7. In: Elliott, G., Timmermann, A. (Eds.), Handbook of Economic Forecasting, vol. 2A. Elsevier, , Amsterdam.

Eggertsson, G.B., Krugman, P., 2012. Debt, deleveraging, and the liquidity trap: a Fisher–Minsky–Koo approach. Quarterly Journal of Economics 127 (3), 1469–1513.

Elliott, G., Timmermann, A., 2013. Handbook of Economic Forecasting, vols. 2A–2B. Elsevier, Amsterdam.

Filipe, J., Adams, G., 2005. The estimation of the Cobb-Douglas function: a retrospective view. Eastern Economic Journal 31 (3), 427–445.

Friedman, M., 1968. The role of monetary policy. The American Economic Review 58 (1), 1–17.

Gechert, S., Will, H., 2012. Fiscal Multipliers: A Meta Regression Analysis, Institut für Makroökonomie und Konjunkturforschung (Macroeconomic Policy Institute), Working Paper 97. http://www.boeckler.de/pdf/p_imk_wp_97_2012.pdf.

Hall, B., Woodward, S., 2008. Options for Stimulating the Economy. http//woodwardhall.wordpress.com/2008/12/08/options-for-stimulating-the-economy.

Hall, B., Woodward, S., 2009. Fiscal Stimulus: More Needed? https://woodwardhall.wordpress.com/2009/02/01/fiscal-stimulus-more-needed.

Heim, J., 2008. The consumption function. Review of Business Research 8 (2), 18–36.

Heim, J., 2012. Does crowd out Hamper government stimulus programs in recessions? Journal of Applied Business and Economics 13 (2), 11–27.

Herndon, T., Ash, M., Pollin, R., 2013. Does High Public Debt Consistently Stifle Economic Growth? A Critique of Reinhart and Rogoff. Political Economy Research Institute, Working Paper Series 322. University of Massachusetts, Amherst.

International Monetary Fund, 2009. The State of Public Finances: Outlook and Medium-term Policies After the 2008 Crisis. International Monetary Fund, Washington.

Ilzetzki, E., Mendoza, E.G., Végh, C.A., 2013. How big (small?) are fiscal multipliers? Journal of Monetary Economics 60 (2), 239–254.

Jeffreys, H., Jeffreys, B., 1988. Lagrange's interpolation formula. In: Methods of Mathematical Physics. Cambridge University Press, Cambridge, England.

Johansen, S., 1995. Likelihood-based Inference in Cointegrated Vector Autoregression Model. Oxford University Press, Oxford.

Keynes, J.M., 1936. The General Theory of Employment, Interest, and Money. Hareourt, Brace and Company, New York.

Keynes, J.M., 1998. The Collected Writings of John Maynard Keynes. Cambridge University Press, Cambridge.

Klein, L., 1950. Economic Fluctuations in the United States 1921–1941. Wiley, New York.

Krugman, P., August 11, 2010. Reinhart and Rogoff are confusing me. New York Times.

Krugman, P., August 20, 2011. Fancy theorists of the world unite. The New York Times.

Kumar, M.S., Woo, J., 2010. Public Debt and Growth, IMF Working Paper No.10/174.

Litterman, R., 1986. Forecasting with Bayesian vector autoregressions. Five years of experience. Journal of Business & Economic Statistics 4, 25–38.

Lucas Jr., R., 1972. Expectations and the neutrality of money. Journal of Economic Theory 4, 103–124.

Lucas, R.E., 1987. Models of Business Cycles. Basil Blackwell, New York.

Malinvaud, E., 1977. The theory of unemployment reconsidered. In: Yrjö Jahnsson Lectures. Blackwell, Oxford.

Mankiw, G., 2008. Spending and Tax Multipliers, Greg Mankiw's Blog. http://www.aei.org/publication/spending-and-tax-multipliers.

Mateescu, G., 2008. Polynomial interpolation and applications to autoregressive models. Romanian Journal of Economic Forecasting 1, 119–129.

Mountford, A., Uhlig, H., 2009. What Are the Effects of Fiscal Policy Shocks? Journal of Applied Econometrics 24 (6), 960–992.

Nickel, C., Tudyka, A., 2013. Fiscal Stimulus in Times of High Debt: Reconsidering Multipliers and Twin Deficits, Working Paper Series, 1513. European Central Bank.

Nickel, C., Vansteenkiste, I., 2008. Fiscal Policies, the Current Account and Ricardian Equivalence. European Central Bank, Working Paper Series, No. 935. http://www.ecb.europa.eu/pub/pdf/scpwps/ecbwp935.pdf.

Panizza, U., Presbitero, A., 2012. Public Debt and Economic Growth: Is There a Causal Effect? MoFiR Working Paper, No. 65.

Perotti, R., 1999. Fiscal policy in good times and bad. Quarterly Journal of Economics 114 (4), 1399–1436.

Poterba, J., Rotemberg, J., Summers, L., 1986. A tax-based test for nominal rigidities. The American Economic Review 76 (4), 659–675.

Ramey, V.A., 2011. Can government purchases stimulate the economy? Journal of Economic Literature 49 (3), 673–685.

Reinhart, C.M., Rogoff, K.S., 2009. This Time Is Different: Eight Centuries of Financial Folly. University Press, Princeton, NJ.

Reinhart, C.M., Rogoff, K.S., 2010. Growth in a time of debt. The American Economic Review: Papers and Proceedings 100 (2), 573–578.

Romer, C., Bernstein, J., 2009. The Job Impact of the American Recovery and Reinvestment Plan. http://otrans.3cdn.net/45593e8ecbd339d074_l3m6bt1te.pdf.

Romer, C., Romer, D., 2010. The macroeconomic effects of tax changes: estimates based on a new measure of fiscal shocks. The American Economic Review 100, 763–801.

Ross, W.D., 1957. Aristotelis Politica. Oxford University Press, Oxford.

Simon, H.A., Levy, F.K., 1963. A note on the Cobb-Douglas function. The Review of Economic Studies 30, 93–94.

Sims, C., 1980. Macroeconomics and reality. Econometrica 48, 1–48.

Stock, J., Watson, M., 2001. Vector autoregressions. The Journal of Economic Perspectives 15, 101–115.

Tsay, R., 2001. Analysis of Financial Time Series. John Wiley & Sons, New York.

Woodford, M., 2011. Simple analytics of the government expenditure multiplier. American Economic Journal: Macroeconomics 3 (1), 1–35.

Yanushevsky, R., 2011. Guidance of Unmanned Aerial Vehicles. Taylor & Francis, New York.

CHAPTER TWO

Fiscal Stimulus Policy

Contents

A promise made is a debt unpaid.

Proverb

2.1 INTRODUCTION

The literature on the relationship between government debt and economic growth is scarce. However, the findings of both Herndon et al. (2013) and Reinhart and Rogoff (2009) are suggestive, rather than conclusive, because they operate with historic data. It is dangerous to build future financial policy by using blindly such findings because pictures of the world economy are changing with time, and statistics of the past may not apply to a current or future economic situation in a country. More reliable mathematical models should be developed.

Although constraints on spending and borrowing have grown, many governments have been emphasizing the importance of infrastructure in assisting economic growth. A number of countries have explicitly recognized this as part of their stimulus packages. As mentioned in Chapter 1, $840 billion stimulus package enacted by the US Congress contained $105 billion for infrastructure, which is significantly less than $2.5 trillion worth of stimulus launched by the Chinese government, most of which went to special purpose vehicles to build rail, bridges, airports, condo buildings, etc. Many economists consider the overinvestment undertaken in China as an attempt to avert an economic slowdown.

Applied Macroeconomics for Public Policy
ISBN: 978-0-12-815632-2
https://doi.org/10.1016/B978-0-12-815632-2.00002-X

49

Paul Krugman believes that $105 billion for infrastructure was insufficient to ignite the economy. He argued that the stimulus was too small to have a major impact, and he pushed for more stimulus. Krugman questioned the validity of the aforementioned finding related to the linkage between government debt and economic growth (Krugman, 2012). He criticized the conclusion that stepping over the 90% "border" of the debt to GDP ratio is harmful for growth and believed that increasing government debt can increase growth, if the money is invested well, which he links to infrastructure spending (Krugman, 2012). Although the impact of government spending programs in the past that were intended to increase economic growth by using infrastructure-focused stimulus packages was very modest and did not restore economic activity, Krugman (2012) states that "fiscal expansion will be even better for America's future if a large part of the expansion takes the form of public investment — of building roads, repairing bridges and developing new technologies, all of which makes the nation richer in the long-run." For him, big government spending is a solution of problems of high unemployment and low GDP growth: "But the essential point is that what we really need to get out of this current depression is another burst of government spending."

Krugman believes that it is the debt to GDP ratio that matters and not the debt itself. In Krugman (2009) he wrote: "How, then, did America pay down its debt? Actually, it didn't… But the economy grew, so the ratio of debt to GDP fell, and everything worked out fiscally… Which brings me to a question a number of people have raised: maybe we can pay the interest, but what about repaying the principal? …But why would we have to do that? Again, the lesson of the 1950s — or, if you like, the lesson of Belgium and Italy, which brought their debt-GDP ratios down from early 90s levels — is that you need to stabilize debt, not pay it off; economic growth will do the rest." Being a supporter of Keynesian economic doctrine, he believes that it is governments' role to create jobs—more teachers, construction workers for public works projects, etc.—when the private sector cannot, and that such a strategy results in economic growth, so the ratio of debt to GDP should fall, and everything should work out fiscally.

Research results related to the debt to GDP ratio were based mostly on analysis of the existing statistical economic data. Different conclusions and the following disputes reflect different interpretations by economists of the available statistical material. Using regression models and/or the existing historic data, most of the aforementioned publications examined the impact of government spending to stimulate the economy on GDP or analyzed the influence of the debt to GDP ratio on economic growth. However, they did not establish the direct relationship between the GDP, the related government spending, and the debt to GDP ratio.

Models describing the debt to GDP ratio dynamics will be considered to examine the linkage between the GDP growth rate, the related government spending maintained by taxes and government borrowing (its effect is presented by related fiscal multipliers), and the debt to GDP ratio (see also Yanushevsky and Yanushevsky, 2013; Yanushevsky and Yanushevsky, 2014; Yanushevsky and Yanushevsky, 2017). Based on the developed models giving the lower estimate of the debt to GDP ratio, the impact of expansionary fiscal policy intended to reduce unemployment and increase economic growth by using stimulus packages is analyzed. The models are used to analyze whether government stimulus spending or/and tax cuts can improve the economic situation or this policy increases a national debt to such a degree that the debt to GDP ratio becomes dangerously high.

Considering fiscal stimulus policy, we pay main attention to the effect of government investment in infrastructure. This measure increases employment faster than other stimulus spending (e.g., increased spending on welfare). First, the debt to GDP ratio dynamics model describing government stimulus related to investment in infrastructure is considered. It is shown that a similar model can be used to analyze tax cut measures to boost the economy, as well as the combination of the considered separately stimuli—tax cut and investment in infrastructure. A generalized debt to GDP ratio dynamics model is developed to obtain more accurate estimates of the debt to GDP ratio, especially for the case when the considered fiscal stimuli are accompanied by a proper monetary policy.

2.2 THE DEBT TO GDP RATIO DYNAMICS FOR FISCAL EXPENDITURE STIMULUS

The debt dynamics can be described by the following equation:

$$\dot{D}(t) = rD(t) + G(t) - T(t) \qquad (2.1)$$

where $D(t)$ is general government debt; r is the interest rate on debt; $G(t)$ and $T(t)$ are government purchases (expenditure excluding interest payments on debt) and revenues, respectively.

Government revenues are presented in the form

$$T(t) = \tau Y(t) \qquad (2.2)$$

where τ is a tax rate and the Cobb–Douglas function $Y(t)$ represents GDP (in many models, the Cobb–Douglas function is used as the estimation and forecasting of GDP from the supply side).

$$Y(t) = AK^{\alpha}(t)L^{\beta}(t) \tag{2.3}$$

where A is a measure of technology and α and β are the output elasticities of capital K and labor L, respectively.

The Cobb–Douglas functional form of production functions and its modifications are widely used to represent the relationship of an output to inputs in macro- and microeconomic models (see, e.g., Glomm and Ravikumar, 1997). Various economic models, starting from the Solow growth model (see, e.g., Romer, 2006), used the Cobb–Douglas function to examine long-run growth analytically and determine the economy's balanced-growth path. If initially capital was represented by one parameter, later in some models private and public capitals were considered separately (see, e.g., Aschauer's, 1989; Cassou and Lansing, 1998; Glomm and Ravikumar, 1994, 1997; Lynde and Richmond, 1993; Munnell, 1990). Economists began to study the influence of government spending on consumption-savings decisions in models, which allow the possibility of persistent growth; long-run growth models with productive government spending combine several goods and services, such as roads and highways, sewer systems, harbors, and public sector R&D, together into one category called public capital. Government spending is maintained by taxes and government borrowing. To obtain visible analytical results, the mentioned models contain unrealistic assumptions, such as that the government budget is balanced and tax revenues are used only to finance public investment in infrastructure (see Glomm and Ravikumar, 1997).

In contrast to the aforementioned long-run dynamic models operating with private and public capitals, the model developed below belongs to the so-called short-run models (Yanushevsky and Yanushevsky, 2013). It analyzes the situation when a certain government policy focuses to move the economy on a more productive stage. Usually, such a situation is characterized by the unbalanced government budget, significant debt, and unemployment. This situation was during the 2008 economic crisis in the United States and European countries. Because the opinion of economists, mostly only supported by chosen historic examples, diverges whether government spending focused on infrastructure can improve the economic situation, the developed debt to GDP ratio dynamics model focuses to resolve this problem rigorously. It analyzes, under the aforementioned conditions, the relationship between government spending on infrastructure, GDP, and the debt to GDP ratio.

The debt to GDP ratio $d(t) = D(t)/Y(t)$ dynamics can be presented as

$$\dot{d}(t) = \left(\frac{D(t)}{Y(t)} \right)' = \frac{\dot{D}(t)}{Y(t)} - \frac{D(t)}{Y(t)} \frac{\dot{Y}(t)}{Y(t)} = \frac{\dot{D}(t)}{Y(t)} - g d(t) \qquad (2.4)$$

where

$$\dot{Y}(t) = g Y(t) \qquad (2.5)$$

$$g = \alpha \frac{\dot{K}}{K} + \beta \frac{\dot{L}}{L} \qquad (2.6)$$

g is a GDP growth rate (see also Appendix A).

Substituting Eq. (2.1) in Eq. (2.4) and using Eq. (2.2), we obtain

$$\dot{d}(t) = (r - g)d(t) + \frac{G(t)}{Y(t)} - \tau \qquad (2.7)$$

Practical application of Eq. (2.7) requires knowledge of $G(t)$ and $Y(t)$. However, these parameters are interconnected. In reality, we deal with a system of equations because $Y(t)$ depends on $\dot{K}(t)$ and $\dot{L}(t)$ (see Eqs. (2.5) and (2.6)), and Eq. (2.7) should be supplemented with equations describing dynamics of capital K and labor L. Analysis of such a system presents substantial difficulties, especially when it is necessary to predict future values of the debt to GDP ratio. Below we use Eq. (2.7) to build the model that allows us to obtain the analytical solution of the lower estimate of $d(t)$ (see also Yanushevsky and Yanushevsky, 2014).

Let $t = t_0$, $g = g_0 < r$, and $G(t_0) = l_0 T(t_0)$, $l_0 > 1$, (l_0 characterizes the ratio between government expenditure, excluding interest payments on debt, and its revenues, so that $l_0 > 1$ assumes the revenues to be less than the expenditures).

As indicated above, one of the approaches to stimulate GDP growth and employment is the use of additional government spending $\Delta G(t)$ to resuscitate the economy by investing in infrastructure—repair and build roads, bridges, etc. It is assumed that with the increasing number of working people, the consumption will rise and this will stimulate economic growth. This approach was tested in a case of economic recessions—significant decline in the economic activity and high unemployment—and is recommended by many economists as the necessary cure for the economic slump.

The multiple effect of infrastructure spending will be presented by the multiplier $l_1 > 1$, the ratio of a change in the GDP to the change in government spending $\Delta G(t)$ that causes it (see, e.g., Auerbach and Gorodnichenko, 2012a,b; Blanchard and Perotti, 2002; Christiano et al., 2011; Leeper et al., 2010; Ramey, 2011).

Although the mentioned publications analyze the multipliers dynamics, usually in practice, in simulation models, the multiplier is presented as a constant parameter. Because additional government spending contributes to the national debt, it is of importance to determine whether the projected future economic growth (in accordance with a chosen multiplier) is sustained with the resulting national debt.

The model analyzed below corresponds to the case of declining economic activity, substantial debt, and high unemployment. It is assumed that at $t = t_0$ $\dot{L}(t_0) = 0$, and for $t > t_0$, when the government stimulus package focuses infrastructure, the GDP growth rate $g_1 > g_0$ can be achieved by increasing employment, i.e., in Eq. (2.6) for $t > t_0$, $\dot{L}(t) > 0$.

The assumption that the rate change is implemented immediately, i.e., the related government spending takes effect without delay, which usually contradicts reality (inevitable delays may produce even the opposite effect), will allow us to consider the obtained debt to GDP ratio estimate as optimistic.

Assuming that the taxes remain unchanged, the additional government spending $\Delta G(t)$ at $t \geq t_0$ to increase $Y(t)$ and make it growing with the rate $g_1 > g_0$, i.e.,

$$Y(t) = Y(t_0)e^{g_1(t-t_0)}, \quad t \geq t_0 \tag{2.8}$$

should be

$$\Delta G(t) = l_G^{-1}\left(e^{g_1(t-t_0)} - e^{g_0(t-t_0)}\right)Y(t_0) \tag{2.9}$$

(the above equation follows directly from the definition of the fiscal multiplier l_G).

As indicated earlier, the assumption that the rate change is implemented immediately will allow us to obtain an optimistic estimate of the debt to GDP ratio. In addition, we assume that the basic government spending $G(t) = l_3 Y(t)$ is not only frozen at $t = t_0$ (as a percent of GDP; see Eq. (2.2)), but for $t > t_0$ it will decrease by $\Delta G_1(t)$ because of the increase in employment, which can be evaluated by using Eq. (2.6) and considering the derivative of $L_1(t)/L_0(t)$, where L_1 and L_0 characterize employment for the GDP growth rates g_1 and g_0, respectively, i.e.,

$$\left(\frac{L_1}{L_0}\right)' = \frac{g_1 - \alpha \dfrac{\dot{K_1}}{K_1}}{\beta} \frac{L_1}{L_0} - \frac{g_0 - \alpha \dfrac{\dot{K_0}}{K_0}}{\beta} \frac{L_1}{L_0}$$

$$= \frac{g_1 - g_0 - \alpha \left(\dfrac{\dot{K_1}}{K_1} - \dfrac{\dot{K_0}}{K_0}\right)}{\beta} \frac{L_1}{L_0}, \quad \frac{L_1(t_0)}{L_0(t_0)} = 1 \qquad (2.10)$$

where K_i is capital corresponding to g_i, $i = 0, 1$.

Neglecting the term in parenthesis that describes the growth rate of capital and solving Eq. (2.10), we obtain the upper estimate of $\Delta G_1(t)$ (this term can only decrease the value of L_1/L_0) as

$$\Delta G_1(t) = d_2 G(t_0)\left(e^{\frac{g_1 - g_0}{\beta}(t - t_0)} - 1\right) \qquad (2.11)$$

where l_2 characterizes the percent of welfare-related spending at $t = t_0$; the values of $c > 0$ reflect a country's welfare policy and structure; because the mentioned term can only decrease the value of L_1/L_0, to simplify the model, we ignore this term and operate with the increased rate of employment $(g_1 - g_0)\beta^{-1}$ (this simplification, as well as that mentioned earlier, gives an optimistic estimate of the debt to GDP ratio).

Based on Eqs. (2.8), (2.9), and (2.11), the model describing the debt to GDP ratio dynamics under the government strategy to decrease unemployment $(\dot{L} > 0)$ and boost the economy (increase the growth rate from g_0 to g_1) by investing in infrastructure has the form

$$\dot{d}(t) = (r - g_1)d(t)$$

$$+ \frac{G(t_0) - d_2\left(G(t_0)e^{\frac{g_1 - g_0}{\beta}(t - t_0)} - 1\right) + l_G^{-1}\left(e^{g_1(t - t_0)} - e^{g_0(t - t_0)}\right)Y(t_0)}{Y(t_0)e^{g_1(t - t_0)}} - \tau,$$

$$t > t_0$$

$$(2.12)$$

or (see Eqs. (2.7) and (2.9)) the above equation can be transformed to

$$\dot{d}(t) = (r - g_1)d(t) + e^{-g_1(t - t_0)}\left(l_3 - d_2 l_3\left(e^{\frac{g_1 - g_0}{\beta}(t - t_0)} - 1\right)\right)$$

$$+ l_G^{-1}\left(1 - e^{-(g_1 - g_0)(t - t_0)}\right) - \tau, \quad t > t_0$$

$$(2.13)$$

because $G(t_0) = l_3 Y(t_0)$.

The solution of Eq. (2.13) has the form (Yanushevsky and Yanushevsky, 2013)

$$d(t) = d(t_0)e^{(r-g_1)(t-t_0)} + a_4 e^{(r-g_1)(t-t_0)} + a_3 e^{-g_1(t-t_0)} + a_2 e^{-(g_1-g_0)(t-t_0)}$$
$$+ a_1 e^{\left(-g_1 + \frac{g_1-g_0}{\beta}\right)(t-t_0)} + a_0$$

(2.14)

where

$$a_0 = \frac{\tau l_1 - 1}{l_G(r - g_1)},$$

$$a_1 = -\frac{c l_3 l_2 \beta}{g_1 - g_0 - r\beta},$$

$$a_2 = \frac{1}{l_G(r - g_0)},$$

$$a_3 = -\frac{l_3(1 - c l_2)}{r},$$

$$a_4 = -a_0 - a_1 - a_2 - a_3$$

The considered model assumes that the government fiscal policy (excluding investment in infrastructure) remains unchanged. To analyze the efficiency of the policy combining investment in infrastructure with decreasing other government spending, we assume that government spending not related to the considered stimulus decreases with a rate h, i.e., instead of the term $G(t_0)$ in Eq. (2.12) we have (Yanushevsky and Yanushevsky, 2013)

$$G(t) = G(t_0)e^{-h(t-t_0)}, \quad t > t_0 \tag{2.15}$$

so that the solution of the modified Eqs. (2.12) and (2.13) has the form (2.14) with the term $a_3 e^{-g_1(t-t_0)}$ changed to $a_{31} e^{-(g_1+h)(t-t_0)} + a_{32} e^{-g_1(t-t_0)}$, where

$$a_{31} = -\frac{l_3}{r + h}, \quad a_{32} = \frac{c l_3 l_2}{r}.$$

Finally, we consider the situation when at $t > t_0$ the government fiscal policy results in a conditionally balanced budget (revenues equal expenditure, excluding stimulus spending). This corresponds to $l_3 e^{-g_1(t-t_0)} - \tau = 0$, $t > t_0$, in Eq. (2.13); $a_3 = \frac{c l_3 l_2}{r}$ and $\tau = 0$ in the expression for a_0 in Eq. (2.14).

The developed model (2.13) offers several observations for discussion. As seen from Eqs. (2.13) and (2.14), the government fiscal policy, characterized by the level of spending l_3 and the tax rate τ, has a direct impact on the debt to GDP ratio; and higher values of l_3 and smaller values of τ contribute to an increase of $d(t)$.

Because the employment growth in the considered model is $(g_1 - g_0)$ β^{-1} (see Eq. (2.11)), it is valid only for a finite time interval. Taking into account the population growth, the current and admissible levels of unemployment, as well as reasonable values of g_1 and g_0, it is easy to conclude that the results obtained from the analysis of Eq. (2.13) are valid for the time interval of approximately 10–15 years.

Although the solution of Eq. (2.13) is given for a constant tax rate τ, in reality, τ depends on time. However, in the case of the unchanged government tax policy and absence of sharp economic turns, the $\tau-$ changes are small. For example, the US tax revenues have averaged about 18.3% of GDP over 1970–2008. In 2009, it dropped to 15.1% and grew slowly to 15.8% in 2012. Because we operate with the lower estimate of the debt to GDP ratio, in the below examples, τ is chosen to satisfy this requirement.

It is an inconvenient reality that the literature provides a wide range of multiplier estimates (see, e.g., Auerbach and Gorodnichenko, 2012a,b). As mentioned earlier, the reason is that the impact of fiscal multipliers depends on the environment in which it is implemented, as well as data quality and the assumptions of related regression models; that is, there exist many factors that may cause economic effects and the size of the multiplier to vary both in the short and long run.

2.3 THE DEBT TO GDP RATIO DYNAMICS FOR FISCAL STIMULUS POLICY

We rewrite the debt to GDP ratio dynamics Eq. (2.7)

$$\dot{d}(t) = (r - g)d(t) + \frac{G(t)}{Y(t)} - \tau \qquad (2.7)$$

As earlier, let $t = t_0$, $g = g_0 < r$, and $G(t_0) = l_0 T(t_0)$, $l_0 > 1$.

The model analyzed below corresponds to the case of declining economic activity, substantial debt, and high unemployment. Tax cuts allow consumers to have more money to spend and producers to increase production and hire more working force. A less tax burden and higher employment will increase demand. The above factors should stimulate economic growth.

As earlier, it is assumed that at $t = t_0$, $\dot{L}(t_0) = 0$, and for $t > t_0$, when the government decreases taxes, the GDP growth rate $g_1 > g_0$ can be achieved by increasing employment, i.e., for $t > t_0$, $\dot{L}(t_0) > 0$.

The additional tax decrease $\Delta\tau(t)$ at $t \geq t_0$ that increases $Y(t)$ and makes it growing with the rate $g_1 > g_0$, i.e., $Y(t) = Y(t_0)e^{g_1(t-t_0)}$ (see Eq. (2.8)), in the short run will decrease the tax revenues by

$$\Delta T(t) = l_T^{-1}\left(e^{g_1(t-t_0)} - e^{g_0(t-t_0)}\right)Y(t_0) \tag{2.16}$$

(the above equation follows directly from the definition of the tax multiplier l_T).

As a result, the new government revenues $T(t)$ will be

$$T(t) = \tau Y(t_0)e^{g_0(t-t_0)} - l_T^{-1}\left(e^{g_1(t-t_0)} - e^{g_0(t-t_0)}\right)Y(t_0) \tag{2.17}$$

(Here τ corresponds to the old tax policy, where $T_{old}(t) = \tau Y(t_0)e^{g_0(t-t_0)}$).

As a result of increased employment, we assume that the component of government spending G_0 related to unemployment decreases by $\Delta G_1(t)$. (We use Eq. (2.11) to determine the lower limit of $d(t)$; however, in this case the exponential term in Eq. (2.11) can be increased to reflect the change in capital K, but this change is insignificant (see Eq. (2.10)).

Based on Eqs. (2.8), (2.11), and (2.17), the model describing the debt to GDP ratio dynamics (2.7) under the government strategy to decrease unemployment $(\dot{L} > 0)$ and boost the economy (increase the growth rate from g_0 to g_1) by decreasing taxes has the form

$$\dot{d}(t) = (r - g_1)d(t)$$

$$+ \frac{G(t_0) - d_2\left(G(t_0)e^{\frac{g_1-g_0}{\beta}(t-t_0)} - 1\right) + l_T^{-1}\left(e^{g_1(t-t_0)} - e^{g_0(t-t_0)}\right)Y(t_0)}{Y(t_0)e^{g_1(t-t_0)}} - \tau,$$

$$t > t_0$$

$$\tag{2.18}$$

i.e., the above equation is similar to Eq. (2.12). (To estimate the lower limit of $d(t)$ and make Eq. (2.18) look like Eq. (2.12), we do not use τ corresponding to the stimulus policy and neglect the factor $e^{(g_0-g_1)(t-t_0)}$ in the last term of Eq. (2.18). However, a more accurate estimates of the lower limit of $d(t)$ can be obtained from Eq. (2.18) with $\tau(t) = \tau e^{(g_0-g_1)(t-t_0)}$.)

The models developed to evaluate the effect of stimulus packages focused on investment in infrastructure (increased government spending) and the effect of tax cuts are qualitatively identical. However, in the case of tax cuts, the growth rate g_1 can be higher than that for a spending stimulus because of the decreased corporate taxes. Eqs. (2.12)–(2.15) can be used in both cases for properly chosen multipliers l_G and l_T.

Moreover, if the growth rate g_1 is reached by a combined strategy—stimulus spending and tax cuts, it is easy to conclude that in the developed model, the multiplier should be used:

$$l_{\sum} = \left(\rho_1 l_G^{-1} + l_T^{-1} \rho_2 \right)^{-1} \tag{2.19}$$

where the coefficients $\rho_1 + \rho_2 = 1$ reflect the share of each considered measure presented by the corresponding multiplier (see Eqs. (2.9) and (2.16)).

2.4 DISCRETE DEBT TO GDP RATIO DYNAMICS MODELS FOR FISCAL STIMULUS POLICY

The discrete debt dynamics model can be described by the following equation:

$$D_{t+1} - D_t = r D_t + G_{t+1} - T_{t+1} \tag{2.20}$$

where D is general government debt; r is the interest rate on debt; G and T are government purchases (expenditure excluding interest payments on debt) and revenues, respectively; the lower index indicates discrete time in years.

It describes more precisely (see terms G_{t+1} and T_{t+1} in Eq. (2.20)) than the continuous model (2.1) the real process of the data gathering and reporting. Although both discrete and continuous models give very close results, algorithms accompanying discrete models are simpler than for continuous models.

Below the discrete analog of the continuous model, Eq. (2.18) is considered.

Similar to Eq. (2.2), government revenues are presented in the form

$$T_t = \tau Y_t \tag{2.21}$$

where τ is a tax rate and the Cobb–Douglas function Y_t represents GDP (see Eq. (2.3))

$$Y_t = AK_t^{\alpha}L_t^{\beta} \qquad (2.22)$$

The debt to GDP ratio d_t dynamics can be presented as

$$d_{t+1} - d_t = \frac{D_{t+1}}{Y_{t+1}} - \frac{D_t}{Y_t} = \frac{D_t + rD_t + G_{t+1} - T_{t+1}}{Y_t(1+g)} - \frac{D_t}{Y_t}$$

$$= \frac{r - g}{1 + g}d_t + \frac{G_{t+1} - T_{t+1}}{Y_{t+1}} \qquad (2.23)$$

where

$$Y_{t+1} - Y_t = AK_t^{\alpha}L_t^{\beta}\left[\left(\frac{K_{t+1}}{K_t}\right)^{\alpha}\left(\frac{L_{t+1}}{L_t}\right)^{\beta} - 1\right] = gY_t \qquad (2.24)$$

$$g = (1 + g_K)^{\alpha}(1 + g_L)^{\beta} - 1, \qquad (2.25)$$

and

$$K_{t+1} = (g_K + 1)K_t, \quad L_{t+1} = (g_L + 1)L_t \qquad (2.26)$$

Practical application of Eq. (2.23) requires knowledge of G_{t+1} and Y_{t+1}. However, these parameters are interconnected. In reality, we deal with a system of equations because Y_{t+1} depends on K_{t+1} and L_{t+1} (see Eqs. (2.24) and (2.25)), and Eq. (2.23) should be supplemented with equations describing dynamics of capital K and labor L. Analysis of such a system presents substantial difficulties, especially when it is necessary to predict future values of the debt to GDP ratio.

Below we use Eq. (2.23) to build the model that allows us to obtain the analytical solution of the lower estimate of d_t.

Let $t = t_0$, $g = g_0 < r$, and $G_0 = l_0 T_0$, $l_0 > 1$. As indicated above, one of the approaches to stimulate GDP growth and employment is the use of additional government spending ΔG_t.

Similar to the above continuous model, it is assumed that at $t = t_0$ $\dot{L}_{t_0} = 0$ and for $t > t_0$, when the government stimulus package focuses infrastructure, the GDP growth the rate $g_1 > g_0$ can be achieved by increasing employment, i.e., in Eq. (2.25) for $t > t_0$ $\dot{L}_t > 0$.

For simplicity, we consider the initial moment $t_0 = 0$, so that $t = 0, 1, 2, \ldots$.

Assuming that the taxes remain unchanged, the additional government spending ΔG_{t+1} at $t \geq t_0$ to increase Y_t and make it growing with the rate $g_1 > g_0$, i.e.,

$$Y_{t+1} = (1 + g_1)Y_t, \tag{2.27}$$

should be

$$\Delta G_{t+1} = l_G^{-1}\left[(g_1 + 1)^{t+1} - (g_0 + 1)^{t+1}\right]Y_0 \tag{2.28}$$

(the above equation follows directly from the definition of the fiscal multiplier).

As in the continuous case, we also assume that the basic government spending $G_t = l_3 Y_t$ is not only frozen at $t = t_0$ (as a percent of GDP; see Eq. (2.21)), but for $t > t_0$ it will decrease by $\Delta G_{1,t+1}$ owing to the increase in employment (see Eq. (2.26); upper indices "0" and "1" correspond to g_0 and g_1, respectively)

$$\frac{L_{t+1}^1}{L_{t+1}^0} = \frac{\left(1 + g_L^1\right)^{t+1}}{\left(1 + g_L^0\right)^{t+1}} = \frac{\left(1 + g_K^0\right)^{\alpha(t+1)/\beta}}{\left(1 + g_K^1\right)^{\alpha(t+1)/\beta}} \frac{\left(1 + g_1\right)^{(t+1)/\beta}}{\left(1 + g_0\right)^{(t+1)/\beta}}, \quad \frac{L_0^1}{L_0^0} = 1$$
$$\tag{2.29}$$

As in the continuous case, we will ignore the influence of the capital component in Eq. (2.29) (either the values of g_K^0 and g_K^1 are close so that the first fraction in Eq. (2.29) is either close to 1 or less than 1 and we increase the value of Eq. (2.29)) to obtain an optimistic estimate of the debt to GDP ratio by increasing the term

$$\Delta G_{1,t+1} = d_2\left(\frac{(1 + g_1)^{\frac{t+1}{\beta}}}{(1 + g_0)^{\frac{t+1}{\beta}}} - 1\right)G_0 \approx d_2\left(e^{\frac{g_1 - g_0}{\beta}(t+1)} - 1\right)G_0 \tag{2.30}$$

where the exponential term that equals approximately $(1 + g_1)^{\frac{t+1}{\beta}}\big/(1 + g_0)^{\frac{t+1}{\beta}}$ (it follows immediately from $e^g \approx 1 + g$) is more convenient to be used in computational algorithms. It can be obtained also from Eq. (2.11) and reflects the step g-rate change in Eq. (2.25). To simplify the model, we ignore the influence of the capital component in Eq. (2.25) and operate with the increased rate of employment approximately equal to $(g_1 - g_0)\beta^{-1}$. Both expressions Eq. (2.30) for $\Delta G_{1,t+1}$ can be used (see Eqs. (2.48) and (2.49)).

Based on Eqs. (2.27)–(2.30), the model describing the debt to GDP ratio dynamics in the case of the government stimulus spending to decrease unemployment $(\dot{L} > 0)$ and boost the economy (increase the growth rate from g_0 to g_1) has the form

$$d_{t+1} = \frac{1+r}{1+g_1}d_t$$

$$+ \frac{G_0 - d_2\left(e^{\frac{g_1 - g_0}{\beta}(t+1)} - 1\right)G_0 + l_G^{-1}\left[(g_1 + 1)^{t+1} - (g_0 + 1)^{t+1}\right]Y_0}{(1 + g_1)^{t+1}Y_0} - \tau,$$

$$t = 0, 1, 2, \ldots$$

$$(2.31)$$

or because $G_0 = l_3 Y_0$, the above equation can be transformed to

$$d_{t+1} = \frac{1+r}{1+g_1}d_t$$

$$+ \frac{l_3 - d_2 l_3\left(e^{\frac{g_1 - g_0}{\beta}(t+1)} - 1\right) + l_G^{-1}\left[(g_1 + 1)^{t+1} - (g_0 + 1)^{t+1}\right]}{(1 + g_1)^{t+1}} - \tau$$

$$t = 0, 1, 2, \ldots$$

$$(2.32)$$

Eq. (2.31) is a recursion formula that specifies a recursive procedure for determining d_{t+1} based on d_t, $t = 0, 1, 2, \ldots$

As it was shown for the continuous model, in the case of tax cuts and for the general case of the fiscal policy stimulus measures, the following discrete model can be used (see Eq. (2.19)):

$$d_{t+1} = \frac{1+r}{1+g_1}d_t$$

$$+ \frac{l_3 - d_2 l_3\left(e^{\frac{g_1 - g_0}{\beta}(t+1)} - 1\right) + l_\Sigma^{-1}\left[(g_1 + 1)^{t+1} - (g_0 + 1)^{t+1}\right]}{(1 + g_1)^{t+1}} - \tau$$

$$t = 0, 1, 2, \ldots$$

$$(2.33)$$

Similar to the continuous model, in the case of tax cuts, a more precise value of the last term is

$$\tau(t) = \tau(1 + g_0)^{t+1} / (1 + g_1)^{t+1}, \quad t = 0, 1, 2, \ldots$$

To analyze the efficiency of the government fiscal policy combining the considered stimulus with decreasing other government spending, we assume that government spending not related to the stimulus decreases with a rate h, i.e., instead of the term G_0 in Eq. (2.31) should be G_t that is the solution of the equation

$$G_{t+1} = (1 - h)^{t+1} G_t, \quad t = 0, 1, 2, \ldots \quad (2.34)$$

so that the modified Eqs. (2.31)−(2.33) should have instead of the terms G_0 and l_3 the terms $(1 - h)^{t+1} G_0$ and $(1 - h)^{t+1} l_3$, respectively, i.e.,

$$d_{t+1} = \frac{1 + r}{1 + g_1} d_t$$

$$+ \frac{(1 - h)^{t+1} l_3 - d_2 l_3 \left(e^{\frac{g_1 - g_0}{\beta}(t+1)} - 1 \right) + l_{\Sigma}^{-1} \left[(g_1 + 1)^{t+1} - (g_0 + 1)^{t+1} \right]}{(1 + g_1)^{t+1}} - \tau$$

$$t = 0, 1, 2, \ldots$$

$$(2.35)$$

Finally, for the case when at $t > t_0$ the government fiscal policy results in a conditionally balanced budget (revenues equal expenditure, excluding stimulus components), which corresponds to $(1 + g_1)^{-(t+1)} l_3 - \tau = 0$ in Eq. (2.31), we have

$$d_{t+1} = \frac{1 + r}{1 + g_1} d_t$$

$$+ \frac{d_2 l_3 \left(1 - e^{\frac{g_1 - g_0}{\beta}(t+1)} \right) + l_{\Sigma}^{-1} \left[(g_1 + 1)^{t+1} - (g_0 + 1)^{t+1} \right]}{(1 + g_1)^{t+1}}$$

$$t = 0, 1, 2, \ldots$$

$$(2.36)$$

In the considered model (Eqs. (2.7)−(2.13)), we assume that investment in infrastructure is the only factor that resulted in the increased growth rate g_1. It means that the chosen 10-year period may be unrealistic because according to Eq. (2.9) with time the required level of additional government spending $\Delta G(t)$ increases, and at a certain time t_r, government may be unable to satisfy the requirement $\Delta G(t_r)$. In this case, the simulation results should be used for the period of time $[t_0, t]$, $t < t_r$. Starting at t_r, a modified model should be used reflecting a new situation, and other factors that influence GDP should be included in the model.

The model describing the effect of tax cuts on the debt to GDP ratio was built similar to Eqs. (2.7)—(2.13). It is assumed that tax cuts are the only factor changing the GDP growth rate g_1. However, in contrast to the model (2.7)—(2.13), the assumption that tax cuts act during the whole considered time interval is not accurate. Usually, tax cuts are one-step action; it is implemented at a certain year and remains valid for a long period of time. That is why it is reasonable for evaluating the lower limit of the debt to GDP ratio to use the $\Delta T(t_0 + 1)$ value $l_T^{-1}(e^{g_1} - e^{g_0}) Y(t_0) \approx l_T^{-1}(g_1 - g_0) Y(t_0)$ (see Eq.(2.16)).

To emphasize the similar effect of the spending and tax multipliers, we prefer to keep in the equations describing the developed model the components $\Delta G(t)$ and $\Delta T(t)$ as they presented in Eqs. (2.9) and (2.16).

In the above considered models, we analyzed the effect of infrastructure spending and tax cuts on the debt to GDP ratio assuming that the related changes in $G(t)$ and $T(t)$ are the only factors influencing the GDP growth. The considered stimuli were characterized by the spending and tax multipliers.

As indicated in Section 1.5, numerical estimates of the value of fiscal multipliers vary significantly across model classes; within each class of models, they vary a lot with the economic and policy environment. In reality, it is difficult to imagine a "pure" multiplier effect because there exist related factors that interact with the stimulus actions. This fact explains a sizeable range of multiplier estimates, and the efficiency of the considered models depends on the properly chosen values of the fiscal multipliers.

In addition, stimulus measures can be accompanied by additional government actions $S(t)$ (S_t) that would increase GDP independently (for example, the decrease of trade deficit; see Eq. (1.1))—the actions not related directly to the main control actions $G(t)$ and $T(t)$ of the considered models. In this case, to present properly the effect of stimulus actions by using the multipliers l_G and l_T, the effect of $S(t)$ should be extracted, that is, for example, for the spending multiplier, instead of Eqs. (2.9) and (2.28) we have

$$\Delta G(t) = l_G^{-1}\left(\left(e^{g_1(t-t_0)} - e^{g_0(t-t_0)}\right) Y(t_0) - S(t)\right); \qquad (2.9a)$$

$$\Delta G_{t+1} = I_G^{-1} \left(\left[(g_1 + 1)^{t+1} - (g_0 + 1)^{t+1} \right] Y_0 - S_{t+1} \right) \qquad (2.28a)$$

2.5 GENERALIZED DEBT TO GDP RATIO DYNAMICS MODEL

The above considered models estimating the lower debt to GDP ratio limit that can be achieved by the government stimuli are described by differential and difference equations with constant coefficients. The main components of these models, fiscal multipliers, do not change in time and start acting immediately. In reality, a real effect of stimuli becomes visible at least about a year later. As a rule, stimulus is injected into the economy by steps; its implementation is distributed in time. The latest studies (see, e.g., Christiano et al., 2011) show that the stimulus impact is more substantial when fiscal policy is accompanied with a proper monetary policy. In this case, the fiscal multiplier is higher at the initial period, when it starts working, and then, with the increase in the GDP growth rate, its impact decreases significantly.

Below we consider the debt to GDP ratio dynamics model with time-varying parameters, which estimates more precisely the debt to GDP ratio than the above described models (see Yanushevsky and Yanushevsky, 2017).

The earlier used assumption that stimuli change the GDP growth from g_0 to g_1 enables us to evaluate roughly the efficiency of the considered stimulus policies for high debt to GDP ratios. However, a sharp change of a growth rate at $t = t_0$ is a rather strong assumption to obtain the debt to GDP ratio estimate very close to reality. The reaction to stimuli is more complicated. The GDP growth rate is not constant and it is influenced by many other factors, not included in the model, that require special government actions reflected in its spending and revenues.

In contrast to the previously considered models, we assume that the government spending $G(t)$ is not limited by $G(t_0)$ (at the moment of stimuli actions), so that $\tau(t)$ and $l_3(t)$ are functions of time. It means that the model

$$\dot{d}(t) = (r(t) - g_0(t))d(t) + l_3(t) - \tau(t) \qquad (2.37)$$

evaluates $d(t)$ on a finite interval $t \in [t_0, t_f]$ under a certain economic policy (e.g., the policy $G(t)$ and $T(t)$ that created an economic crisis with a high unemployment), and the problem is to evaluate the efficiency of stimulus measures that would produce the GDP growth $g(t) > g_0(t)$ and decrease unemployment.

For the time-varying GDP growth rate, instead of Eq. (2.8) we have

$$Y(t) = Y(t_0)e^{\int_{t_0}^{t} g(t)\,dt}, \quad t \geq t_0 \tag{2.38}$$

The spending and tax multipliers effect (Eqs. (2.9) and (2.16)) can be presented, respectively, by

$$\Delta G(t) = l_G^{-1}(t)\left(e^{\int_{t_0}^{t} g(t)\,dt} - e^{\int_{t_0}^{t} g_0(t)\,dt}\right)Y(t_0), \tag{2.39}$$

and

$$\Delta T(t) = l_T^{-1}(t)\left(e^{\int_{t_0}^{t} g(t)\,dt} - e^{\int_{t_0}^{t} g_0(t)\,dt}\right)Y(t_0), \tag{2.40}$$

Instead of Eq. (2.11) we have

$$\Delta G_1(t) = d_2 G(t_0)\left(e^{\int_{t_0}^{t} \frac{g(t)-g_0(t)}{\beta}(t-t_0)\,dt} - 1\right), \tag{2.41}$$

(Here, for simplicity, we neglect the growth rate of capital (see Eq. (2.10)) because this component is small and the weight of the term in Eq. (2.41) is significantly smaller than terms in Eqs. (2.39) and (2.40)).

The generalized debt to GDP ratio dynamics is described by the following equation:

$$\dot{d}(t) = (r(t) - g(t))d(t) - \tau(t)\, e^{\int_{t_0}^{t}(g_0(t)-g(t))\,dt}$$

$$+ \frac{G(t) - d_2 G(t_0)\left(e^{\int_{t_0}^{t} \frac{g(t)-g_0(t)}{\beta}\,dt} - 1\right) + l_\Sigma^{-1}(t)\left(e^{\int_{t_0}^{t} g(t)\,dt} - e^{\int_{t_0}^{t} g_0(t)\,dt}\right)Y(t_0)}{Y(t_0)e^{\int_{t_0}^{t} g(t)\,dt}},$$

$$t > t_0$$

$$\tag{2.42}$$

where $G(t) = l_3(t)Y(t)$ is the unrelated stimulus part of spending and, in the case of tax cuts, $\tau(t)$ is not a real tax to GDP ratio and corresponds to the old tax policy (see Eqs. (2.16)–(2.18)).

The above equation can be transformed to

$$\dot{d}(t) = (r(t) - g(t))d(t) + l_3(t) - d_2 l_3(t_0)e^{-\int_{t_0}^{t} g(t)\,dt}\left(e^{\int_{t_0}^{t} \frac{g(t)-g_0(t)}{\beta}\,dt} - 1\right)$$

$$+ l_\Sigma^{-1}(t)\left(1 - e^{-\int_{t_0}^{t}(g(t)-g_0(t))\,dt}\right) - \tau(t)\, e^{\int_{t_0}^{t}(g_0(t)-g(t))\,dt}, \quad t > t_0$$

$$\tag{2.43}$$

(If only stimulus spending is considered, the last term of Eq. (2.43) is equal to $\tau(t)$.)

To analyze the efficiency of the policy combining fiscal stimuli with decreasing other government spending, we assume that government-projected earlier spending $G(t)$ not related to the considered stimuli decreases with a rate h, that is, in Eq. (2.40), it should be $G(t)e^{-h(t-t_0)}$ instead of $G(t)$

$$\dot{d}(t) = (r(t) - g(t))d(t) + e^{-h(t-t_0)}l_3(t)$$

$$- d_2 l_3(t_0)e^{-\int_{t_0}^t g(t)dt}\left(e^{\int_{t_0}^t \frac{g(t)-g_0(t)}{\beta}dt} - 1\right) + l_\Sigma^{-1}(t)\left(1 - e^{-\int_{t_0}^t (g(t)-g_0(t))dt}\right)$$

$$- \tau(t)\,e^{\int_{t_0}^t (g_0(t)-g(t))dt}, \quad t > t_0$$

(2.44)

Formally, the $l_3(t)$ values reflect the level of government spending, so that if the forecasted data about future government spending are close to reality, the model (2.43) can be used also to estimate the effect of decreased government spending if spending cuts are expected in the future.

The solution of Eqs. (2.43) and (2.44) enables one to analyze the efficiency of fiscal and monetary policies focused on improving a country's economy. However, the reliability of the obtained results depends on the properly chosen multipliers and the accuracy of the forecasting parameters of the model.

For practical purposes the discrete analog of the above equations is more preferable. The following equivalents of the continuous model (2.34)−(2.41) should be included in the discrete model:

$$Y_{t+1} = (1 + g_{t+1})Y_t, \quad t = 0, 1, 2, \ldots \quad (2.45)$$

where g_{t+1} is the GDP growth rate in the $(t + 1)$ year.

The multipliers effect Eqs. (2.28), (2.39), and (2.40) can be presented by

$$\Delta G_{t+1} = l_{1t}^{-1}\left[\prod_{i=1}^{t+1}(g_i + 1) - \prod_{i=1}^{t+1}(g_{0i} + 1)\right]Y_0, \quad (2.46)$$

and

$$\Delta T_{t+1} = l_{Tt}^{-1}\left[\prod_{i=1}^{t+1}(g_i + 1) - \prod_{i=1}^{t+1}(g_{0i} + 1)\right]Y_0 \quad (2.47)$$

Instead of Eqs. (2.30) and (2.41) we have

$$\Delta G_{1,t+1'} = d_2 G_0 \left[\left(\prod_{i=1}^{t+1} (g_i + 1) \Big/ (1 + g_{0i}) \right)^{\frac{1}{\beta}} - 1 \right] \qquad (2.48)$$

The discrete analog of the model (2.42) has the following form:

$$d_{t+1} = \frac{1 + r_{t+1}}{1 + g_{t+1}} d_t - \tau_{t+1} \frac{\displaystyle\prod_{i=1}^{t+1}(g_{0i} + 1)}{\displaystyle\prod_{i=1}^{t+1} (g_i + 1)}$$

$$+ \frac{G_{t+1} - d_2 G_0 \left[\left(\displaystyle\prod_{i=1}^{t+1} (g_i + 1) \Big/ (1 + g_{0i}) \right)^{\frac{1}{\beta}} - 1 \right] + l^{-1}\sum_{t+1} \left[\displaystyle\prod_{i=1}^{t+1} (g_i + 1) - \displaystyle\prod_{i=1}^{t+1}(g_{0i} + 1) \right] Y_0}{\displaystyle\prod_{i=1}^{t+1} (g_i + 1) Y_0}$$

$$t = 0, 1, 2, \ldots$$

$$(2.49)$$

or because $G_t = l_{3t} Y_t$, the above equation can be transformed to

$$d_{t+1} = \frac{1 + r_{t+1}}{1 + g_{t+1}} d_t + l_{3,t+1} - \tau_{t+1} \frac{\displaystyle\prod_{i=1}^{t+1}(g_{0i} + 1)}{\displaystyle\prod_{i=1}^{t+1} (g_i + 1)}$$

$$- \frac{d_2 l_{30} \left[\left(\displaystyle\prod_{i=1}^{t+1} (g_i + 1) \Big/ (1 + g_{0i}) \right)^{\frac{1}{\beta}} - 1 \right] - l^{-1}\sum_{t+1} \left[\displaystyle\prod_{i=1}^{t+1} (g_i + 1) - \displaystyle\prod_{i=1}^{t+1}(g_{0i} + 1) \right]}{\displaystyle\prod_{i=1}^{t+1} (g_i + 1)}$$

$$t = 0, 1, 2, \ldots$$

$$(2.50)$$

where for the case of tax cuts, similar to the continuous model (see (Eq. 2.42)), τ_{t+1} does not present a real tax to GDP ratio; in the case of only spending stimulus, the tax component of the above equations is equal to τ_{t+1}.

The efficiency of the government fiscal policy combining the considered stimuli with decreasing (with a rate h) other government spending (see Eqs. (2.35) and (2.44)) is described by the following equation:

$$d_{t+1} = \frac{1 + r_{t+1}}{1 + g_{t+1}} d_t + (1 - h)^{t+1} l_{3,t+1} - \tau_{t+1} \frac{\prod\limits_{i=1}^{t+1}(g_{0i} + 1)}{\prod\limits_{i=1}^{t+1}(g_i + 1)}$$

$$- \frac{d_2 l_{30} \left[\left(\prod\limits_{i=1}^{t+1}(g_i + 1) \Big/ (1 + g_{0i}) \right)^{\frac{1}{\beta}} - 1 \right] - \sum\limits_{t+1}^{-1} \left[\prod\limits_{i=1}^{t+1}(g_i + 1) - \prod\limits_{i=1}^{t+1}(g_{0i} + 1) \right]}{\prod\limits_{i=1}^{t+1}(g_i + 1)}$$

$$t = 0, 1, 2, \ldots$$

$$(2.51)$$

As mentioned in the case of the continuous model (2.43), the $l_{3,t+1}$ values $(t = 0, 1, 2\ldots)$ reflect the level of government spending, so that formally Eq. (2.51) can be used also to describe the effect of decreased government spending (in the case of only spending stimulus, the tax component of the above equations is equal to τ_{t+1}).

The expressions (2.50) and (2.51) are written similar to Eqs. (2.42) and (2.43). However, taking into account that the stimulus measures are implemented in steps and distributed over a certain time interval, it is reasonable to consider the following relation between the g_{0i} and g_i: $g_{0i} = g_{i+1}$ $(i = 2, 3, \ldots)$, which means that the system dynamics on the ith time interval starts from the projected growth rate for the previous interval. In this case, Eqs. (2.50) and (2.51) can be presented in the form

$$d_{t+1} = \frac{1 + r_{t+1}}{1 + g_{t+1}} d_t + l_{3,t+1} - \tau_{t+1} \frac{g_{01} + 1}{g_{t+1} + 1}$$

$$- \frac{d_2 l_{30} \left[\left(\prod\limits_{i=1}^{t+1}(g_i + 1) \Big/ (1 + g_{0i}) \right)^{\frac{1}{\beta}} - 1 \right] - \sum\limits_{t+1}^{-1} \left[\prod\limits_{i=1}^{t+1}(g_i + 1) - \prod\limits_{i=1}^{t+1}(g_{0i} + 1) \right]}{\prod\limits_{i=1}^{t+1}(g_i + 1)}$$

$$t = 0, 1, 2, \ldots$$

$$(2.52)$$

$$d_{t+1} = \frac{1 + r_{t+1}}{1 + g_{t+1}} d_t + (1 - h)^{t+1} l_{3,t+1} - \tau_{t+1} \frac{g_{01} + 1}{g_{t+1} + 1}$$

$$- \frac{d_2 l_{30} \left[\left(\prod_{i=1}^{t+1} (g_i + 1) \middle/ (1 + g_{0i}) \right)^{\frac{1}{\beta}} - 1 \right] - l_{t+1}^{-1} \left[\prod_{i=1}^{t+1} (g_i + 1) - \prod_{i=1}^{t+1} (g_{0i} + 1) \right]}{\prod_{i=1}^{t+1} (g_i + 1)}$$

$$t = 0, 1, 2, \ldots$$

(2.53)

(In the case of only spending stimulus for some time intervals, the tax component of the above equations is equal to τ_{t+1}; if tax cuts stimulus starts at $t = k$, the tax component contains g_{0k} instead of g_{01}.) The described model can be applied to the case of countries that are more dynamic and with less bureaucracy than leading industrial countries. Of course, other possible scenarios for g_i can be considered that would simplify Eqs. (2.50) and (2.51).

The considered debt to GDP ratio dynamics models with time-varying parameters can be used successfully only if the time-varying coefficients are predicted properly. Otherwise, the models of the previous sections are preferable. As mentioned earlier, in the case of many uncertain parameters, simpler models can produce better results.

2.6 THE CONSEQUENCES OF HIGH NATIONAL DEBT

The below examples are given for several multipliers examined in the literature (e.g., Auerbach and Gorodnichenko, 2012a; Blanchard and Perotti, 2002; Christiano et al., 2011; Leeper et al., 2010; Mankiw, 2008; Ramey, 2011; Romer and Romer, 2010). As indicated earlier, many researchers believe that tax multipliers are higher than spending multipliers. However, some papers show that the spending multiplier can be high (e.g., in Christiano et al. (2011) the multipliers value equals 3.8). That is why in the examples we do not specify whether it is spending or tax multiplier and use two multipliers $l_G = 1.59$ (recommended by Mark Zandi, the chief economist of Moody's Analytics) and $l_G = 3.8$ (see, e.g., Christiano et al., 2011).

Table 2.1 presents the debt to GDP ratio estimate for the 10-year period based on the solution of Eq. (2.33) for the following parameters: $d_0 = 0.99$; $c = 1$; $r = 0.026$; $\tau = 0.15$; $\beta = 0.69$; $l_3 = 0.194$; and $l_2 = 0.13$ (they are

Table 2.1 Simulation results for the 2012 debt to GDP ratio dynamics model for $l_G = 1.59$

Year	1	2	3	4	5	6	7	8	9	10
Debt/GDP $g_1 = 0.03$	1.03	1.07	1.10	1.14	1.17	1.21	1.24	1.28	1.31	1.34
Debt/GDP $g_1 = 0.04$	1.03	1.06	1.11	1.15	1.20	1.25	1.3	1.36	1.41	1.47

very close to the data characterizing the US economy in 2012 taken from the websites www.usgovernmentspending.com, www.usgovernmen trevenue.com, etc., and also United States Government Accountability Office, 2012). The table is built for $g_0 = 0.022$, $g_1 = 0.03$, and $g_0 = 0.022$, $g_1 = 0.04$, respectively. The chosen multiplier is $l_G = 1.59$. As seen from Table 2.1, the considered multiplier increases the debt to GDP ratio more than 30% in 10 years. For $g_1 = 0.04$, it can be significantly higher because to reach such a growth rate with a relatively small multiplier would require more spending than that for the multiplier $l_G = 3.8$.

Because this and similar estimates of multipliers values are not supported by rigorous mathematics and their validity is argued by many economists, in Table 2.2 we presented the debt to GDP ratio estimate for $l_1 = 3.8$. As seen from Tables 2.1 and 2.2, the lower values of d_t correspond to the multiplier with the higher value, and for $l_G = 3.8$ and $g_1 = 0.04$, we can at least expect that the debt to GDP ratio will not increase significantly.

Of course, the GDP growth rate g_1 depends on many factors including tax policies and the state of the world economy. Some economists—advocates of stimulus spending packages—prefer to ignore these factors and attribute economic growth only to spending stimulus measures. Taking into account that since the second quarter of 2000 the US GDP rate has never reached the 5% level, we consider also the rosy scenario and evaluate the debt to GDP ratio for $g_1 = 0.05$ and $l_G = 3.8$. The results presented in

Table 2.2 Simulation results for the 2012 debt to GDP ratio dynamics model for $l_G = 3.8$

Year	1	2	3	4	5	6	7	8	9	10
Debt/GDP $g1 = 0.03$	1.02	1.05	1.08	1.1	1.12	1.13	1.14	1.15	1.16	1.17
Debt/GDP $g1 = 0.04$	1.01	1.03	1.05	1.07	1.08	1.09	1.09	1.1	1.1	1.1

Table 2.3 Simulation results for the 2012 debt to GDP ratio dynamics model for $l_G = 3.8$

Year	1	2	3	4	5	6	7	8	9	10
Debt/GDP	1.0	1.02	1.03	1.03	1.04	1.04	1.04	1.05	1.05	1.05
g1 = 0.05										

Table 2.3 show that even for this case in 10 years the debt to GDP ratio can increase by more than 5%. The reason of inefficiency of the described stimulus policy is a very high (about 100% of GDP) initial debt and a high level of the federal government spending (including the interest on debt, it is about 22% of GDP). As to the rosy scenario, it is worthwhile to indicate that President Reagan managed only 4% growth four times in 8 years; President Clinton did it five times in 8 years, but no president in the American history has averaged 4% growth over the course of his presidency.

The simulation results in Tables 2.1 and 2.2 show that the debt to GDP ratio increases with time if the government fiscal policy (excluding stimulus measures) remains unchanged. Tables 2.4 and 2.5 contain the simulation results for the government policy combining stimulus with a decrease in

Table 2.4 Simulation results for the 2012 debt to GDP ratio dynamics model for $l_G = 1.59$

Year	1	2	3	4	5	6	7	8	9	10
Debt/GDP	1.02	1.05	1.07	1.09	1.11	1.12	1.13	1.14	1.15	1.16
g1 = 0.03										
Debt/GDP	1.02	1.05	1.08	1.11	1.14	1.17	1.2	1.23	1.27	1.31
g1 = 0.04										

Table 2.5 Simulation results for the 2012 debt to GDP ratio dynamics model for $l_G = 3.8$

Year	1	2	3	4	5	6	7	8	9	10
Debt/GDP	1.02	1.03	1.04	1.05	1.05	1.05	1.4	1.02	1.0	0.98
g1 = 0.03										
Debt/GDP	1.01	1.01	1.02	1.02	1.02	1.01	0.99	0.98	0.96	0.94
g1 = 0.04										

Table 2.6 Simulation results for the 2012 debt to GDP ratio dynamics model for $l_G = 3.8$ and the conditionally balanced budget assumption

Year	1	2	3	4	5	6	7	8	9	10
Debt/GDP	0.99	0.99	0.99	1.0	1.01	1.01	1.02	1.04	1.05	1.06
g1 = 0.03										
Debt/GDP	0.98	0.98	0.98	0.99	1.0	1.01	1.03	1.05	1.07	1.1
g1 = 0.04										

government spending not related to stimulus (see Eqs. (2.15), (2.34), and (2.35); $h = 0.02$ is chosen to get about a 20% decrease in the government spending in 10 years). As expected, the debt to GDP ratio estimate is less than in Tables 2.1 and 2.2, respectively. However, the debt to GDP ratio is still above its initial value for $l_G = 1.59$.

The simulation results in Table 2.6 relate to the government fiscal policy with a conditionally balanced budget (see Eqs. (2.16) and (2.36); revenues equal frozen expenditures, excluding stimulus components). As mentioned earlier, this corresponds to the case when the budget is conditionally balanced, but the debt to GDP ratio is high; the stimulus policy focuses to increase GDP and employment. The data in Table 2.6 show that the considered stimulus measures are insufficient to decrease substantially the debt to GDP ratio; the ratio can only grow.

The interest rate on debt r in the above equations and the related calculations is considered constant. However, it is a time-varying parameter that influences significantly the considered estimates. Table 2.7 shows the parameters of the considered model for 2014 and 2015, in the period during which many economists call a slow recovery.

Compared with the data used in the 2012 model, the parameters τ, l_2, and l_3 changed 8%−15%. We repeat the calculations for Tables 2.1−2.6 for the model with the parameters corresponding to 2015 for the GDP growth rate $g_0 = 0.026$ and $d_0 = 1.01$.

Table 2.7 Economic data for 2014 and 2015

Year	GDP, trillion $, Y	Debt, trillion $, d	Spending, excluding interest on debt, G_0 trillion $	Debt/ GDP	Revenue, trillion $, T	Interest on debt billion, $	Interest rate on debt, r	τ	l_2	l_3
2014	17.4	17.8	3.1	1.03	3.02	430.8	0.0242	0.174	0.12	0.177
2015	18.04	18.1	3.3	1.01	3.25	402.4	0.0235	0.181	0.11	0.18

Table 2.8 Simulation results for the 2015 debt to GDP ratio dynamics model for $l_G = 1.59$

Year	1	2	3	4	5	6	7	8	9	10
Debt/GDP $g_1 = 0.03$	1.0	0.99	0.97	0.96	0.94	0.93	0.91	0.89	0.87	0.86
Debt/GDP $g_1 = 0.04$	1.0	0.99	0.98	0.98	0.98	0.98	0.98	0.99	1.0	1.02

In 2015, the US unemployment level was around 5%. However, this number is deceptive because the labor force participation rate, the percentage of people more than 16 who either have a job or are actively searching for one, is very low, about 65%. Compared with the above considered 2012 model, in 2015, revenues are very close to expenditures (excluding the interest on debt); they exceed them by about $50 billion. Moreover, the assumption that expenditures G_0 are frozen enables us to expect, with the GDP growth, a more visible impact of revenues so that in this case the effect of the spending multiplier can be substantial. However, a high GDP growth ($g_1 = 0.04$ or $g_1 = 0.05$) reached by government spending programs can generate significant debt, and especially for small spending multiplier values, the expectations of a significantly lower debt to GDP ratio would not be realized (see Table 2.8). As to the conditionally balanced budget assumption, the results in Tables 2.6 and 2.13 are close because in this case the debt to GDP ratio dynamics is determined mostly by the close values of r and g_1.

Formally, the results of Tables 2.8—2.12 give a hope that the debt to GDP ratio will decrease. Its lower limit in most cases is significantly below 100%.

However, because the model determines the lower limit, it is only logical to assume that the real debt to GDP ratio will be less than that for

Table 2.9 Simulation results for the 2015 debt to GDP ratio dynamics model for $l_G = 3.8$

Year	1	2	3	4	5	6	7	8	9	10
Debt/GDP $g1 = 0.03$	0.99	0.98	0.95	0.93	0.9	0.87	0.84	0.8	0.76	0.72
Debt/GDP $g1 = 0.04$	1.01	0.96	0.93	0.9	0.87	0.84	0.8	0.76	0.73	0.69

Table 2.10 Simulation results for the 2015 debt to GDP ratio dynamics model for $I_G = 3.8$

Year	1	2	3	4	5	6	7	8	9	10
Debt/GDP	0.98	0.94	0.91	0.87	0.84	0.8	0.77	0.73	0.69	0.66
g1 = 0.05										

Table 2.11 Simulation results for the 2015 debt to GDP ratio dynamics model for $I_G = 1.59$

Year	1	2	3	4	5	6	7	8	9	10
Debt/GDP	0.99	0.97	0.94	0.92	0.88	0.85	0.81	0.77	0.73	0.68
g1 = 0.03										
Debt/GDP	0.99	0.97	0.95	0.94	0.92	0.9	0.89	0.88	0.87	0.87
g1 = 0.04										

Table 2.12 Simulation results for the 2015 debt to GDP ratio dynamics model for $I_G = 3.8$

Year	1	2	3	4	5	6	7	8	9	10
Debt/GDP	0.99	0.96	0.93	0.89	0.84	0.79	0.74	0.68	0.62	0.55
g1 = 0.03										
Debt/GDP	0.98	0.94	0.9	0.86	0.81	0.76	0.71	0.65	0.6	0.54
g1 = 0.04										

Table 2.13 Simulation results for the 2015 debt to GDP ratio dynamics model for $I_G = 3.8$ and the conditionally balanced budget assumption

Year	1	2	3	4	5	6	7	8	9	10
Debt/GDP	1.01	1.0	1.0	1.0	1.0	1.0	1.01	1.02	1.03	1.03
g1 = 0.03										
Debt/GDP	1.0	1.0	1.0	1.0	1.0	1.01	1.02	1.04	1.05	1.07
g1 = 0.04										

the 2012 model. More precise estimates can be obtained from the model considered in Section 2.5.

The government-reported economic data are often revised, and in the 2012 model we used the revised interest payment (see United States Government Accountability Office, 2012). As indicated by Sargent and Hall (2010) (as well as Eisner, 1986; Bohn, 1992, and others), the net interest on federal debt in the number, the government reports, does not correspond to the interest payments that economists put in the government budget constraint; instead it is the sum of all the coupon payments on the Treasury notes and bonds and the capital gains of the zero-coupon Treasury bills. They believe that the misreporting of US government borrowing costs leaves open the possibility of manipulation. Such arithmetic mismeasures the government interest payments by failing to account properly for real capital gains and losses government creditors receive because of changes in inflation, interest rates, and the maturity structure of the debt; coupon payments should not be viewed as pure interest payments—they are part principal repayments and part interest payments.

Interest expense consists of (1) interest accrued and paid on debt held by the public or credited to accounts holding intragovernmental debt during the fiscal year, (2) interest accrued during the fiscal year but not yet paid on debt held by public or credited to accounts holding intragovernmental debt, and (3) net amortization of premiums and discounts.

Debt held by the public and intragovernmental debt holdings are very different. Debt held by the public represents a burden on today's economy as borrowing from the public absorbs resources available for private investment and may put upward pressure on interest rates. This debt is paid in cash and represents a burden on current taxpayers. In contrast, intragovernmental debt holdings typically do not require cash payments from the current budget or represent a burden on the current economy.

Intragovernmental debt holdings represent federal debt owed by Treasury to federal government accounts—primarily federal trust funds such as Social Security and Medicare—that typically have an obligation to invest their excess annual receipts (including interest earnings) over disbursements in federal securities. Most federal government accounts invest in special nonmarketable Treasury securities that represent legal obligations of the Treasury and are guaranteed for principal and interest by the full faith and credit of the US government. The majority of intragovernmental debt holdings are Government Account Series (GAS) securities, which consist of par-value securities and market-based securities with terms ranging from on demand out to 30 years. Par-value securities are issued and redeemed at par (100% of the face value), regardless of current market conditions. Market-based securities can be issued at a premium or discount and are redeemed at par value on the maturity date or at market value if redeemed before the maturity date.

The federal government uses the federal government accounts' invested cash surpluses to assist in funding other federal government operations. Unlike debt held by the public, intragovernmental debt holdings are not shown as balances on the federal government's consolidated financial statements because they represent loans from one part of the federal government to another. Under generally accepted US accounting principles, when the federal government financial statements are consolidated, those offsetting balances are eliminated. In addition, from the perspective of the budget as a whole, Treasury's interest payments to federal government accounts are entirely offset by the income received by such accounts.

The intragovernmental debt and related interest reflects a burden on taxpayers and the economy in the future. Of the fiscal year 2012 increase, $1143 billion was from the increase in debt held by the public and $135 billion was from the increase in intragovernmental debt holdings. The considered 2012 and 2015 models deal with the total national debt and use the federal debt data revised by the Bureau of the Public Debt of the US Government Accountability Office.

Some American economists support the use of the public debt (the total national debt minus intragovernmental debt; in many other countries, terms *public debt* and *national debt* are identical) as the right measure of the economic health, more accurate than the total national debt. They argue that a large increase of the public debt can increase the amount of future interest payments that the federal government must make to lenders outside of the United States, which reduces Americans' income, whereas intragovernmental debt has no such effects (at least now) because it is simply money that the federal government owes (and pays interest on) to itself.

According to the Congress Budget Office (CBO), interest payments on debt represent a large and rapidly growing expense of the federal government. Federal debt held by the public reached about $13 trillion at the end of 2014 fiscal year, an amount that equals 74% of GDP. According CBO's baseline projections, it would climb to $20.6 trillion, or 77% of GDP, in 2024 (in reality, it reached the 77% level in 2016). Currently, the government interest costs on the public debt are around $250 billion a year, a sum that is low owing to the era of low interest rates. According to the CBO forecast, interest rates will gradually rise and can reach in 10 years nearly $800 billion or 3.0% of GDP—the highest ratio since 1996 (see Edelberg, 2014).

Table 2.14 Simulation results for the 2012 debt to GDP ratio dynamics model for $l_G = 1.59$

Year	1	2	3	4	5	6	7	8	9	10
Debt/GDP g1 = 0.03	0.72	0.74	0.76	0.77	0.78	0.79	0.79	0.8	0.8	0.8
Debt/GDP g1 = 0.04	0.72	0.75	0.77	0.80	0.82	0.85	0.88	0.91	0.94	0.97

Table 2.15 Simulation results for the 2012 debt to GDP ratio dynamics model for $l_G = 1.59$

Year	1	2	3	4	5	6	7	8	9	10
Debt/GDP g1 = 0.03	0.72	0.73	0.72	0.72	0.72	0.70	0.69	0.67	0.64	0.61
Debt/GDP g1 = 0.04	0.72	0.73	0.74	0.75	0.76	0.77	0.78	0.79	0.80	0.81

Taking into account the aforementioned and the future intention of the American government to improve the country's infrastructure, we use the considered earlier model Eqs. (2.12)–(2.15), (2.18), and (2.19) [(2.31)–(2.36)] to estimate the public debt to GDP ratio for the next decade.

The below results are obtained for the following parameters: $l_G = 1.59$, $d_0 = 0.703$; $r = 0.0217$; $\tau = 0.16$; $c = 1$; $\beta = 0.69$; $l_3 = 0.194$; and $l_2 = 0.13$ (they are very close to the data characterizing the US economy in 2012; compared with the data of Tables 2.1–2.6, the value of τ was increased slightly to reflect the delayed effect of stimulus in the previous years). Tables 2.14 and 2.15 are built for $g_0 = 0.026$ and $g_1 = 0.03$, and $g_0 = 0.026$ and $g_1 = 0.04$, respectively.

Table 2.14 shows that the government investment in infrastructure will increase more than 14% the public debt to GDP ratio. As seen from Table 2.14, the $d(t)$ estimate reaches 77% significantly earlier than it was projected by CBO. Only a drastic cut of government spending can improve the economy. Table 2.15 contains the simulation results for the government policy combining stimulus with a decrease in government spending; $h = 0.02$ as in the earlier related tests. However, as it was mentioned earlier, using spending stimulus to rear high GDP growth rates can increase, rather than decrease, the debt to GDP ratio even if it is accompanied with some spending cuts not related to the stimulus programs.

The above simulation results show the lower limit of the debt to GDP ratio obtained for the models with constant parameters. As mentioned earlier, the combination of government fiscal and monetary policy is more effective than a pure fiscal policy, and the fiscal multiplier changes significantly during the recovery process (see, e.g., Christiano et al., 2011). Here we use the model (2.50) to examine the debt to GDP trajectory for this case.

We consider here the effect of an increase in government spending for monetary policy near zero and at the zero lower bound. This increase leads to a rise in output and expected inflation. With the nominal interest rate near zero, the rise in expected inflation drives down the real interest rate, which drives up private spending. This rise in spending leads to a further rise in output and expected inflation and a further decline in the real interest rate. The net result is a large rise in output and a large fall in the rate of deflation. In effect, the increase in government consumption counteracts the deflationary spiral associated with the zero-bound state. An important practical objection to using fiscal policy to counteract a contraction associated with the zero-bound state is that there are long lags in implementing increases in government spending. Motivated by this consideration, Christiano et al. (2011) studied the size of the government spending multiplier in the presence of implementation lags. As indicated earlier, when the nominal interest rate is zero or near zero, then there is a large effect on current output and the fiscal multiplier is about 3.8. However, in future periods, in which the nominal interest rate is positive and higher, the effect on government spending is smaller, and the government spending multiplier becomes close to 1.

We analyze the debt to GDP ratio change from 2009 to 2015 based on the model (2.52) with the GDP growth rate $g_0 = -0.014$, $d_0 = 0.7354$, $l_{30} = 0.18$, and $l_2 = 0.11$ that correspond to the US government data related to the fourth quarter of 2008 and the first two quarters of 2009. Because now the economic data of 2009–2015 are available, we use the model (2.50) to evaluate the effect of the US financial and monetary policies starting with February 2009 American Recovery and Reinvestment Act. The g_0 value was determined based on the GDP four quarters data back from March 2009; d_0 corresponds to the fourth quarter of 2008; the growth rate in 2009 was determined based on the GDP growth at the second part of the year (when the stimulus started generating growth). The other parameters of the model correspond to the 2009–2015 data (see Table 2.16). The stimulus spending amounts were subtracted from the government

Table 2.16 Simulation results for the debt to GDP ratio dynamics model (2.50)

Year	2009	2010	2011	2012	2013	2014	2015
$g_{t+1}\%$	0.34	2.532	1.6	2.223	1.678	2.37	2.6
τ_{t+1}	0.15	0.16	0.16	0.16	0.175	0.175	0.185
$l_{3,t+1}$	0.182	0.144	0.15	0.155	0.141	0.14	0.138
$r\%$	3.35	3.05	2.89	2.588	2.43	2.4	2.35
$l_{\sum}$	0.5	1.0	2.0	3.5	3.8	3.8	3.8
Debt/GDP ratio d	(0.8236)	(0.904)	(0.9515)	(0.9935)	(1.003)	(1.03)	(1.038)
	0.8262	0.8766	0.9299	0.976	1.0043	1.032	1.061

Table 2.17 Simulation results for the debt to GDP ratio dynamics model (2.51)

Year	2009	2010	2011	2012	2013	2014	2015
Debt/GDP ratio d	0.8190	0.8609	0.9023	0.9334	0.9454	0.9542	0.963

spending data, and the calculated $l_{3,t+1}$ values are used in the model. In the same way the τ_{t+1} values (increased by the tax cuts amount, which was significantly lower than the stimulus spending) were determined.

Table 2.17 shows the simulation results for the debt to GDP ratio dynamics model (2.51) assuming that the 2009—2015 government stimulus fiscal policy, accompanied with near-zero monetary policy, implemented also austerity measures—spending cuts (as it has been done earlier, $h = 0.02$ is chosen to get about a 20% decrease in the government spending in 10 years). In this case, the debt to GDP ratio in 2015 can be decreased by about 10%.

The simulation results are very close to the real US government data (see Table 2.16, the debt to GDP ratio values in parenthesis). The errors are, to some extent, the result of insufficient and reliable information concerning the US stimulus available now. According to many economists, the $800 billion American Recovery and Reinvestment Act does not present the real amount of money pumped into the economy during 2008—2015, which is much higher. According to the Cato Institute estimates, the United States has dumped at least $2.5 trillion of fiscal stimulus into the economy since 2008. Art Laffer, an economist and former economics adviser to President Ronald Reagan, also puts the true amount of stimulus spending much higher than $800 billion—at more than $4 trillion. The health-care costs related to the President's care program jumped significantly in 2014 and 2015; the government financing of solar energy incentive programs is also increased in 2015. These and other factors (e.g., government constantly corrects economic data; the economic data provided by different respectful organizations may differ significantly) make it difficult to use very efficiently the generalized model. However, the presented simulations reached the main goal and showed that the financial multiplier under the coordinated fiscal and monetary policy can be high, as it was indicated by Christiano et al. (2011). The effect of the 2008–2015 tax cuts is significantly lower than the stimulus spending. That is why $l_{\Sigma,t+1}$ should be close to $l_{G,t+1}$ and we tested $l_{\Sigma,t+1} \geq 3.5$, $t = 4$–7 and $l_{\Sigma,1} = 0.5$ because the 2009 stimulus formally started acting only in the last two quarters of 2009.

As seen from the previous material, many economists believe (their research supports their opinion) that in the period of financial crises, financial multipliers are low, around 1. Different models are built to prove that (see e.g., Auerbach and Gorodnichenko, 2012a; b; Blanchard and Perotti, 2002; Heim, 2012; Ilzetzki et al., 2013; Mankiw, 2008). The considered generalized model, totally different from the mentioned models, can be used to determine the multipliers $l_{G,t+1}$ or $l_{T,t+1}$ if in Eq. (2.50) [(2.43)] we consider $l_{G,t}$ ($l_{T,t}$) as a function that minimizes, for example, $\sum_{t=1}^{n} (d_t - d_{t0})^2$ subject to $const1 < l_{G(T),t} < const2$, where d_{t0} ($t = 1,\ldots, n$) are known values of the debt to GDP ratio (in the above example, these are the 2009–2015 data). This problem belongs to the class of inverse problems and bears all difficulties of solving such problems (e.g., unrobustness of the solution, its high sensitivity to the accuracy of the used data, and the need of regularization used for solving ill-posed problems). Some aspects of this problem are discussed in Appendix B.

The US Federal Reserve kept interest rates near zero for more than 7 years, and many economists believe that the near-zero interest rates policy is toxic for financial stability because it forces retired persons to curtail spending and discourages young people from saving for retirement. Extended periods of ultralow rates also make it more difficult for families to build precautionary reserves. This policy does not stimulate economic growth. These economists explain the anemic economic growth in 2009–2016 by the ineffectiveness of the ultralow interest rates rather than the high debt to GDP ratio. This contradicts to the research results of Reinhart and Rogoff (2009).

The above examples show how dangerous to start government stimulus programs in countries with a high debt to GDP ratios. They also show that the assumptions of relatively high growth rates are nonrealistic. As mentioned earlier, according to Reinhart and Rogoff (2009), who analyzed the national debt, the GDP growth rates usually do not exceed 1%–2%. It is also reasonable to conclude that the analysis of the national, rather than public, debt gives a more plausible picture of the economy and the model dealing with the national debt is more reliable.

The Cobb–Douglas functions (2.3) and (2.22) are considered for a constant A, i.e., it is assumed that a period of economic downturn is not accompanied with technological innovation that can ignite economic and job growth. For example, at the end of the 20th century, the Internet and information technology became accelerators of the economy in many countries. In the late 1990s, the US government moved into fiscal surplus and the debt to GDP ratio fell from 66% in 1995 to 56% in 2000. However, it is too risky to spend lavishly, for example, on infrastructure with a hope of Internet-type miracles in the future.

The above analysis shows that government spending stimulus (investment in infrastructure) alone cannot decrease the debt to GDP ratio and boost the economy. It shows that Krugman and some other economists are wrong in their belief that the ratio of debt to GDP will fall and "everything worked out fiscally." However, Krugman is right by saying "increasing government debt can increase growth, if the money is invested well." The problem is what should be considered as a good investment. Public–private partnerships and individual and corporate contributions to infrastructure financing are innovative ways to seek new funding mechanism to prevent deficits from rising. Such programs are potential mechanisms through which public spending on infrastructure can be more efficient. Government spending on infrastructure may lead to a declining debt to GDP ratio when a balanced budget approach is followed at the same time. To boost the economy, investment should focus on areas that would bring a substantial profit and growth of capital, i.e., $\dot{K} > 0$ in Eq. (2.6). Government stimulus programs related to these areas can increase growth and decrease the debt to GDP ratio. However, usually, the private sector (less bureaucratic and more dynamic than the public one) is more sophisticated and faster than the government in finding and investing in such areas. Reforms to encourage private investment are the proper financial policies to restore economic health. As mentioned earlier, the existing publications focus mostly on investigating how efficient investment in infrastructure is and how dangerous high debt to GDP ratios are for economic growth, and more precisely, how they influence the GDP growth rate. The above simulation results show (see also Yanushevsky and Yanushevsky, 2013; Yanushevsky and Yanushevsky, 2014; Yanushevsky and Yanushevsky, 2017) that economic growth reached by government investment in infrastructure can increase its debt to such a degree that the debt to GDP ratio becomes dangerously high. The crises in Greece and Ireland show the consequences of high debt to GDP ratios for countries with previously fast-growing economies.

The role of public policy is to enhance economic growth and development. Infrastructure investments including roads, bridges, water supply, and infrastructure for public health and education are all factors that determine the quality of life in a country and influence the economy's ability to function and grow. That is why during crises the most important infrastructure projects should be implemented. Public policy should create favorable conditions for businesses to participate in the infrastructure projects. Private investments can be encouraged by tax cuts. Moreover, now an overwhelming number of economists believe that monetary policy is a dominant factor in guiding the economy out of recession.

However, for a very high level of debt and a high debt to GDP ratio, it is unlikely that stimulus measures alone can restore the economic health even if they are accompanied by proper monetary policy.

REFERENCES

Aschauer, D., 1989. Is public expenditure productive. Journal of Monetary Economics 23 (2), 177−200.

Auerbach, A.J., Gorodnichenko, Y., 2012a. Fiscal multipliers in recession and expansion. In: Alesina, A., Giavazzi, F. (Eds.), Fiscal Policy after the Financial Crisis. University of Chicago Press, Chicago.

Auerbach, A.J., Gorodnichenko, Y., 2012b. Measuring the output responses to fiscal policy. American Economic Journal: Economic Policy 4, 1−27.

Blanchard, O., Perotti, R., 2002. An empirical characterization of the dynamic effects of changes in government spending and taxes on output. Quarterly Journal of Economics 117 (4), 1329−1368.

Bohn, H., 1992. Budget deficits and government accounting. Carnegie-Rochester Conference Series On Public Policy 37, 1−83.

Cassou, S., Lansing, K., 1998. Optimal fiscal policy, public capital, and the productivity slowdown. Journal of Economic Dynamics and Control 30 (9−10), 1445−1489.

Christiano, L., Eichenbaum, M., Rebelo, S., 2011. When is the government spending multiplier large? Journal of Political Economy 119 (1), 78−121.

Eisner, R., 1986. How Real Is the Federal Deficit? The Free Press, New York.

Edelberg, W., 2014. CBO's Projection of Federal Interest Payments. ww.cbo.gov/publication/45684.

Glomm, G., Ravikumar, B., 1994. Public investment in infrastructure in a simple growth model. Journal of Economic Dynamics and Control 8 (8), 173−1887.

Glomm, G., Ravikumar, B., 1997. Productive government expenditures and long-run growth. Journal of Economic Dynamics and Control 1 (1), 183—204.

Hall, G., Sargent, T., 2010. Interest Rate Risk and Other Determinants of Post-WWII U.S. Government Debt/GDP Dynamics. NBER Working Paper 15702.

Heim, J., 2012. Does crowd out Hamper government stimulus programs in recessions? Journal of Applied Business and Economics 13 (2), 11—27.

Herndon, T., Ash, M., Pollin, R., 2013. Does High Public Debt Consistently Stifle Economic Growth? A Critique of Reinhart and Rogoff. Political Economy Research Institute, Working Paper Series 322. University of Massachusetts, Amherst.

Ilzetzki, E., Mendoza, E.G., Végh, C.A., 2013. How big (small?) are fiscal multipliers. Journal of Monetary Economics 60 (2), 239—254.

Krugman, P., 2012. End This Depression Now! W.W. Norton and Company, New York.

Krugman, P., August 28, 2009. The burden of debt. The New York Times.

Leeper, E., Walker, T., Yang, S., 2010. Government Investment and Fiscal Stimulus. IMF Working Papers, pp. 1—30.

Lynde, C., Richmond, J., 1993. Public capital and total factor productivity. International Economic Review 401—444.

Mankiw, G., 2008. Spending and Tax Multipliers, Greg Mankiw's Blog. http://www.aei.org/publication/spending-and-tax-multipliers.

Munnell, A., September/October 1990. How does public infrastructure affect regional performance? New England Economic Review 1, 1—32.

Ramey, V.A., 2011. Identifying government spending shocks: it's all in the timing. Quarterly Journal of Economics 126 (1), 1—50.

Reinhart, C.M., Rogoff, K.S., 2009. This Time Is Different: Eight Centuries of Financial Folly. University Press, Princeton, NJ.

Romer, C.D., Romer, D.H., 2010. The macroeconomic effects of tax changes: estimates based on a new measure of fiscal shocks. The American Economic Review 100, 763—801.

Romer, D.H., 2006. The Solow Growth Model, Advanced Macroeconomics, third ed. McGraw—Hill, New York.

United States Government Accountability Office, 2012. Schedules of Federal Debt, Financial Audit-Bureau of the Public Debt's Fiscal Years 2012 and 2011. GAO-13-114. http://www.treasurydirect.gov/govt/reports/pd/feddebt/feddebt_ann2012.pdf.

Yanushevsky, C., Yanushevsky, R., 2013. Spending and growth: a modified debt to GDP dynamic model. International Journal of Economic Sciences and Applied Research 6 (3), 21—33.

Yanushevsky, C., Yanushevsky, R., 2014. Is infrastructure spending an effective fiscal policy. Metroeconomica 65 (1), 123—135.

Yanushevsky, C., Yanushevsky, R., 2015. Stimulus or austerity: which policy is a road to a healthy economy? Chapter 4. In: Amo-Yartey (IMF), C. (Ed.), Fiscal Policies: International Aspects. Short and Long-term Challenges and Macroeconomic Effects. Nova Science Publishers, New York.

Yanushevsky, C., Yanushevsky, R., 2017. Evaluation of the efficiency of stimulus measures. London Journal of Research in Humanities and Social Sciences 17 (1), 1—9.

How Dangerous Is National Debt

Contents

Out of debt, out of danger.

Proverb

3.1 INTRODUCTION

The 2008 financial crisis and the resulting substantial increase of debt levels have reignited the debate about economic austerity and economic policies implemented with the aim of reducing government budget deficits. The theoretical justification for austerity was apparently academic research by Reinhart and Rogoff (2009), analyzing historical relationship between debt and economic growth. Austerity conditions imposed on Greece (its debt to GDP ratio exceeded 90%) by the terms of its bailout required sharp cuts of government spending. Growing fears of a Greek default soon raised concerns about the ability of other Eurozone countries—Portugal, Ireland, Italy, and Spain—to manage their mounting deficits. The European Central Bank (ECB) and the International Monetary Fund (IMF) imposed tough austerity measures as a condition for their financial support. It looks like demands for austerity were an intuitive rather than well-thoughtful reaction to a severe crisis situation.

Ideas about austerity are not new. They are linked to the national debt, which, in its modern form, is about 300 years old. Following World War I, the debate about austerity economics rose to the top of the policy agenda as a consequence of the high levels of public debt accumulated during the war and the economic challenges of the interwar years. The debate did not produce any agreement among economists. However, a very successful model of austerity, based on the classical theory, at least in response to a recession,

Applied Macroeconomics for Public Policy
ISBN: 978-0-12-815632-2
https://doi.org/10.1016/B978-0-12-815632-2.00003-1

occurred in the United States between 1920 and 1921. Classical economics stress the importance of reducing government borrowing and balancing the budget because there is no benefit from higher government spending; lower taxes can increase economic efficiency.

Antiausterity views are linked to Keynesian theory that was a guidance of American economic policy during the Great Depression. John Keynes argued that "The boom, not the slump, is the right time for austerity at the Treasury."

During the 2008 financial crisis, from 2010 to 2011, many European countries embarked on austerity programs, reducing their budget deficits relative to GDP.

Struggling to meet tax revenue goals under a rescue program overseen by the European Union and the International Monetary Fund, Greece decreased its budget deficit from 10.4% of GDP in 2010 to 9.6% in 2011. However, its debt to GDP ratio increased from 143% in 2010 to 165% in 2011. The EU-IMF loan program, which Ireland entered in December 2010, had severely constrained domestic budgetary discretion, and in 2010, Ireland had a record low of 32.3% deficit of GDP. In 2011 it was 12.6%. However, the debt to GDP ratio jumped from 86.8% in 2010 to 109.1% in 2011. Italy's budget deficit of GDP was 4.5% in 2010 and 3.8% in 2011, whereas the debt to GDP ratio did not change significantly: it was 115.3% and 116.4%, respectively. However, in 2013, when deficit was almost zero, it jumped to 123.3%. Spain decreased its budget deficit from 9.24% of GDP in 2010 to 8.9% in 2011. However, its debt to GDP ratio increased from 60.1% in 2010 to 69.5% in 2011 and reached about 100% in 2015. Being under the pressure of the EU-IMF program, Portugal decreased its budget deficit from 11.2% of GDP in 2010 to 7.4% in 2011, whereas its debt to GDP ratio jumped from 92.6% to 111.4%.

Despite declining budget deficits in each of the above indicated country, GDP growth was not sufficient to support a decline in the debt to GDP ratio. Budget deficit cuts slowed economic activity, which in turn further depressed revenues and intensified the effort required to reduce budget deficits. It is almost obvious that such means to fight deficits as tax hikes and spending cuts are recessionary. Cuts in wages and employment in the government sector of economy, the suppression of the salary bonuses for public employees, legislative adjustments to raise the retirement age in the public sector, pensions reduction, rises in VAT (value-added tax), and the wealth tax—such types of austerity measures were used in the aforementioned countries—decrease consumer confidence, reduce household disposable income, and thus reduce spending and consumption and slow down the economy.

However, an important objective of a policy of economic austerity is the maintenance of investor confidence in the government's ability to manage its finances and to restore the economy. The implementation of austerity measures often leads to a drastic decrease in the social and economic situation. Rising unemployment rates and decreasing household budgets, as an effect from lower wages, cuts in welfare payments, and social services, result in a recession. That weakens employment and consumption, causing lower tax income, that is, government revenues and a further increase in a country's debt.

Wolf (2012) analyzing the relationship between GDP growth in 2008–12 and total reduction in budget deficits due to austerity policies in several European countries concluded, "In all, there is no evidence here that large fiscal contractions budget deficit reductions bring benefits to confidence and growth that offset the direct effects of the contractions. They bring exactly what one would expect: small contractions bring recessions and big contractions bring depressions."

Similarly, Paul Krugman (2012) analyzed the relationship between GDP and reduction in budget deficits for several European countries and concluded that austerity was slowing the growth. He wrote: "this also implies that 1 euro of austerity yields only about 0.4 euros of reduced deficit, even in the short run. No wonder, then, that the whole austerity enterprise is spiraling into disaster."

Because the EU–IMF austerity policy did not work, as it was expected, in October 2012, the IMF released a report that stated the Eurozone austerity measures may have slowed economic growth and worsened the debt crisis. The International Monetary Fund admitted that its forecasts for countries that implemented austerity programs have been consistently overoptimistic, suggesting that tax hikes and spending cuts have been doing more damage than expected and that countries that implemented fiscal stimulus, such as Germany and Austria, did better than expected. However, the EU defended the measures, saying they restored confidence in how countries were being managed.

Despite the previously described gloomy results of austerity policy, Latvia, a small European country, succeeded in implementing austerity measures. Latvia's economy returned to growth in 2011 and 2012, outpacing the 27 nations in the EU, while implementing significant austerity measures. Its budget deficit dropped from 8.1% in 2010 to 3.6% in 2011 and the debt to

GDP ratio dropped from 44.1% to 41.9%, respectively. The IMF/EU and other international donors provided substantial financial assistance to Latvia. The IMF/EU program successfully concluded in December 2011. In 2015 the country has a small, less than 1%, budget deficit and the debt to GDP ratio 35.7%. Advocates of austerity argue that Latvia represents an empirical example of the benefits of austerity.

However, Latvia's 2015 unemployment rate around 10% exceeds its 6%−8% unemployment rate in 2006−07. When a country is trying to get out of recession, then lowering government spending and laying off workers usually increase unemployment.

The aforementioned US economic policy during 1920−21 recession, as well as Latvia's austerity "phenomena," demonstrates that it is difficult and maybe even impossible to create a rigorous macroeconomic theory as a reliable guidance for decision-making. The important economic term *consumer confidence*, a basis for many substantial results in economic theory, may look incompatible with human irrationality. Behavior of people of different countries and their confidence in government depend on the cultural level of population and influence of religion and traditions on their actions. This can explain nonidentical reaction to austerity policy in some countries. Of course, additional factors, such as the structure of economy and the level of debt, should be taken into account during the decision-making process concerning austerity policy.

It is not disputable that the situation with constantly growing budget deficit and increasing accumulated debt threatens to a country's sovereignty. At a certain moment, austerity measures should be implemented. However, the timing of austerity measures is everything. Contemporary Keynesian and New Keynesian economists argue that budget deficits are appropriate when an economy is in recession to reduce unemployment and help stimulate GDP growth. According to Reinhart and Rogoff (2013), "Austerity seldom works without structural reforms—for example, changes in taxes, regulations and labor market policies—and if poorly designed, can disproportionately hit the poor and middle class. Our consistent advice has been to avoid withdrawing fiscal stimulus too quickly, a position identical to that of most mainstream economists." Many economists believe that the best time for austerity measures is when the economy is in the expansion phase of the business cycle. They will slow down the growth to a healthy 2%−3% rate and reassure investors that the government is fiscally responsible. Austerity measures have wide economic, political and social motivations and consequences, and agreement about the particular measures chosen, and the pace at which debts are to be decreased should be reached based on a sophisticated decision-making process including political negotiation.

The terms *debt* and *deficit* are often used almost interchangeably in fiscal policy debates. Many economists argue that budget deficit, rather than debt, explains decreasing economic growth because federal borrowing directly linked with budget deficit. An increase in the federal budget deficit makes the government increase borrowing money from its own citizens as well as from international investors. These actions may produce a crowd-out effect and a decline in investment, that is, a decrease of future growth rates. Note that the size of the nation's outstanding *debt* plays no role in this account of borrowing and subsequent growth. So long as current flows of savings are not being claimed by government borrowing, no crowding-out occurs. Comparing the US mid-1980s and mid-1990s economic data, researchers noticed that the average debt to GDP ratio was clearly higher but annual deficits were lower in the latter period. This allows them to claim a high correlation between budget deficits and crowding-out. However, such an insufficient (only one country and two time periods were compared without a thorough causal analysis) and absolutely nonrigorous analysis (unfortunately, it is typical for many economic "theories") cannot be taken seriously. Moreover, some economists have made the claim that rising debt levels can produce financial crises (the reasons of crises in Greece and Ireland were mentioned earlier).

Usually, persons who borrow money and pay their debts are considered as perspective; however, persons in a high debt, who continue borrowing, are not trusted with money. Which type of the mentioned persons is more preferable to deal with? It is unlikely to give a definite answer. However, if a person with a high debt possesses outstanding qualities that allow him to make debt payment and maintain a high level of living, such a person has no difficulties to get money.

The United States is a powerful country. The market for US treasuries is the most liquid and transparent market in the financial world. It is very unlikely that investors would refuse to hold US debt. However, it is irresponsible to make any theoretical statements based on the experience of only one powerful country as the United States. Moreover, the experience of the 2008 financial crisis, which started in the United States and spread all over the world, shows how dangerous for the world is any unstable economic situation in the United States, which for the past 8 years accumulated debt about $12 trillion—twice more than that for all previous years added by 43 presidents combined. Surprisingly, some economists continue to assert there is no solid evidence that the country is approaching a tipping point and the current level of the US national debt is not a problem.

The literature related to debt reduction focuses mostly on the impact of fiscal policy on growth (e.g., the size of fiscal multipliers, expansionary fiscal contraction). A limited number of studies have analyzed debt reduction episodes and their impact on long-term growth (Alesina, 2009). However, the material still lacks a comprehensive analysis of the factors that explain the time needed to reduce debt to sustainable levels. The analysis focuses on how growth and interest rates can affect the likelihood of debt reduction and vice versa. (Unfortunately, economic theory is not conclusive in determining whether federal government debt raises interest rates, and if it does, by how much (see, e.g., Miller et al., 1996).) Kumar and Woo (2010) use a regression-based model to explore the impact of high national debt on potential economic growth and show that a 10 percentage point increase in the initial debt to GDP ratio is associated with a slowdown in annual real per capita GDP growth of around 0.2 percentage points per year, with the impact being somewhat smaller in advanced economies, so that reducing debt from high levels can be good for growth. However, it is not clear what is the best way to reduce national debt. The existing papers analyze influence of past fiscal policies on debt reduction. Moreover, some economists believe that the historical fiscal policy would bring the current high debt ratio back to its normal level of 0.35 over the coming decade (Hall, 2013). There is no surprise that the debt to GDP ratio forecast based on the stochastic model of Hall (2013) differs significantly from the debt to GDP ratio projections obtained by the US Congressional Budget Office, the fact indicated by the mentioned author, because initial assumptions of the paper are questionable.

Difficulty in solving the debt problem is in the uncertainty surrounding the accumulation of debt. Future business cycles are inherently impossible to forecast. Because high debt creates greater uncertainty about prospects and policies, it is difficult to build reliable models that would produce reliable results. As shown in Guichard et al. (2007), the policy with fiscal adjustments that reform entitlements and increase the share of spending for capital projects is more likely to succeed and affect positively growth. However, regaining fiscal control by reducing national debt will not be easy because of the large size of consolidation needs estimated for many countries and the uncertain global outlook (IMF, 2010a).

Political economy variables are important in explaining the duration of debt consolidations, given that debt reductions are politically controversial and governments face electoral constraints when designing their debt reduction strategies. Political economy constraints may also limit the implementation of needed reforms to reduce fiscal deficits. Studies have shown that the likelihood of debt consolidation could be lowered by institutional weaknesses, lack of political cohesion, and government fragmentation (see, e.g., Buti and Van den Noord, 2003). An assessment of past fiscal adjustment plans shows that, in many cases, implementation of planned spending cuts was problematic and had to be reversed (IMF, 2010b). This could jeopardize the initial fiscal objectives and undermine the sustainability of the debt reduction strategy.

Usually, politicians establish long-term financial goals and formulate the future fiscal policy to realize these goals (e.g., planned spending cuts, revenue-enhancing measures, structural fiscal reform on entitlements). These goals are supported by simulation results using complex economic models with many uncertain parameters. As a result, in many cases, long-term economic forecasts are not attainable.

As mentioned earlier, at the initial stages of resolving complex problems, more simple models give more reliable estimates than complex dynamic models that contain many uncertain parameters. Below we will show how to use the optimal theory approach to evaluate whether the proposed economic plans are political or practical. Based on the mentioned goals, two types of optimal problems are formulated. The obtained solutions provide yearly information about the necessary debt policy to reach the goals and depend on the chosen criterion and its parameters. First, the optimal debt reduction policy is considered assuming that substantial debt cuts can be carried out. Then a more moderate policy of balancing budget by a specific year is considered. Although usually optimal solutions are rarely realized precisely in practice, the obtained optimal yearly debt estimates help to evaluate how realistic is a proposed economic policy related to debt reduction and how efficiently it is realized. They are intermediate yearly goals to reach the long-term goal.

3.2 OPTIMAL APPROACH TO THE DEBT REDUCTION PROBLEM

As shown in the previous chapter, the government policy focused on investment in infrastructure or tax cuts to boost the economy is not an efficient strategy, which can lead to serious consequences and create dangerous problems. Here we discuss what can be reached by using austerity measures focused on decreasing the national debt. Without analyzing the related concrete policies, we will estimate how realistic are long-term goals established by politicians and in what intermediate yearly goals the long-term goals can be translated. Such an approach can help to estimate realistically the proposed austerity policy. The yearly goals are obtained from the solution of the quadratic optimal terminal problem. Its solution determines the yearly debt estimates as optimal subgoals linked to a public policy goal proposed by politicians to reduce national debt by a certain amount for a projected period. Any policy with the yearly debt (debt to GDP ratio) significantly different from the obtained optimal values would question the ability to achieve the final goal or would cause one to assume that it would require later more painful economic policies than in the optimal case.

The debt dynamics was presented in Chapter 2 in the form

$$\dot{D}(t) = rD(t) + G(t) - T(t) \qquad (3.1)$$

By introducing the new variable, the difference between the government purchases and revenues,

$$u(t) = G(t) - T(t) \qquad (3.2)$$

and considering it as control, Eq. (3.1) reduces to the form typical for control theory

$$\dot{D}(t) = rD(t) + u(t), \quad D(t_0) = D_0 \qquad (3.3)$$

where $D(t)$ is a state variable with the initial value D_0 and $u(t)$ is control.

The problem of decreasing the national debt is formulated as the optimal control problem of choosing u_t that minimizes the quadratic performance index

$$2J = D^2(t_f) + \int_{t_0}^{t_f} cu^2(t)dt \qquad (3.4)$$

subject to Eq. (3.3), where c is a coefficient and $t = 0$ and $t = t_f$ are initial and final times, respectively.

The performance index (3.4) can be considered as a result of Lagrangian constrained optimization: $min\ D^2(t_f)$ under limited resources $\int_{t_0}^{t_f} u^2(t)dt \leq$ $const$. Formally, a more precise representation of the goal and constraint is $min\ D^2(t_f)$ and $\int_{t_0}^{t_f} |u(t)|dt \leq const$, respectively. However, because $u(t)$ is not positive in the debt reduction problem and it is simply impossible to indicate reliable values of the above $const$, the used constraint with $u^2(t)$ is similar, in many practical cases, to the constraint with $|u(t)|$, and the quadratic functional (3.4) with a properly chosen c reflects the goal—to reduce the debt over a certain period of time. The presence of the integral $\int_{t_0}^{t_f} cu^2(t)dt$ in Eq. (3.4) reflects the fact that government expenditure and revenue are limited; the value of this term depends on the coefficient c, which choice will be explained later. Minimization of this term shows the required interconnection between spending and revenue policies.

The solution of the formulated problem is (see, e.g., Chow, 1986; Kwakernaak and Sivan, 1972; Yanushevsky, 2011)

$$u(t) = -\frac{1}{c}W(t)D(t) \qquad (3.5)$$

and the optimal debt dynamics is described by the following equation:

$$\dot{D}(t) = rD(t) - \frac{1}{c}W(t)D(t), \quad D(t_0) = D_0 \qquad (3.6)$$

where $W(t)$ satisfies the Riccati equation

$$\dot{W} = -2rW + \frac{1}{c}W^2, \quad W(t_f) = 1 \qquad (3.7)$$

The solution of Riccati equations presents certain difficulties, and it is impossible in the general case to obtain the analytical solution. However, this can be done for the particular case (3.7).

The Riccati equation (3.7) can be written as

$$\frac{dW}{W(c^{-1}W - 2r)} = dt$$

The result of its integration can be presented the form

$$\ln\frac{W - 2rc}{W} = 2rt + const$$

or

$$W(t) = \frac{-2rc}{const \cdot e^{2rt} - 1}$$

where the constant of integration is determined from the condition $W(t_f) = 1$, i.e.,

$$1 = \frac{-2rc}{const \cdot \exp(2rt_f) - 1}$$

so that

$$const = (1 - 2rc)\exp(-2rt_f)$$

Its substitution to the above expression for $W(t)$ gives us

$$W(t) = \frac{\exp[2r(t_f - t)]}{1 - \frac{1}{2rc}\{1 - \exp[2r(t_f - t)]\}} \tag{3.8}$$

The expressions (3.5) and (3.7) follow immediately from the solution of the optimal control problem for the quadratic performance index (3.4) (see, e.g., Kwakernaak and Sivan, 1972; Yanushevsky, 2011). The coefficient c should be chosen to satisfy realistic budgetary constraints and the debt reduction goal.

The debt to GDP ratio dynamics is presented by the following equation (see Eq. (2.4)):

$$\dot{d}(t) = \frac{\dot{D}(t)}{Y(t)} - gd(t) \tag{3.9}$$

By substituting Eq. (3.6) in Eq. (3.9), we have

$$\dot{d}(t) = \left(r - g - \frac{1}{c}W(t)\right)d(t), \quad d(t_0) = d_0 \tag{3.10}$$

Assuming that optimal debt cuts are accompanied by the GDP gross rate $g = g_o$, the solution of Eq. (3.10) gives an estimate of the GDP to debt ratio for the optimal law (3.5).

The above considered optimal solution requires at least a balanced budget as a necessary condition to implement in practice the described optimal policy or the policy close to the recommendations following from the optimal solution (Eqs. (3.6) and (3.7)). However, usually, there are many obstacles, political and economic, to implement in practice the considered optimal policy. For example, even if the highly indebted countries set up severe austerity programs, they are far from achieving a budget surplus; they would already be happy enough if the deficit does not increase any further and could be moderately decreased in the next few years.

Below we consider the debt to GDP ratio optimal problem, which can be more appropriate for implementation in many countries than the debt minimization problem (3.4).

Assuming the average expected GDP gross rate during the period $t_f - t_0$ equals g, Eq. (3.9) can be written as

$$\dot{d}(t) = (r - g)d(t) + \frac{G(t) - T(t)}{Y(t)} = (r - g)d(t) + \frac{u(t)}{Y(t)} \tag{3.11}$$

By introducing the control

$$v(t) = \frac{G(t) - T(t)}{Y(t)} \tag{3.12}$$

and the performance index

$$2J_1 = d^2(t_f) + \int_{t_0}^{t_f} cv^2(t)\,dt \tag{3.13}$$

analogous to Eqs. (3.2) and (3.4), we get the optimal solution

$$v(t) = -\frac{1}{c} W_0(t) d(t) \tag{3.14}$$

where W_0 satisfies the Riccati equation

$$\dot{W}_0 = -2(r - g) W_0 + \frac{1}{c} W_0^2, \quad W_0(t_f) = 1 \tag{3.15}$$

The solution of the Riccati equation (3.15) is analogous to Eq. (3.8)

$$W_0(t) = \frac{\exp[2(r - g)(t_f - t)]}{1 - \dfrac{1}{2(r - g)c}\{1 - \exp[2(r - g)(t_f - t)]\}} \tag{3.16}$$

The optimal debt to GDP ratio dynamics is described by the equation similar to Eq. (3.10), and the procedure of determining the optimal policy in accordance with the criterion (3.13) is similar to that considered earlier for the criterion (3.4). However, the coefficient c and $W_0(t)$ are different than those in Eqs. (3.4)–(3.7). The coefficient c should be chosen to achieve a certain reduction of the debt to GDP ratio in $t_f - t_0$ years.

In contrast to the above considered problem demonstrating the optimal policy to reach a certain debt reduction in $t_f - t_0$ years, we consider a more modest goal—to balance budget by a t_f year.

From Eq. (3.1) the condition of balancing budget at $t = t_f$ can be written as

$$rD(t_f) + G(t_f) - T(t_f) = 0 \tag{3.17}$$

and transformed (divided by $Y(t_f)$ and using Eqs. (3.13) and (3.14)) to

$$r - c^{-1} W_0(t_f) = 0 \tag{3.18}$$

so that

$$c = r^{-1} \tag{3.19}$$

The solution of the optimal problem, minimization of the performance index including the debt to GDP ratio, under the condition (3.19) determines the debt policy to balance the budget by a specific year. Based on the chosen performance index, the obtained optimal solution establishes yearly debt level goals that can be realized by an appropriate fiscal policy of the government assuming that such goals can be achieved.

However, the same condition can be used for a more aggressive policy—the balancing budget policy accompanied by debt decrease—if the optimal policy (3.5) is used. The condition (3.17) is equivalent to

$$rD(t_f) + u(t_f) = 0 \qquad (3.20)$$

and substituting Eq. (3.5) into Eq. (3.20) (taking into account that $W(t_f) = 1$) gives immediately Eq. (3.19).

3.3 SPECIFICS OF THE DISCRETE OPTIMIZATION MODEL

As mentioned earlier, in many cases, discrete models are more convenient for development of computational algorithms. Taking into account that optimal problems for models described by difference equations have specific features, we consider in detail a discrete variant of the problem presented in the previous section.

By introducing the new variable, the difference between the government purchases and revenues is

$$u_t = G_{t+1} - T_{t+1}, \qquad (3.21)$$

and considering it as control, Eq. (2.21) reduces to the form

$$D_{t+1} - D_t = rD_t + u_t, \quad t = 0, 1, 2, \dots \qquad (3.22)$$

where D_t is a state variable with the initial value D_0 and u_t is control.

The problem of decreasing the national debt is formulated as the optimal control problem of choosing u_t that minimizes the quadratic performance index

$$2J = D_N^2 + \sum_{t=0}^{N-1} cu_t^2 \qquad (3.23)$$

subject to Eq. (3.22), where c is a coefficient and $t = 0$ and $t = N$ are initial and final times, respectively.

As in the continuous case, the performance index (3.23) can be considered as a result of Lagrangian constrained optimization: $min\ D_N^2$ under limited resources $\sum_{t=0}^{N-1} cu_t^2 \leq const$ or $min\ \sum_{t=0}^{N-1} cu_t^2$ under limited D_N^2. Formally, a more precise representation of the goal and constraint is $min\ D_N^2$ and $\sum_{t=0}^{N-1} c|u_t| \leq const$, respectively.

Similar to the continuous case, the presence of the sum expression cu_t^2 in Eq. (3.23) reflects the fact that government expenditure and revenues are limited; the value of this term depends on the coefficient c, which choice will be explained later. Minimization of this term shows the required interconnection between spending and revenue policies.

The solution of the formulated problem is (see e.g., Chow, 1986; Kwakernaak and Sivan, 1972; Yanushevsky, 2011)

$$u_t = -(c + W_{t+1})^{-1}(r+1)W_{t+1}D_t \qquad (3.24)$$

and the optimal debt dynamics is described by the following equation:

$$D_{t+1} - D_t = rD_t - (c + W_{t+1})^{-1}(r+1)W_{t+1}D_t, \quad t = 0,\ 1,\ 2,\ldots \qquad (3.25)$$

where W_t satisfies the Riccati equation

$$W_t = (1+r)^2 W_{t+1}(c + W_{t+1})^{-1}, \quad W_N = 1 \qquad (3.26)$$

The expressions (3.24) and (3.26) follow immediately from the solution of the optimal control problem for the quadratic performance index (3.23) (see, e.g., Murata, 1978).

The debt to GDP ratio d_t dynamics (see Eqs. (3.21), (3.22), and (2.23)) can be presented as

$$d_{t+1} - d_t = \frac{r-g}{1+g}d_t + \frac{G_{t+1} - T_{t+1}}{Y_{t+1}} = \frac{r-g}{1+g}d_t + \frac{u_t}{(1+g)Y_t} \qquad (3.27)$$

By substituting Eq. (3.24) in Eq. (3.27), we have

$$d_{t+1} - d_t = (1+g)^{-1}\left[r - g - (c + W_{t+1})^{-1}(r+1)W_{t+1}\right]d_t, \quad d(0) = d_0 \qquad (3.28)$$

Assuming that optimal debt cuts are accompanied by the GDP gross rate $g = g_0$, the solution of Eq. (3.28) gives an estimate of the GDP to debt ratio. For example, for $d(t_0) = 1$, $g_0 = 0.03$, $r = 0.026$, and the optimal strategy

(3.24), we can reach in a 10-year period the GDP to debt ratio equal to 0.55, i.e., almost twice less than its initial value. As mentioned earlier, the practical implementation of the optimal policy (3.24) is limited.

Assuming the average expected GDP growth rate during the period $t_f - t_0$ equals g and introducing the control

$$v_t = \frac{G_{t+1} - T_{t+1}}{Y_{t+1}} \tag{3.29}$$

we present (2.23) in the form similar to Eq. (3.21)

$$d_{t+1} - d_t = \frac{r - g}{1 + g}d_t + v_t \tag{3.30}$$

and consider the optimal problem of minimizing the performance index

$$2J_1 = d_N^2 + \sum_{t=0}^{N-1} cv_t^2 \tag{3.31}$$

Analogous to Eqs. (3.22) and (3.23), we get the solution

$$v_t = -(c + W_{t+1})^{-1}(1 + g)^{-1}(r + 1)W_{t+1}d_t \tag{3.32}$$

where W_t satisfies the Riccati equation

$$W_t = \frac{(1 + r)^2}{(1 + g)^2}W_{t+1}(c + W_{t+1})^{-1}, \quad W_N = 1 \tag{3.33}$$

The optimal debt to GDP ratio dynamics is described by the equation

$$d_{t+1} - d_t = \frac{r - g}{1 + g}d_t - (c + W_{t+1})^{-1}(1 + g)^{-1}(r + 1)W_{t+1}d_t \tag{3.34}$$

and the procedure of determining the optimal policy in accordance with the criterion (3.28) is similar to that considered earlier for the criterion (3.23). However, the coefficient c and W_t are different than those in Eqs. (3.23)–(3.26).

Similar to the continuous model, from Eq. (2.20) the condition of balancing budget at $t_f = N$ can be written as

$$rD_{N-1} + G_N - T_N = 0 \tag{3.35}$$

and transformed (divided by Y_N) to

$$r(1 + g)^{-1}d_{N-1} + v_{N-1} = 0 \tag{3.36}$$

As in the continuous case (see Eqs. (3.18) and (3.19)) by substituting Eq. (3.32) in Eq. (3.36) and taking into account that $W_N = 1$, we have

$$r(1+g)^{-1}d_{N-1} - (c+1)^{-1}(1+g)^{-1}(r+1)d_{N-1} = 0 \qquad (3.37)$$

The condition (3.19) follows immediately from Eq. (3.37).

Similar to the continuous case, the same condition can be used for a more aggressive policy—balancing budget and debt decrease—if the optimal policy (3.24) is used. The condition (3.35) is equivalent to

$$rD_{N-1} + u_{N-1} = 0 \qquad (3.38)$$

and substituting Eq. (3.24) into Eq. (3.38) (taking into account that $W_N = 1$) gives immediately Eq. (3.19).

Various governmental accounting systems follow the established accounting standards. Different standards may require the presence of an additional term $F(t)$ $[F_{t+1}]$ in the basic debt equation (3.1) [Eqs. (3.21) and (3.25)], reflecting the so-called other means of financing (see Appendix D), i.e.,

$$\dot{D}(t) = rD(t) + G(t) - T(t) + F(t) \qquad (3.39)$$

$$D_{t+1} - D_t = rD_t + G_{t+1} - T_{t+1} + F_{t+1}, \quad t = 0, 1, 2, \dots \qquad (3.40)$$

Respectively, the additional term $f(t) = F(t)/Y(t)$ $[f_{t+1} = F_{t+1}/Y_{t+1}]$ will be in the debt to GDP equations, i.e.,

$$\dot{d}(t) = (r-g)d(t) + \frac{G(t) - T(t)}{Y(t)} + f(t) \qquad (3.41)$$

$$d_{t+1} - d_t = \frac{r-g}{1+g}d_t + \frac{G_{t+1} - T_{t+1}}{Y_{t+1}} + f_{t+1} \qquad (3.42)$$

The solution of the considered optimal problems will contain the additional terms dependent on $F(t)$ and $f(t)$ $[F_{t+1}$ and $f_{t+1}]$. The corresponding expressions are given in Appendix C.

Finally, formally the developed dynamic models do not account for inflation. However, the interest rates and the GDP growth rates reflect the effect of inflation. We did not specify how to choose their values, which can be presented in the nominal or real numbers. Usually, the real, adjusted for inflation, GDP growth rates are commonly used to measure the size and growth of a country's economy. As to the basic debt equation, the interest rates correspond to nominal prices. Usually, the symbol i, rather than r, is used, so that the balanced budget condition (3.19) should be

$$c = i^{-1} \qquad (3.43)$$

The debt to GDP ratio models use the real interest rates r and GDP growth rates g, but the debt values are determined by using the GDP nominal values (see details in Appendix D).

3.4 OPTIMIZATION PROCEDURE AND DEBT ESTIMATES

The given examples relate to the existing concrete proposals prepared by American politicians and use the US economic data.

Understanding the urgency in resolving the US debt problem, the proposal crafted by a bipartisan group of senators known as the "Gang of Six" called for $500 billion in immediate savings and for reducing the deficit by $3.7 trillion over the coming decade. Democrats and Republicans agreed on approximately $4 trillion in long-term deficit reductions over the next decade or so, but how to get there is the major point of contention.

The proposals of several bipartisan commissions (starting with the Bowles—Simpson Commission) focused on deficit reduction but differed in their changes to taxation, entitlement programs, defense spending, and research funding. Considering various scenarios of cuts and using macroeconomic simulation models, they presented the debt estimates in 10—30 years (in some reports as a percent of the future GDP). Although such forecasting models are very unreliable, politicians prefer to use them to defend their position avoiding responsibility for mistakes, which can be rigorously proved only in 10—30 years.

Here we consider two goals offered to resolve the US debt problem: to decrease debt by $4 trillion and to balance budget in 10 years. First we consider the optimal strategy to minimize the national debt in 10 years, i.e., the optimal problem with the performance index (3.4) (Eq. (3.20)). For the discrete model (3.23), the solution follows from Eqs. (3.24) and (3.26).

First, we consider the 2012 data: D_0 equals $16.05 trillion and $r = 0.026$. The coefficient c is chosen to satisfy realistic budgetary constraints and the $4 trillion debt reduction. For $r = 0.026$ and $c = 17.5$, the solution of the system (3.22), (3.25), and (3.26) (for the continuous model—Eqs. (3.4), (3.5), and (3.6)), i.e., the debt for each consecutive year (and yearly cuts), is presented in Table 3.1.

Table 3.1 Optimal solution for the performance index (3.4) [(3.23)] for the 2012 data

Year	1	2	3	4	5	6	7	8	9	10
Debt	15.6	15.17	14.74	14.32	13.91	13.52	13.13	12.74	12.37	12.01
Debt cuts	0.45	0.43	0.43	0.42	0.41	0.39	0.39	0.39	0.37	0.36

Table 3.2 Optimal solution for the performance index (3.4) [(3.23)] for the 2014 data

Year	1	2	3	4	5	6	7	8	9	10
Debt	17.35	16.92	16.49	16.08	15.67	15.27	14.88	14.5	14.13	13.77
Debt cuts	0.45	0.43	0.43	0.41	0.41	0.4	0.39	0.39	0.37	0.36

Using the 2014 and 2015 debt data (see Table 2.7; the reliability of this information was discussed earlier), the coefficient c is determined: $c = 19.5$ for $r = 0.0242$ and $c = 20.2$ for $r = 0.0235$.

The optimal debt reduction based on the 2014 and 2015 data is presented in Tables 3.2 and 3.3.

As seen from Tables 3.1–3.3, the optimal debt cuts are very close. Assuming that optimal debt cuts are accompanied by the GDP gross rate $g = g_o$, the solution of Eqs. (3.8) and (3.10) [Eqs. (3.28) and (3.26)] gives an estimate of the GDP to debt ratio. For example, for $d(t_0) = 1.01$, $g_o = 0.03$, and $r = 0.0235$ in a 10-year period, the optimal strategy (3.5) [Eq. (3.21)] can reduce the debt to GDP ratio to 0.59.

Many economists believe that, assessing the economic impact of federal debt, debt held by the public (not gross national debt) is the more correct measure because it shows the degree to which the federal government must rely on private savings to finance borrowing. As indicated earlier, most of the difference between these two measures is accounted for by the large surplus generated by Social Security and held in the Social Security Trust Fund; this is money that the government is borrowing from itself, so it does not crowd out potential private borrowers. The optimal debt policy related to the US public debt is based on the 2015 data: D_0 equals \$13.15 trillion and $r = 0.0227$. The coefficient c is chosen to satisfy realistic budgetary constraints and the \$4 trillion debt reduction. For $r = 0.0227$

Table 3.3 Optimal solution for the performance index (3.4) [(3.23)] for the 2015 data

Year	1	2	3	4	5	6	7	8	9	10
Debt	17.66	17.23	16.82	16.41	16.01	15.62	15.23	14.86	14.49	14.13
Debt cuts	0.44	0.43	0.41	0.41	0.4	0.39	0.39	0.37	0.37	0.36

Table 3.4 Optimal solution for the performance index (3.4) [(3.23)] for the 2015 data

Year	1	2	3	4	5	6	7	8	9	10
Debt	12.72	12.3	11.89	11.48	11.07	10.67	10.28	9.89	9.51	9.14
Debt cuts	0.43	0.42	0.41	0.41	0.41	0.4	0.4	0.39	0.39	0.37

and $c = 15.4$, the solution of the system (3.22), (3.25), and (3.26) is given in Table 3.4.

The debt cuts for the considered case are very close to the optimal national debt cuts. For $d(t_0) = 0.73$ and $g_o = 0.03$ in a 10-year period, the optimal strategy (3.5) [(3.21)] can reduce the debt to GDP ratio to 0.37.

As mentioned earlier, the optimal solution (3.5) [(3.21)] requires at least a balanced budget as a necessary condition to implement the described optimal policy. In the case of a high debt and a budget deficit, it is highly unrealistic to expect that the established yearly cuts can be realized in practice.

In contrast to the previously considered example demonstrating the optimal policy to reach the $4 trillion debt reduction in 10 years, here we consider a more modest goal—to balance budget by a t_f year.

In the United States, the annually balanced budget was the goal until the Great Depression in the 1930s. Keynesian economics believe that this is a bad approach because during a recession a sharp fall in levels of consumer and business confidence can result in a rapid fall in investment. In a recession, as tax revenues fall, the only way for government to balance the budget is to raise taxes and lower spending. However, most economists believe that such a policy only would worsen recession. In their opinion, deficit spending is allowed during a recession period; too much deficit reduction is harmful to an economy that is not at full strength.

Usually, that deficit is around 3% of GDP. During the 2008, financial crisis deficit in 2009 reached 9.8% of the economy, but in 2015 it became about average again, at 3.2%. It means that this is a time to start improving the economy despite a very high national debt.

A reasonable question is how to find a balanced approach—a plan that both would help the economy to grow and would address the growing debt. The budget process, focused on balancing the budget, should include annual budget targets toward meeting future fiscal goals to reduce the national debt.

Table 3.5 Optimal solution for the performance index (3.13) [(3.31)] (budget balance in 10 years)

Year	1	2	3	4	5	6	7	8	9	10
Debt/GDP	0.967	0.944	0.921	0.898	0.875	0.852	0.829	0.807	0.784	0.761
Debt	16.15	16.24	16.32	16.39	16.45	16.5	16.54	16.57	16.58	16.58
Debt change	0.1	0.09	0.08	0.07	0.06	0.05	0.04	0.03	0.01	0

Table 3.6 Optimal solution for the performance index (3.13) [(3.31)] (budget balance in 10 years)

Year	1	2	3	4	5	6	7	8	9	10
Debt/GDP	1.006	0.982	0.958	0.93	0.91	0.89	0.86	0.84	0.81	0.79
Debt	17.91	18.0	18.09	18.17	18.24	18.29	18.33	18.36	18.38	18.38
Debt change	0.11	0.09	0.09	0.08	0.07	0.05	0.04	0.03	0.02	0

Table 3.5 contains the debt to GDP ratio and the debt data for each consecutive year calculated based on Eqs. (3.10)−(3.16) [(3.28)−(3.34)] for $t_0 = 0$, $t_f = 10$, and $D_0 = 16.051$ (as in the earlier example) and $d_0 = 0.99$, $g_o = 0.03$, $r = 0.026$, and $c = r^{-1} = \frac{1}{0.0224} = 38.46$. As seen from Table 3.5, the strategy based on minimization of the debt to GDP ratio with the goal to balance the budget in 10 years is more moderate than the strategy to decrease debt by $4 trillion and the debt cuts are significantly less.

Tables 3.6 and 3.7 are built similar to Table 3.5 for the 2014 and 2015 data, respectively. Using the 2014 and 2015 debt data (see Table 2.7; the reliability of this information was discussed earlier), the coefficient c was determined: $c = 41.32$ for $r = 0.0242$ and $c = 42.55$ for $r = 0.0235$.

The described policy can decrease the debt to GDP ratio only by about 20% (for $g_o = 0.03$, the optimal reduction policy (3.5) [(3.23)] considered earlier can decrease the debt to GDP ratio by about 60%) and does not accumulate any significant new debt.

Table 3.7 Optimal solution for the performance index (3.13) [(3.31)] (budget balance in 10 years)

Year	1	2	3	4	5	6	7	8	9	10
Debt/GDP	0.986	0.963	0.939	0.916	0.892	0.869	0.845	0.822	0.799	0.776
Debt	18.2	18.3	18.39	18.47	18.54	18.59	18.64	18.67	18.68	18.68
Debt change	0.1	0.1	0.09	0.08	0.07	0.05	0.05	0.03	0.01	0

Table 3.8 Simulation results for the time-varying growth rate with average g = 0.03

Year	1	2	3	4	5	6	7	8	9	10
g	1.9	2.2	2.5	3	3.1	3.3	3.5	3.5	3.5	3.5
Debt/GDP	0.987	0.972	0.953	0.929	0.905	0.878	0.85	0.823	0.796	0.768
Debt	16.15	16.24	16.32	16.39	16.45	16.5	16.54	16.57	16.58	16.58
Debt change	0.1	0.09	0.08	0.07	0.06	0.05	0.04	0.03	0.01	0

In contrast to Table 3.5 that corresponds to the optimal strategy (3.14)−(3.16) [(3.32) and (3.33)] and the constant growth rate $g_o = 0.03$, Table 3.8 is built for time-varying growth rate with its average value 0.03 and the same optimal strategy (3.14)−(3.16) [(3.32) and (3.33)] for the 2012 data. The same values of $d(10)$ (approximately for the discrete model, which in contrast to the continuous model has the $(\cdot)$ $(t+1)$ terms) in the mentioned tables follow immediately from the analytical expression of the solution of Eq. (3.11) [(3.29)]; the same debt levels (approximately for the discrete model) follow from comparison of Eqs. (3.14) and (3.5) [(3.32) and (3.24)]. (The optimal laws for the considered models are valid for time-varying parameters; however, because of unreliable forecasts, the examples are given for more realistic scenarios.)

Analogous to the balanced budget for the national debt to GDP ratio model, the solution for the case of the public debt to GDP ratio model and the performance index (3.13) [(3.31)] is given in Table 3.9 for the 2015 data.

The balance budget condition was obtained for the criterion minimizing the debt to GDP ratio at a certain chosen period of time. It is obvious that for a lower time period t_f, we should expect a larger $d(t_f)$. However, as seen from Table 3.10 obtained for the optimal strategy to balance budget in 5 years, this value is less than that at the same time for the optimal solution corresponding to a larger period to balance budget.

Table 3.9 Optimal solution for the performance index (3.13) [(3.31)] (the 2015 data and budget balance in 10 years)

Year	1	2	3	4	5	6	7	8	9	10
Debt/GDP	0.713	0.696	0.679	0.662	0.645	0.628	0.611	0.594	0.577	0.56
Debt	13.22	13.3	13.36	13.42	13.46	13.5	13.53	13.56	13.57	13.57
Debt change	0.07	0.08	0.06	0.06	0.04	0.04	0.03	0.03	0.01	0

Table 3.10 Optimal solution for the performance index (3.13) [(3.31)] (the 2015 data and budget balance in 5 years)

Year	1	2	3	4	5
Debt/GDP	0.7108	0.6917	0.6735	0.6535	0.6345
Debt	13.1888	13.2187	13.2393	13.25	13.25
Debt change	0.0388	0.0299	0.0206	0.0107	0

As seen from Tables 3.5—3.10, in the case of the balanced budget obtained from the debt to GDP ratio criterion, the debt increases are significantly less than those in the case of the $4 trillion debt reduction.

Formally, the models (3.10)—(3.16) [(3.28)—(3.34)] can be used, similar to the models (3.1), (3.3)—(3.7), to decrease the debt to GDP ratio over a certain period of time, and the coefficient c should be chosen to satisfy the projected $d(t_f)$. However, it is logical to combine the two considered optimal problems: first, use the optimal policy to balance budget and then make the optimal debt cuts.

As indicated earlier (see Eq. (3.5) [(3.20)] and Eq. (3.24) [(3.38)]), optimization of the performance index (3.4) [(3.23)] under the balanced budget condition (3.19) presents a more aggressive strategy than minimization of the criterion (3.13) [(3.23)] because in this case we operate directly with the budget deficit (more precisely, with its main part—we cannot influence interest debt payments on debt) rather than with its ratio to the GDP—as in the case of the debt to GDP ratio model. Tables 3.11—3.13 are built for the optimal strategy (3.5) [(3.20)] and the balanced budget condition (3.19) for the US 2012, 2014, and 2015 data, respectively, similar to Tables 3.5—3.7. As seen from these tables, under the more aggressive fiscal policy, both the debt to GDP ratio and debt are less than those in the case of fiscal policy based on optimization of the debt to GDP ratio criterion (3.13) ([(3.31)]. This policy is accompanied with debt cuts; however, debt cuts are significantly less than those when the goal is to decrease the debt by $4 trillion in 10 years (see Tables 3.1—3.3).

Of course, a proper fiscal policy is determined by a concrete situation in a country and should reflect its resources that government can use to carry out an efficient economic policy.

The document prepared by the US House Budget Committee (see Price, 2016) focuses on balancing the budget and achieving $7 trillion in deficit reduction over the next decade. Using the 2016 debt data ($D_0 = 19.36$; $d_0 = 1.048$; $r = 0.0222$; and $g_0 = 0.027$) and assuming the future GDP growth rate g = 3.5, in Tables 3.14 and 3.15 we presented the results of the optimal austerity policies to decrease the debt in 10 years by $7 trillion (in Eq. (3.4) [(3.23)], $c = 12.92$) and to balance the budget in 10 years (see Eq. (3.13) [(3.31)]). The significantly different debt and debt to GDP ratio values in these tables show that the policy goals are not formulated properly.

Table 3.11 Optimal solution for the performance index (3.4) [(3.23)] (budget balance in 10 years)

Year	1	2	3	4	5	6	7	8	9	10
Debt/GDP	0.965	0.923	0.892	0.863	0.835	0.808	0.783	0.759	0.737	0.715
Debt	15.96	15.87	15.8	15.74	15.69	15.65	15.62	15.6	15.59	15.59
Debt cuts	0.09	0.09	0.07	0.06	0.05	0.04	0.03	0.02	0.01	0

Table 3.12 Optimal solution for the performance index (3.4) [(3.23)] (budget balance in 10 years)

Year	1	2	3	4	5	6	7	8	9	10
Debt/GDP	0.995	0.962	0.93	0.9	0.87	0.84	0.818	0.793	0.77	0.741
Debt	17.71	17.63	17.56	17.5	17.45	17.41	17.38	17.36	17.35	17.35
Debt cuts	0.09	0.08	0.07	0.06	0.05	0.04	0.03	0.02	0.01	0

Table 3.13 Optimal solution for the performance index (3.4) [(3.23)] (budget balance in 10 years)

Year	1	2	3	4	5	6	7	8	9	10
Debt/GDP	0.976	0.943	0.91	0.88	0.85	0.828	0. 8	0.78	0.756	0.734
Debt	18.01	17.94	17.87	17.81	17.76	17.73	17.7	17.68	17.67	17.67
Debt cuts	0.09	0.07	0.07	0.06	0.05	0.03	0.03	0.02	0.01	0

Table 3.14 Optimal solution for the performance index (3.4) [(3.23)] for the 2016 data

	1	2	3	4	5	6	7	8	9	10
Debt/GDP	0.97	0.9	0.84	0.78	0.72	0.66	0.61	0.56	0.52	0.47
Debt	18.62	17.9	17.18	16.47	15.76	15.07	14.38	13.7	13.03	12.36
Debt cuts	0.74	0.72	0.72	0.71	0.69	0.69	0.69	0.68	0.67	0.67

Table 3.15 Optimal solution for the performance index (3.13) [(3.31)] for the 2016 data

Year	1	2	3	4	5	6	7	8	9	10
Debt/GDP	1.02	0.99	0.96	0.93	0.91	0.88	0.85	0.82	0.8	0.77
Debt		19.5	19.62	19.74	19.84	19.92	20.0	20.05	20.09	20.11	20.11
Debt change	0.14	0.12	0.12	0.1	0.08	0.08	0.05	0.04	0.02	0

Some economists believe that balanced budget amendments are silly because deficits not necessarily add to the debt to GDP ratio and deficits are a normal part of life. Kleinbard (2015) explains: "Imagine that the federal debt-to-GDP ratio is 50 percent and the economy is growing at 4 percent a year. If the federal government runs a deficit equal to 2 percent of GDP, the debt-to-GDP ratio will remain a constant 50 percent — the denominator goes up by 4 percent, and the numerator by 2 percent (from, say 50/100 to 52/104). Many economists, therefore, do not lose sleep over the deficit that average no more than 2 percent of GDP over the long haul; if one assumes that the long-term US economy growth rate hovers around 3.5 percent per annum, this would imply a stable debt-to GDP ratio in the neighborhood of 60 percent."

Unfortunately, the author frivolously manipulates with numbers closing eyes to reality. In 2017, the deficit was 3.5% of GDP, and for the debt to GDP ratio equal to 70%, the GDP growth rate should be 5%; for $d(t) = 1$, the growth rate should be 3.5%. This follows immediately from Eq. (2.7) if its left part equals zero. More accurate relation between the deficit to GDP ratio $def_t = g d_t/(1 + g)$ follows from Eq. (2.23). Moreover, the above examples prove nothing. The presence of deficit shows that debt is growing and spending cannot be unlimited. Despite the mistake in Reinhart and Rogoff (2009) and insufficient reliability of conclusions based on the correlation analysis, the historical data analysis should not be ignored; it should serve at least as a warning. A huge country's debt undermines its solvency and surely increases the price paid by the country to borrow. For the United States, with dollar as the global reserve currency, it is inadmissible to be even close to the situation of being branded noncreditworthy.

REFERENCES

Alesina, A., Ardagna, S., 2009. Large changes in fiscal policy: taxes versus spending. In: Tax Policy and the Economy, vol. 24. National Bureau of Economic Research Tax policy and the Economy.

Buti, M., Van den Noord, P., 2003. What is the impact of tax and welfare reforms on fiscal Stabilisers? A simple model and an application to EMU. In: European Economy-economic Papers, vol. 187. Directorate General Economic and Monetary Affairs, European Commission, Brussels.

Chow, G.C., 1986. Analysis and Control of Dynamic Economic Systems. Krieger Publ. Co., Malabar, FL.

Guichard, S., Kennedy, M., Wurzel, E., Andre, C., 2007. What Promotes Fiscal Consolidation: OECD Country Experiences, OECD Economics Department Working Paper, No. 533.

Hall, R.E., 2013. Fiscal Stability of High-debt Nations under Volatile Economic Conditions, NBER Working Paper 18797.

International Monetary Fund, 2010a. Fiscal Exit: From Strategy to Implementation, IMF Fiscal Monitor. International Monetary Fund, Washington.

International Monetary Fund, 2010b. Strategies for Fiscal Consolidation in the Post-Crisis World. International Monetary Fund, Washington.

Kleinbard, E., 2015. We Are Better than This: How Government Should Spend Our Money. Oxford University Press, New York.

Krugman, P., April 24 , 2012. Austerity and growth, (again). New York Times.

Kumar, M.S., Woo, J., 2010. Public Debt and Growth, IMF Working Paper, No.10/174.

Kwakernaak, H., Sivan, R., 1972. Linear Optimal Control Systems, first ed. Wiley-Interscience, Hoboken, NJ.

Miller, S.M., Frank, S., Russek, F., 1996. Do federal deficits affect interest rates? Evidence from three econometric methods. Journal of Macroeconomics 18 (3), 403–428.

Murata, Y., 1978. Optimal Control Methods for Linear Discrete-time Economic Systems. Springer Verlag, New York.

Price, T., March 2016. A Balanced Budget for a Stronger America. House Budget Committee. www.Budget.House.Gov/FY2017.

Reinhart, C.M., Rogoff, K.S., 2009. This Time Is Different: Eight Centuries of Financial Folly. University Press, Princeton, NJ.

Reinhart, C.M., Rogoff, K.S., April 25 , 2013. Debt, growth and the austerity debate. New York Times.

Wolf, M., April 12, 2012. The impact of fiscal austerity in the Eurozone. Financial Times.

Yanushevsky, R., 2011. Guidance of Unmanned Aerial Vehicles. Taylor & Francis, New York.

CHAPTER FOUR

Realization of Established Goals

Contents

A statesman is a politician who places himself at the service of the nation.

A politician is a statesman who places the nation at his service.

Georges Pompidou

4.1 INTRODUCTION

Spending and taxing are two main instruments of fiscal policy, an important part of government public policy, which goals are reflected in the constitution of democratic countries. In an eloquent form, fiscal policy is defined as the art of government spending and taxing. According to the famous phrase of the Nobel Prize—winning economist Milton Friedman, a key advisor to President Reagan, government spending is the true tax—as a direct payment or in a form of borrowing: "Keep your eye on one thing and one thing only: how much government is spending, because that's the true tax … If you're not paying for it in the form of explicit taxes, you're paying for it indirectly in the form of inflation or in the form of borrowing. The thing you should keep your eye on is what government spends, and the real problem is to hold down government spending as a fraction of our income, and if you do that, you can stop worrying about the debt."

Applied Macroeconomics for Public Policy
ISBN: 978-0-12-815632-2
https://doi.org/10.1016/B978-0-12-815632-2.00004-3

The above aphorism can be interpreted as the economic analog of Newton's third law (for every action, there is an equal and opposite reaction). By productive spending, government performs its constitutional obligations, and taxation policy focuses to raise the necessary revenues to support this spending. Supporting reduction of tax rates, Friedman believed that without reduced spending, there were no real tax cuts. However, in the early 1980s, he did not endorse austerity and immediate spending cuts. Experiments with austerity in several countries showed that austerity tanked their economy; governments became unpopular and were voted out.

The US current level of debt is significantly higher than it was in the 1980s, and now there are examples of the efficiency of austerity measures. They are supported by a growing number of economists. However, the fear of their unpopularity among the population kept many 2016 Republican presidential candidates from including them in their economic platform; they preferred to emphasize only tax proposals.

The solution of the optimal problems considered in the previous chapter (minimization of the performance indices including debt and the debt to GDP ratio) determines the austerity policies focused to reduce debt by a certain year and to balance the budget by a specific year.

1-year forecasts, required in the offered procedure, are more reliable and accurate than, for example, 10-year forecasts that accompany the earlier mentioned proposals to handle the national debt. Any mistakes in yearly forecasts corresponding to the chosen policy can be taken into account in the next year strategy; a corrected debt at the end of the kth year can be considered as the initial condition for the chosen optimal problem, and it can be solved again to obtain the corrected optimal strategy in the following years. As to the debt to GDP ratio, its $d(t_f)$ estimate using an average GDP growth rate g forecast for the considering period can be also corrected. Usually, its range of changes is not too big, and the $d(t_f)$ estimates can be obtained for the maximal and minimal values of the g estimates. Such a procedure makes the offered approach to optimal debt policy more reliable; the intermediate debt goals make the debt reduction policy easier to analyze and correct, if it is necessary, than the approaches based on long-term financial goals and unreliable forecasts.

We did not consider any concrete measures to reach the formulated goals. However, any fiscal policy with the yearly debt (debt to GDP ratio) values, which are significantly different from the obtained optimal yearly values, would question the ability to achieve the final goal and would allow one to assume that it would require later more painful economic policies than in the optimal case. The established yearly optimal debt cuts allow one to judge whether the proposed austerity policy can be realized in practice. Because the effect of a real debt policy can be evaluated and compared with the projected debt estimates at the end of each consecutive year, the ability to make yearly corrections in the described procedure (that makes it adaptive), which requires only 1-year forecasts of the effect of debt-related actions that change government purchases and revenues, makes the debt policy based on the offered approach more realistic and more flexible than the policy based on the long-term economic forecasts.

As indicated earlier, the debt to GDP ratio is an important indicator of a country's economy. High GDP values send an alarming signal to the government indicating that the country does not live within its means: it is spending more than earning and, as a result, going deeper into debt. This is a warning that the country's fiscal and monetary policies should be changed. The consequences of high debt to GDP ratios were analyzed by Reinhart and Rogoff (2009, 2010).

In Chapter 2, we considered the effects of the fiscal policy (government stimulus packages and tax reduction) on the debt to GDP ratio and effects of the monitory policy being embedded in the multiplier values. In Chapter 3, the optimal approach to the debt to GDP ratio reduction was proposed based on the formulated final terminal goals. Here the debt to GDP ratio dynamics is considered assuming that dynamics of the GDP and its main components capital K and labor force L are known. The obtained theoretical results are applied below to evaluate the proposals of the 2016 presidential candidates focused on improving the US economy. The considered proposals were tested by using the Taxes and Growth Model developed by the Tax Foundation, the tax policy research organization.

In contrast to the considered above models, the whole economy output (2.3), the static model of the US economy developed by the mentioned organization contains three outputs—the outputs of the private business sector, the household and institutions, and the government enterprises. The input—output relationship of these economic sectors is presented similar to (2.3). The model contains equations related to capital and labor stocks. The production function computes how the tax-induced changes in labor and capital inputs affect economic output.

The components of the model, as many other economic models, describe relationships obtained by using regression analysis. As a result, the accuracy of the forecasting depends significantly on the accuracy of the regression models. In addition, taking into account that tax cuts are the base of most Republican proposals, the value of tax multipliers used in the model influences considerably the reliability of the forecasts.

The Taxes and Growth Model does not take into account the fiscal or economic effects of interest on debt. It also does not account for the potential macroeconomic effects of any spending cuts that may be required to finance the plan. All this makes the indicated estimates as a road to a healthy economy very unreliable. Below some forecasts from the proposals based on this model are used to test these proposals—to determine the future values of the debt to GDP ratio.

4.2 ANALYSIS OF PROPOSALS FOCUSED ON IMPROVING THE ECONOMY

To evaluate the future debt to GDP ratio based on the research results obtained by using the Tax Foundation's Taxes and Growth Model, we consider the following system of differential equations (see Eqs. (2.5), (2.6), and (3.11)):

$$\dot{d}(t) = (r - g)d(t) + \frac{G(t) - T(t)}{Y(t)} \tag{4.1}$$

where

$$\dot{Y}(t) = gY(t) \tag{4.2}$$

$$g = \alpha \frac{\dot{K}}{K} + \beta \frac{\dot{L}}{L}, \quad \dot{K} = g_K K, \quad \dot{L} = g_L L, \tag{4.3}$$

for the continuous model (see Eqs. (2.24)−(2.26), and (3.27)) and

$$d_{t+1} - d_t = \frac{r - g}{1 + g}d_t + \frac{G_{t+1} - T_{t+1}}{Y_{t+1}} \tag{4.4}$$

$$Y_{t+1} - Y_t = gY_t \tag{4.5}$$

where

$$g = (1 + g_K)^{\alpha}(1 + g_L)^{\beta} - 1 \tag{4.6}$$

and

$$K_{t+1} = (g_K + 1)K_t, \quad L_{t+1} = (g_L + 1)L_t \tag{4.7}$$

for the discrete model.

The initial conditions for the indicated equations correspond to the 2015 data of Table 2.7, that is, $Y(0) = 18$; $D(0) = 18.2$; $d(0) = 1.01$; $r = 0.0223$; $T(0) = 3.2$; $G(0) = 3.7$; the 2015 growth rate $g = 0.021$. In addition, capital income in current dollars is \$7880.619 billion and labor cost is 10,973.320 billion (the latest corrected data of the Bureau of Economic Analysis); the labor force equals 153.64 million (full- and part-time jobs) that is equivalent to 125.5 million full-time employees.

Because the GDP growth rate depends on the labor L and capital K dynamics, it is possible to analyze $d(t)$ by solving the system of equations describing the K and L dynamics and Eqs. (4.1)−(4.3) [Eqs. (4.4)−(4.7)].

As indicated earlier, the considered models are applied below to evaluate the proposals of the 2016 presidential candidates focused on improving the US economy, which were tested and assessed by the Tax Foundation.

The coefficients $\alpha = 0.3051$ and $\beta = 0.6916$ in Eq. (4.3) [Eq. (4.6)] (see Appendix A) are used to determine the GDP growth rates based on the Tax Foundation estimates of the capital and workforce data in the analyzed proposals. Although the Cobb−Douglas function was considered in the dynamic long-term forecasting models (see, e.g., Solow, 1956), its ability to get reliable quantitative predictions is questionable. This function is a static characteristic obtained based on the analysis of the dynamic process. The inverse problem (in our case, back to dynamics), as many inverse mathematical problems, usually is more complicated and requires additional conditions to have a unique solution. The modified aggregate production function (to insert dynamics) contains the time-varying $A(t)$ (A_t) (see Eqs. (2.3) and (2.22)), which changes the GDP growth rate by g_A; $\dot{A} = g_A A$ for the continuous model and $A_{t+1} = (g_A+1)A_t$. In the case $A(t) = Ae^{g_A t}$, the growth rate is constant.

Evaluation of g_A based on the 1987−2014 data (see Appendix A) shows that it could add not more than 1% to the g-rate obtained from Eq. (4.3) [(4.6)]. The analysis of the time-varying g_A based on the economic 1909−49 data (see Solow, 1957) shows an average upward shift of about 1.5% per year.

Understanding that the temptation of the Tax Foundation economists was to be optimistic and to give an estimate that the politicians wanted to hear, we use an optimistic estimate of the debt to GDP ratio by choosing in Eq. (4.1) [(4.3)] the larger of two values: the g-rate determined by the economists evaluated the proposals and the growth rate obtained from Eq. (4.3) [(4.6)] and increased by 1.5%.

Senator Cruz's tax plan would institute a flat 10% tax rate on individual income and replace the corporate income tax and all payroll taxes with a 16% "Business Transfer Tax" or subtraction method value-added tax (VAT). The plan would also lead to a 43.9% larger capital stock, 12.2% higher wages, and 4.8 million more full-time equivalent jobs.

According to the Tax Foundation's model (Pomerleau and Schuyler, 2015), it would cut taxes by $3.6 trillion over the next decade on a static basis (federal revenue would be reduced by $3.6 trillion on a static basis); on average, for all taxpayers, taxes would be cut by 9.2%. The US federal government would raise 71% of all revenues from the new broad-based VAT. However, as a result of the expected economic growth that the plan would produce, federal revenues would decline by $768 billion over the next decade (the larger economy would increase wages, which would narrow the revenue lost through the individual income tax by about $700 billion; in addition, the new VAT would end up raising $2.2 trillion more over the next decade owing to growth of the economy).

By reducing significantly marginal tax rates and the cost of capital, the plan would lead to a 13.9% higher GDP over the long term, provided that the tax cut could be appropriately financed. This increase in GDP would translate into the above indicated 12.2% higher wages and 4.8 million new full-time equivalent jobs. Accounting for economic growth, all taxpayers would see an increase in after-tax income of at least 14% at the end of the decade.

The indicated 43.9% increase of the capital stock and 4.8 million new jobs are equivalent to $g_K = 0.0439$ and $g_L = 0.00381$ (see Eq. 4.4 [(4.6)]), and the average 10-year GDP growth rate g according to Eq. (4.3) [(4.6)] with 1.5% correction is about 2.9%. Based on the analysis of Pomerleau and Schuyler (2015), the average growth rate would be around 3.4%.

As mentioned earlier, the Taxes and Growth Model does not take into account the fiscal or economic effects of interest on debt. It also does not require budgets to balance over the long term nor does it account for the potential macroeconomic effects of any spending cuts that may be required to finance the plan. In economics, the measure of a "long-term" time frame is not fixed; it is more of a concept than an actual length of time. Of course, the indicated additional 13.9% of the GDP for 10 years would mean a slow (on average 1.33% additional annual economic growth) economic recovery and increased federal debt.

With the additional annual 1.33% increase of the GDP growth rate, it is impossible to expect in this case (see, e.g., Eq. (2.6)) the decreasing federal debt, which is the main factor undermining the health of the US economy. It is also unrealistic to expect a high annual GDP growth rate. Based on the US economic data after World War II, it is difficult to assume that the GDP growth rate would exceed 5% during 10 years period, so that the simulation results of Table 2.3 show that the federal debt would increase with all negative economic consequences.

Understanding that, Senator Cruz's proposal includes elimination/reduction of four departments (Department of Education with $67.1 billion budget in 2015, Department of Energy with $27.4 billion budget, Department of Commerce with $8.6 billion budget, and Department of Housing and Urban Development with $35 billion budget) and the IRS (with $12 billion budget), which, as he estimated, would save over $500 billion over 10 years.

As to the mentioned amount $500 billion, this is not enough to satisfy the conclusions of the "Gang of Six", which called for $500 billion in immediate savings and for reducing the deficit by $3.7 trillion over the coming decade (see Table 3.3 and Eq. 3.4 [(3.23)]). The enormous debt, according to Reinhart and Rogoff (2010), would be also an obstacle to reach the indicated growth rate.

According to Senator Cruz's tax plan and the results of the Taxes and Growth Model, for the models (4.1)−(4.7), assuming that spending $G(t) = G(0)$ is frozen and the $3.2 trillion revenue $T(0)$ is decreased yearly by average $76.8 billion and $g = 0.034$, we have $T(t) = 3.2 − 0.0768t$ and $Y(t) = 18\exp(0.034t)$ [$T_{t+1} = T_t − 0.0768$, $T_0 = 3.2$ and $Y_{t+1} = (1 + 0.034)Y_t$, $Y_0 = 18$].

The simulation results reflecting only tax cuts are given in Table 4.1.

Assuming that the offered additional $500 billion spending cuts are realized uniformly during the next 10 years, in the considered models, $G(t) = 3.7 − 0.05t$ [$G_{t+1} = G_t − 0.05$; $G_0 = 3.7$]. The simulation results are given in Table 4.2.

Table 4.1 Effect of Cruz's tax cuts proposal

Year	1	2	3	4	5	6	7	8	9	10
Debt/GDP	1.0296	1.0479	1.065	1.081	1.0959	1.1097	1.1225	1.1343	1.1452	1.1552

Table 4.2 Effect of Cruz's tax cuts and decreasing the government size proposal

Year	1	2	3	4	5	6	7	8	9	10
Debt/ GDP	1.0269	1.0426	1.0573	1.0709	1.0836	1.0953	1.106	1.1159	1.125	1.1332

The simulation results show that the considered proposal cannot significantly improve the US economy. The debt to GDP ratio remains in the dangerous above 100% area, and even the intermediate goal—balanced budget—cannot be reached.

Senator Rand Paul proposed the "Flat and Fair Tax" that would move to a 14.5% tax rate on all types of income (including wages paid by governments and nonprofit organizations) with a sizable deduction and exemption, eliminate the corporate tax to create a 14.5% business transfer tax paid by businesses on profits and wages, introduce full expensing for investments in capital, and eliminate the payroll tax on both the employer and employee. According to the Tax Foundation analysis (Lundeen and Schuyler, 2015), his plan would grow the economy by 12.9% in the long run, create 4.3 million jobs, and cost $1.8 trillion over 10 years on a static basis and raise $737 billion when accounting for economic growth.

Based on the Taxes and Growth Model, Senator Paul's tax reform proposal would increase GDP by 12.9% by the end of roughly 10 years (it may be shorter or longer depending on how long it takes for business to pull permits for new buildings, supply chains to adjust, etc.). This is equivalent to average additional growth of about 1.24 percentage points per year. These tax changes result in an increase of the capital stock of 40.5% by the end of the adjustment period and result in higher after-tax wages of 5.5%. Additionally, the tax cut on wage income to 14.5% also increases the incentive to work and results in 3.5% additional private business hours of work. This is equivalent to 4.3 million full-time jobs. On a dynamic basis, the plan would increase after-tax incomes by a total 16% for all income groups.

On a static basis, Senator Paul's tax reform plan would lose nearly $2 trillion over a 10-year period, with an average annual cost of about $200 billion (in one version (see Pomerleau, 2015) about 300 billion). Taking into account the growth of the economy, over time this would lead to smaller tax costs so that, according to Lundeen and Schuyler (2015) estimate, the plan would end up raising an additional $737 billion over the budget window.

However, similar to Senator Cruz's plan, the 1.24% yearly additional GDP growth during 10 years (the average growth rate around 3.3%) makes the $737 billion estimate look unrealistic. Based on the considered models in Chapter 2 and 3, it is possible to conclude that Senator Paul's plan does not satisfy the conclusions of the "Gang of Six" (see Table 3.3 and Eq. 3.4 [(3.23)]). It is unlikely that the proposed measures may balance the budget over 10 years (see Tables 3.7 and 3.9).

The analysis similar to the previous proposal shows that the indicated 40.5% increase of the capital stock and 4.3 million new jobs are equivalent to $g_K = 0.0405$ and $g_L = 0.00343$ (see Eq. (4.4) [(4.6)]), and the average 10-year GDP growth rate g according to Eq. (4.3) [(4.6)] with 1.5% correction on "technical change" is around 3%.

According to Senator Paul's tax plan and the results of the Taxes and Growth Model, for the models (4.1)–(4.7), assuming that spending $G(t) = G(0)$ is frozen, the $3.2 trillion revenue $T(0)$ is increased yearly by average $73.7 billion, and g = 0.033, we have $T(t) = 3.2 + 0.0737t$ and $Y(t) = 18\exp(0.033t)$ [$T_{t+1} = T_t + 0.0737$, $T_0 = 3.2$ and $Y_{t+1} = (1 + 0.033)Y_t$, $Y_0 = 18$].

The simulation results reflecting only the tax cuts are given in Table 4.3.

Although the proposed tax cuts look a little bit more efficient than those in the earlier considered proposal, they still cannot move the economy in a healthier direction.

Senator Santorum's tax plan (Santorum, 2015) assumes a 20% flat tax on individual and corporate income and repeals a number of complex features in the current tax code. It assumes the tax cut by $3.2 trillion over the next decade on a static basis. As a result, the plan would end up reducing tax revenues by $1.1 trillion over the next decade when accounting for economic growth from increases in the supply of labor and capital. According to the Taxes and Growth Model (Cole, 2015a,b), the plan would significantly reduce marginal tax rates and the cost of capital, which would lead to a 10.2% higher GDP over the long term, provided that the tax cut could be appropriately financed. The plan would also lead to a 29% larger capital stock, 7.3% higher wages, and 3.1 million more full-time equivalent

Table 4.3 Effect of Paul's tax cuts proposal

Year	1	2	3	4	5	6	7	8	9	10
Debt/ GDP	1.0225	1.0341	1.0448	1.0548	1.064	1.0725	1.0803	1.0873	1.0938	1.0995

jobs. On a static basis, the plan would cut taxes by 3% on average for all taxpayers. In addition, it would eliminate the estate tax and the Alternative Minimum Tax. Accounting for economic growth, all taxpayers would see an increase in after-tax income of at least 7.5% at the end of the decade. Because of a large tax cut, the federal government deficit would increase by over $3.2 trillion on a static basis and $1.1 trillion on a dynamic basis. The tax cut in Senator Santorum's plan looks more modest than that in Senators Cruz's and Paul's plans. As a result, the debt to GDP ratio should be larger than that in the considered above proposals.

The analysis similar to the previous proposals shows that the indicated 29% increase of the capital stock and 3.1 million new jobs are equivalent to $g_K = 0.029$ and $g_L = 0.00247$ (see Eq. (4.4) [(4.6)]), and the average 10-year GDP growth rate g according to Eq. (4.3) [(4.6)] with 1.5% correction is about 2.5%, 0.6% less than it follows from the Taxes and Growth Model.

For the models (4.1)−(4.7), assuming that spending $G(t) = G(0)$ is frozen, the $ 1.1 trillion revenue $T(0)$ is decreased yearly by average $110 billion, and $g = 0.026$, we have $T(t) = 3.2 - 0.11t$ and $Y(t) = 18\exp(0.031t)$ [$T_{t+1} = T_t - 0.11$, $T_0 = 3.2$ and $Y_{t+1} = (1 + 0.031)Y_t$, $Y_0 = 18$].

The simulation results reflecting only tax cuts are given in Table 4.4. The offered cut measures are more modest and less efficient than those in the previous proposals.

Similar to the above discussed plans, Senators Lee and Rubio (2015) have developed their plan to reform the individual and corporate income tax codes. It focuses to eliminate many of the income tax system biases against saving and investment. Based on the Taxes and Growth Model estimating the growth and revenue effects of the Rubio−Lee plan (Pomerleau and Schuyler, 2015), the plan would generate a large and positive impact on growth but would also create a large financing need during the first several years. The plan would cut the corporate tax rate to 25%. It would cap the tax rate on noncorporate business income at 25%. The proposal would integrate the corporate and shareholder taxes to remove double taxation, which was

Table 4.4 Effect of Santorum's tax plan

Year	1	2	3	4	5	6	7	8	9	10
Debt/ GDP	1.0343	1.0575	1.0795	1.1004	1.1202	1.139	1.1567	1.1735	1.1893	1.2043

modeled as a zero tax rate on qualifying capital gains and dividends. The proposal would repeal many of the tax increases in the Affordable Care Act (ACA), including its surtaxes on upper-income individuals' wage and investment income. The plan would abolish the estate tax. Several of the draft proposal recommendations would simplify the individual tax code (Schuyler and McBride, 2015). The plan would also require US companies to pay a 6% tax on earnings held abroad by their foreign subsidies (to reduce the short-term revenue cost).

According to the modeling results, the impact of the plan on government revenue would be substantial. In a conventional revenue estimate that ignores the growth effects of tax changes (on a static basis), the plan appears to lower federal revenue by about $414 billion annually. However, in a dynamic revenue estimate that accounts for tax-induced changes in economic activity, the budget would improve over time. Some of these changes are so strongly progrowth (notably expensing of capital investments, the zero tax rate on qualifying capital gains and dividends, and the much lower corporate tax rate) that the model predicts the plan would increase federal revenue by an annual $94 billion in the long run, following an estimated $1.7 trillion revenue loss over the initial 10-year period.

The Taxes and Growth Model predicts "that the tax changes in the Rubio-Lee plan would significantly increase work, saving, and investment incentives in the United States, leading to a decade of rapid growth and a permanently stronger and more prosperous economy than otherwise. The model estimates that after the economy has adjusted to the improved incentives, annual gross domestic product would be 15% higher over the long-run (equivalent to an average of additional annual growth of 1.44% over a 10-year adjustment period and an extra $2.7 trillion annually in terms of 2015's GDP), the stock of capital used in production (equipment, structures, intellectual property, etc.) would be almost 50% larger... and real hourly wages would be 12.5% higher.... The plan would ... raise the level of employment by nearly 2.7 million jobs."

As indicated by McBride (2015), many economists disagree with the Tax and Growth Model prediction that the level of the economy would be increased by 15% after about 10 years (this is even more than that in proposals of Senators Cruz, Paul, and Santorum). He writes: "Some people will reflexively doubt that such growth is even possible. However, putting it into to context, 15 percent growth in GDP over 10 years only requires an additional annual growth of 1.44 percent on top of our currently moribund growth rate of about 2 percent. That is the sort of growth the

U.S. experienced in the 1980s and 1990s. It's not remotely unprecedented." On the one hand, the debt situation in 1980−90s was different and, according to the Taxes and Growth Model, the considered proposal would lead to $1.7 trillion revenue loss over the initial 10-year period. On the other hand, McBride (2015), by referring to the publications of Kotlikoff et al. (1999, 2001, 2002) and Romer (2010), believes that tax multiples can be high. Pomerleau and Schuyler (2015) cautiously state: "These gains would not occur overnight. The model is long-run, and the economy would require several years to adjust. However, while the gains would not be instantaneous, they would take place fairly quickly." Their charts show that in 7 years the debt to GDP ratio would increase by about 8%, but in 2025 the increase would drop to 7%; only in 2040, it would return to the current debt level. According to the material of Chapter 2 (see, e.g., Table 2.2 and 2.3) and the material of Chapter 3, the considered Rubio−Lee plan suffers the drawbacks of the plans of Senators Cruz, Paul, and Santorum.

In addition, similar to the above analyzed proposals, for the Rubio−Lee proposal, we have $g_K = 0.05$ and $g_L = 0.00215$ (see Eq. (4.4) [(4.6)]), and the average 10-year GDP growth rate g according to Eq. (4.3) [(4.6)] with 1.5% correction is around 3.2%, close to the 3.5% estimate obtained by the Tax Foundation based on the Taxes and Growth Model.

For the models (4.1)−(4.7), assuming that spending $G(t) = G(0)$ is frozen and the $1.1 trillion revenue $T(0)$ is decreased yearly by average $110 billion, we have $g = 0.035$; $T(t) = 3.2 - 0.17t$; and $Y(t) = 18\exp(0.035t)$ [$T_{t+1} = T_0 - 0.17$, $T_0 = 3.2$ and $Y_{t+1} = (1 + 0.035)Y_t$, $Y_0 = 18$].

The simulation results reflecting only tax cuts are given in Table 4.5.

The debt to GDP ratio is high and close to that obtained for Santorum's proposal.

According to the Tax Foundation's Taxes and Growth Model (Pomerleau, 2015a), the Governor Jeb Bush's plan would significantly reduce marginal tax rates and the cost of capital, which would lead to a 10% higher GDP over the long term (about extra 0.96% yearly). The plan would also lead to a 28.8% larger capital stock, 7.4% higher wages, and 2.7 million more full-time equivalent jobs. This corresponds to

Table 4.5 Effect of the Rubio−Lee proposal

Year	1	2	3	4	5	6	7	8	9	10
Debt/ GDP	1.0336	1.0556	1.0763	1.0955	1.1134	1.13	1.1454	1.1596	1.1727	1.1847

$g_K = 0.0288$ and $g_L = 0.00215$ (see Eq. (4.4) [(4.6)]), and the average 10-year GDP growth rate g according to Eq. (4.3) [(4.6)] with 1.5% correction is about 2.5%, whereas the estimate based on Taxes and Growth Model gives about 3%.

The Governor's plan would cut taxes by $3.6 trillion over the next decade on a static basis. This plan would reduce individual income tax rates, broaden the income tax base by limiting itemized deductions, and expand the Earned Income Tax Credit for childless taxpayers. The plan would also reform the business tax code by reducing the corporate income tax rate to 20%, moving to full expensing of all capital investment, and moving to a territorial tax system. In addition, the plan would eliminate the Estate Tax, eliminate the Alternative Minimum Tax, change the treatment of interest, and eliminate many other complex features of the current tax code. However, the plan would end up reducing revenue by $1.6 trillion over the next decade when accounting for the additional economic growth created by the plan. Unfortunately, the plan ignores the huge current federal debt and does not offer solution to decrease this debt. According to the material of Chapter 2 (see, e.g., Table 2.2 and 2.3) and the material of Chapter 3, the Jeb Bush's plan suffers the drawbacks of the Santorum's plan, and the debt to GDP ratio is close to the data in Table 4.4.

President's Trump (2015) tax plan focuses on lowering substantially individual income taxes and the corporate income tax and eliminating a number of complex features in the current tax code. According to the Taxes and Growth Model (see Cole, 2015a,b), it would significantly reduce marginal tax rates and the cost of capital, which would lead to an 11% higher GDP over the long term (yearly average is about 1%) provided that the tax cut could be appropriately financed. This plan would reduce individual income tax rates, lowering the top rate from 39.6% to 25% and creating a large zero bracket. The plan would also reform the business tax code by reducing the income tax on all businesses to 15% and eliminate business tax expenditures, including deferral and interest deductions. In addition, the plan would eliminate the Net Investment Income Tax of 3.8%, which was passed as part of the Affordable Care Act, the Estate Tax, and the Alternative Minimum Tax. The plan would also lead to a 29% larger capital stock, 6.5% higher wages, and 5.3 million new full-time equivalent jobs; this corresponds to $g_K = 0.029$ and $g_L = 0.00423$ (see Eq. 4.4 [(4.6)]), and the average 10-year GDP growth rate g according to Eq. (4.3) [(4.6)] with 1.5% correction is around 2.6%, whereas according to the Taxes and Growth Model, it would be about 3% in the long run. President's Trump (2015) plan would cut taxes by $11.98 trillion over the next decade on a static basis. However, according to the Tax Foundation, the plan would increase the federal government deficit by over $10 trillion, both on a static and dynamic basis. Although it is not clear why the static and dynamic estimates coincide, it is obvious that tax reduction alone in this and all the above considered proposals cannot improve the US economy.

All the discussed plans, although each of them contains useful and necessary tax cuts (the optimal size of the tax cut can be analyzed separately), do not deal with the real dangerous economic situation—the US huge federal debt. Senator Cruz's plan only contains an attempt to solve this problem. However, Cruz's attempt to offer a certain structural change—eliminate some federal departments and services—is too timid. Drastic measures penetrating in all sectors of the economy and sophisticated fiscal and monetary policies are needed to restore the economy to its previous might. As to the Senators Lee and Rubio plan that would return the federal debt to its current level in 2040, such proposals cannot be considered as serious ones.

Proposals related to the tax cut, as well as required investments in the infrastructure (e.g., unsafe bridges, broken roads), are useful and necessary. They are steps in a proper direction to restore the economy. However, as it follows from the above analysis, for the existing federal debt, without significant structural changes, it is impossible to expect a significant improvement of the US economy.

Unfortunately, during electoral campaigns, politicians avoid speaking about the need to cut government spending because any discussion about the real cuts to social programs threatens to frighten away their supporters. Moreover, Democrats call for more tax revenues from the wealthy as part of their spending proposals. Regrettably, many politicians think more about the next election rather than about their actual constituents, and economists, who help them to prepare their electoral programs, care more about money they will earn by building a rosy financial picture of the future rather than a realistic analysis of economic issues related to the proposed policies and programs.

4.3 POLITICS AND ECONOMY: PROBLEMS ECONOMISTS EVADE

The parameters of the above considered models characterize an economic policy and its results, which do not necessarily coincide with the established goals formulated by politicians. The aforementioned material shows that economics and politics are interconnected. From the beginning, macroeconomics, the branch of economics that studies the behavior and performance of an economy as a whole, was and remains political. Macroeconomic decision-making is in hands of politicians who usually lack of knowledge in economics and mathematics.

For conservative politicians, terms *supply* and *demand* that characterize the so-called *market forces* are the solution of all economic problems. They do not understand and/or do not want to understand that the ideal (pure) market does not exist. Although market forces are able to stabilize the economic situation, ignoring the government's ability to control the economy is a huge mistake. In turn, liberal politicians believe in the power of government to guide and control the economy. They close eyes on inefficiency of government bureaucracy and inability of the planning economic system to react fast to the changing economic environment. Market forces are a source of self-regulation and stabilization, whereas government actions guide a country's economy in a certain direction. It means that the real economic system is combined; that is, it contains the feedforward (government) and feedback (market) channels. It is well known that such systems are the most sophisticated if both mentioned channels are tuned properly. However, without factually accurate and *well-reasoned* criteria, guidance is useless. Unfortunately, some politicians link the country's wealth criteria with their own benefits criteria (to keep their status, etc.). Many of them, being, for example, lawyers or physicians, are unable to formulate properly the needed criteria so that they substitute them frequently with pure propagandistic statements.

Public policy is important in stimulating and developing the economy. Investment in the infrastructure, education, research, and health-care sectors can have profound economic effects. It is economists' responsibility to provide politicians with necessary information and help them to make proper decisions. Economists do matter in public policy, even though policymakers often ignore their advice. Although politicians listen to economists' recommendations, their decisions are dominated by political concerns and usually they pay attention to advices that agree with their intentions. Only in crisis situations, when politicians are desperately seeking solutions, economists can have direct effect on government policy. However, because of the existence of absolutely opposite approaches to the solution of many macroeconomic problems, politicians prefer to choose economists whose research backs their political views. Now there exist the so-called nonpartisan organizations such as the US Congressional Budget Office that conduct, as they state, objective impartial analysis and hire its employees solely on the basis of professional competence without regard to political affiliation. They do not make policy recommendations; they produce independent analyses of budgetary and economic issues and provide economic estimates. Usually, their estimates are used by political parties to provecorrectness or criticize a policy proposal. However, the used methodologies, based on macroeconomic theory, and the existing forecasting models (see Section 1.6) have not established themselves as reliable practical tools, so that, on the one hand, the estimate correctness can be questionable and, on the other hand, a political majority can simply disregard them.

Individuals involved in decision-making and implementation of the economic policy belong to the so-called political elite. Pareto (1935), who developed the elite theory of politics, introduced the term "elite" as a class of the people "who have the highest indices in their branch of activity" and divided this class into two: "a governing elite, comprising individuals who directly or indirectly play some considerable part in government, and nongoverning elite, comprising the rest." In democratic countries, politicians seek elective positions and then, as a rule, try to keep them. A political elite is motivated by an ambition to obtain money, power, and distinctions. This group benefits from durable privileges and inequalities of access to wealth and income. Such a case, as the resignation of the British Prime Minister David Cameron following Britain's vote to leave the European Union, is beneath common nowadays because the political elite's central concern is achieving and preserving power.

As many analyses have revealed, in actual government decision-making economic and political objectives often do not coincide. That is why it is reasonable to ask: "Who runs the economy—politicians or economists?" The political elite, being the planners and decision-makers, play a very significant role in the country's development, so that in the economic development as well. Unfortunately, only 'pure' economic theory can be nonpolitical. An ideal economist should ignore any political bias or prejudice to provide impartial information and recommendations how to improve the economic performance of a country. Politicians could then evaluate this economic information and make decisions. However, the real picture is different.

President Reagan's words "Are you better off now than you were four years ago? Is it easier for you to go and buy things in the stores than it was four years ago? Is there more or less unemployment in the country than there was four years ago? Is America as respected throughout the world as it was?" establish the main criterion (Are you better off now than you were 4 years ago?) and related subcriteria that should be considered by citizens to evaluate the performance of a political elite. The economic criteria are dominant as the country should be able to feed and clothe its citizen, and the political elite is responsible for economic stability and security of citizens first and foremost. As to the country's international standing, it is largely driven by the strength of the economy.

A belief in the way government should operate within a society characterizes a political ideology of its members. In the United States, most citizens consider themselves liberal, moderate, and conservatives. There are countries where a majority of people are socialists or communists. The political spectrum of a society is usually described along a left—middle—right line: left—liberals, middle—moderate, and right—conservatives. Liberals denounce economic and social inequality. They support unions' rights to organize and strike, progressive taxation, a clear environment, free education, affordable health care, and other social programs. Conservatives believe in a small government, firm law, and strict moral codes.

Fighting for power, politicians support different ideological groups. As a result, the political elite is also ideologically divided, and its members try to present themselves as leaders of separate ideological groups. Most of the politicians lack of serious economic knowledge and use economists to prepare proposals formulating the proposed economic policy containing future promises that, as a rule, are highly unrealistic. Although the performance of the economy is one of the key political battlegrounds, insufficient proficiency in economy makes them unable to be very persuasive in this area, and, trying to jump on the political elite train, they deliberately prioritize other topics (e.g., climate change, pollution, immigration) targeting special group of population (e.g., those who are with low level of education, minorities) to get their votes. However, such an activity only hurts the country, and the damage level depends on the governmental structure, current economic situation, and correlation of political forces in the country.

A slow economic recovery from the 2008 economic crisis in a sophisticated democracy such as the United States vividly demonstrates the importance of pure economists as the main tool to make a country prosperous.

Many economic issues are seen through the eyes of ideology. Different economic theories reflect different political views of their founders. Politicians use those economists and economic research that backs their political view. A precise Pareto (1935) definition "Economics is but a small part of sociology, and pure economics is but a small part of economics" commits pure economists to be honest researchers and advisors rather than obedient (humble) servants of a political elite.

All peoples' lives are affected by the power structures that exist in society, and political ideology influences economic thought. A country's economic health is one of the most important life support products for politicians, the means to prolong their life in politics. In periods of economic crises, they appeal to economists of different political views asking their advice. High unemployment during economic crises is a direct threat to a country's political stability. That is why the Keynesian theory assuming a significant government involvement in the economy continues to be very popular. Of course, final decisions belong to politicians and reflect their political beliefs. Even accepting Keynesian economics, liberal politicians prefer spending increases to tax cuts. Moreover, not infrequently some politicians even insist on increasing taxes for the wealthy. At a certain degree, this reflects a Marxists type of thoughts (government favors the moral order of bourgeois values) and plays well among the low-income population; however, the tax increases only stifle the economic growth and prolong recessions.

In relatively quiet economic periods, the mentioned political strategy proves to be successful in many countries, especially in those where labor unions have a significant power. By supporting such measures, economists promote greater equality in society rather than strengthen a country's economy, which would bring benefits to all members of the society. The enlarged government during the 1929 economic crisis, an increased debt and budget deficits, and stagflation of the 1970s, a phenomenon that contradicted the Keynesian theory, brought to life economic policies focused on reducing government interference in the economy. The so-called supply-side economic policies, mentioned in Section 1.4, include deregulation, privatization, and tax cuts as means to increase the productivity and the efficiency of the economy. Prime Minister Thatcher and President Reagan were great champions of supply-side economists like Milton Friedman, Keith Joseph, and Friedrich Hayek. In the United States, Republicans are adamant supporters of supply-side economics. The aforementioned economists were proponents of monetarism—the view that the chief determinant of economic growth is the supply of money rather than fiscal policy. However, there are many economists (e.g., Paul Krugman) suggesting this is not a good idea.

As indicated earlier, the monetary policy is mostly in hands of the independent central banks rather than government. That is why when answering the question "who runs the economy—politicians or economists?" it is definitely possible to state that politicians determine only fiscal policy. Central bank independence is widely accepted as a necessary prerequisite for successful monetary policies, which proved to be a very important factor of the economic recovery. The main reason for making central banks independent was the necessity of setting inflation-targeting monetary policy, which became urgent after the demise of the gold standard and the period of a high inflation of the 1970s and early 1980s. With independence, the task of stabilizing inflation at low levels looked easier to achieve. However, the 2008 financial crisis extended the scope of monetary policy problems. To lower interest rates and increase the money supply, independent central banks purchased government securities or other securities from the market (the so-called quantitative easing); short-term interest rates were at or approaching zero or even became negative. As mentioned earlier, monetary policy can serve as an amplifier of fiscal policy (multipliers can be several times larger). Maybe economists should be allowed to handle all economic policy? Instead of that, central banks often serve as easy scapegoats for politicians when they decide to escape responsibility for making decisions themselves. For example, during the 2008 crisis, European governments criticized monetary policy of European Central Bank for having overstepped its boundaries. Formally, in the United States and Europe, monetary policy of central banks focuses to offset the deficiencies of fiscal policy. Economists try to repair damage caused by politicians.

Close to elections, politicians are not stingy on promises (e.g., income tax cuts, consumer rebate programs, college affordable programs) to create favorable social conditions that would help the reelection of leaders of their party. The above described Republicans' proposals do not consider how to decrease the US national debt, which presents a real danger for the country's prosperity, and even how to solve the problem of balancing its budget. We did not consider the economic plan of the Democratic candidate Hillary Clinton because her promised spending and tax increase for the rich, according to an analysis by the Tax Foundation, would lower the United States' GDP by 1%, while also reducing incomes for all earners, not just the superwealthy.

Politicians dealing with fiscal and monetary policies try to create before elections a favorable situation for leaders of their party to be reelected. To achieve this goal, it is possible first to increase employment by stimulating the economy and then by carrying out a more rigorous spending policy to decrease inflation, if it would jump up, so that it would be an increased employment under a moderate inflation before the elections. The similar result can be reached by the opposite combination of actions: First it should be a rigorous spending policy to decrease inflation, which can increase unemployment, and then a stimulus policy to decrease unemployment. Therefore, regulation of the levels of inflation and employment focuses to guarantee political victories rather than a sustainable economic growth. As a result, the political process produces economic fluctuations. Promises of politicians, both realized and unrealized, can hurt the economy as well. Unfulfilled promises (e.g., it was determined later that promised tax benefits for investment in special areas or regions would increase budget deficit, so that government decided not to provide such benefits) not only harm the investors but also undermine their belief in government and its economic policy.

During the period of the 2008 financial crisis, instead of focusing on the country's economy the US president spent time fighting for the promised so-called Obamacare to provide health insurance to more than 10 millions of Americans. Health care is the main fiscal problem. Its costs are the main reason for our fiscal malaise. The United States spends today on health care more than any other developed country in the world (measured as a percentage of GDP or per capita). The US-failed affordable health-care system is the result of the absence of a rigorous approach to this complex economic problem. President Obama and his surrounding, having no solid knowledge in basic science, made decisions based on their ideology without understanding that the establishing of an expensive health system in the period of severe economic crises is equivalent to suicide.

Private medicine in the United States is too expensive. Existing channels to maximize physicians' profit are a lure for a possible fraud, which insurance companies would not fight because their profit is the result of a "productive cooperation" with private medicine. It is unrealistic to expect from the government any substantial decrease of private health-care costs. Health insurance companies give healthy donations to political parties.

Without any doubt, all citizens of such a powerful and prosperous country as the United States should have affordable health care (right up to a universal health-care system). However, it is also obvious that the modification of the US current health system would require a significant amount of money the government lacks. During the crisis and a huge debt, the country cannot allow itself such a luxury. It was clear not only to economists (excluding those who decided to make money for fuzzy calculations that enable the president to declare that it will even save government money in the future) but also to any educated person based on common sense. However, politicians involved in this adventure found economists who justified the efficiency of the future affordable health-care system. They stated that the 2010 Affordable Care Act was designed to reduce government spending on health care. Moreover, according to the CBO analysis, the Affordable Care Act would reduce the debt by $143 billion over first 10 years (2010—2019) and by more than $1 trillion in the second decade. However, reality proved the opposite. The program costs and will cost (if it is not abolished) the government more than $100 billion yearly and is one of the reasons of a slow economic recovery.

Professor Gruber, an MIT economist, the director of the Healthcare Program at the National Bureau of Economic Research, and an architect of the Affordable Care Act, cynically admitted that the "stupidity of the American voter" and a "lack of transparency" were key to passing the Affordable Care Act. After 7 years of malfunctioning of the current health system, Republicans, who voted unanimously against the ACA, witnessing its deficiencies, could not agree to offer something better because many of them are slaves of their ideology and self-interests; others are simply unable to think properly.

There are known general characteristics of health system of the leading industrial countries to be compared with the existing US health system. Because the health system contributes significantly to the country's debt, the solution of the health-care problem should start with the admissible amount of money that can be now allocated for the health care. This should be the starting point. Policies and alternative variants of their realization should be discussed and developed after this amount is established. Unfortunately, politicians start with policies and then ask an appropriate organization to estimate costs in 10—20 years. Such future estimates are unreliable and misleading; in addition, they ignore the fact that in the future more money can be allocated and the health system can be improved.

Liberal politicians easily accept, without any serious consideration, such slogans as international cooperation and free trade. They do not want to understand that free-trade agreements are, at a certain degree, equivalent to redistribution of wealth, which is very attractive subject of their constituencies—their base. Countries with lower standard of living and a cheap workforce benefit from free trade compared with countries with higher standard of living and more expensive labor.

For President Bill Clinton, who signed the 1994 North American Free Trade Agreement (NAFTA), which created a free-trade zone between the United States, Canada, and Mexico, this agreement was "a symbolic struggle for the spirit of our country and for how we would approach this very difficult and rapidly changing world dealing with our own considerable challenges here at home." He considered its importance in creating "an economic order in the world that will promote more growth, more equality, better preservation of the environment, and a greater possibility of world peace." For him, this was the first step toward a worldwide trade agreement that "could make the material gains of NAFTA for our country look small by comparison."

The idea of free-trade agreements to reduce trading costs, increase business investment, and help countries be more competitive in the global marketplace was not new. The problem is how to implement such agreements in practice so that they would be equally beneficial for all participants. Despite NAFTA's benefits, its disadvantages were usually discussed during presidential campaigns. In 1992, before the trade agreement was even ratified, Presidential candidate Ross Perot famously warned that "You're going to hear a giant sucking sound of jobs being pulled out of this country." During the 2008 Presidential campaign, Barack Obama and Hillary Clinton blamed NAFTA for growing unemployment. Both candidates promised to either amend or back out of the agreement all together and halt any new ones. However, since becoming President, Obama has not done anything related to NAFTA. Moreover, he and Hillary Clinton tried to push forward Transatlantic Free Trade Agreement. During the 2016 presidential campaign, a successful businessman Donald Trump decisively, as this has never happened before, declared that the country should reconsider all its trade agreements because they not only kill manufacturing jobs and increase unemployment but also are a huge burden for the country's economy (see also Section 4.5).

Politicians like to talk about economic growth. However, they do not work with economists to develop a real efficient economic policy. They are interested only in keeping their elite or pseudoelite positions. The size of the US federal government increased significantly in the past decades, and there is no serious discussion how to decrease it. More bureaucracy means additional funding to support it. However, this does not bother politicians because bureaucracy is a part of their suite, a measure of their power.

The goals characterizing a serious fiscal policy should include increase in the GDP growth rate, reduction of government spending, reduction of the national debt, and reduction to a certain level of the debt to GDP ratio. The above considered models can be helpful to implement such a policy.

4.4 DECISION-MAKING DURING PERIODS OF ECONOMIC DECLINE

Observations of economic processes of different levels (micro and macro) enriched scientists with knowledge about their moving forces, important parameters characterizing them, etc. Reasoning from observations has been important to scientific practice at least since the time of Aristotle. Naturalistic observations help to produce hypotheses and build models and theories about the natural world. Specifics of macroeconomic processes do not allow scientists to design experiments to test thoroughly their hypotheses and theories and to state that the developed macroeconomic theories have a universal character. The last century brought to life about 50 economic theories (supply and demand; classical economics; Keynesian economics; neoclassical economics; monetarism; market socialism; Marxism; rational choice theory; supply-side economics; Phillips curve, etc.). Some of them had a very short life.

Economic crises are a source of new information. They are the tests that allow economic scientists to assess their hypotheses/theories, reconsider and reject obsolete theories, and create the new ones based on an idea or set of ideas that explain new facts or events. The crises also test the politicians' ability to formulate and implement an efficient public policy and their ability to work productively with economists to resolve urgent economic problems.

One of the most important government responsibilities and obligations is to guarantee employment and high (as it is possible) living standards for a county's citizens. Periods of crises, large macroeconomic shocks accompanied with high unemployment, are very difficult for many people, and these times are the best checkup of the government efficiency and its ability to recover the economy. Usually, the country's leader, its president or prime minister, is under high pressure to make proper decisions and to take economic measures that would decease unemployment and in a short time put the country's economy on a wealthy track. As a rule, most of countries' leaders have no even elementary knowledge in economics. Georges Pompidou, Prime Minister of France from 1962 to 1968 and later President of the French Republic from 1969 until his death in 1974, is a rare exclusion from this "rule." Being an economist, he demonstrated his competence that conferred indisputable authority on him and commanded respect. That is why making economic decisions for persons unfamiliar even with economic terminology is an extremely difficult task. Politicians like to discuss economic problems. To learn several economic terms does not present any difficulties. However, to discuss economic problems without a deep understanding of them, that is what we see almost everyday, is irresponsible.

In contrast to the traditional decision-making procedure, in democratic countries the economic policy should be approved by the legislative branch of government containing persons who have their economic advisors and whose political views and strategies can be different than those of the head of the government (in many cases focused to benefit their future career). The leader should not only offer a proper economic policy but also persuade the legislative branch to support this policy and, if necessary, to find a compromise decision. The process to obtain consensus takes time, and making decisions using a consensus approach is not always effective. In crisis situations, loss of time can aggravate the situation to such a degree that a prescribed medicine would not work. The leader's ideology is also a significant factor that may influence decision-making.

Below we analyze three economic crises (the Great Depression of the 1930s, the deep economic malaise of the 1970s, and the 2008 financial crisis) and measures taken to restore the economy.

The period of the Great Depression links to Presidents Herbert Hoover and Franklin Roosevelt.

The stock market dropped almost 30% below the peak of 1929; interest rates dropped to low levels; investment and consumer spending significantly decreased; and prices began to decline causing deflation. A drop in prices (the price level fell 27%) led to a drop in production (US industrial production fell 47%). The period 1929—1933 was the worst owing to the significant drop in real GDP (30%) and prices, as well as an increase in unemployment (it reached 25% in 1933) A slow recovery started in spring of 1933 when the real GDP average growth rate became 9% (excluding 1938 when the real GDP dropped 3.3%), and the crisis ended, what is officially believed, in 1941 with the beginning of World War II (in 1940 the United States still had a 15% unemployment rate, but in 1941 it befitted below 10%).

The US stock market crash of 1929 had devastating effects in many countries. Accompanied by an economic downturn in Germany, and financial difficulties in France and Great Britain, it caused a global financial crisis. Dedication to the gold standard in each of these nations only made the economic situation worse.

Now many economists agree that the reason for the Great Depression was the speculative and unstable foundations of the American financial sector that caused the banking crisis that resulted in vanishing one-third of all banks, a reduction of bank stockholders wealth, and, what is more important, monetary contraction by 35% that caused deflation.

President Hoover had a sufficient experience in business and his close advisors Robert Lamont, Secretary of Commerce, Andrew Mellon, Secretary of the Treasury (1929–1932), and Odgen Mills, first Under Secretary of the Treasury and then Secretary of the Treasury (1932–1933), had plenty of experience in business and finance. They also believed in a small government and a responsible balanced budget economic policy. Hoover and Mellon supported the opinion of genuine free-market economists that the self-regulating economic process is able to stabilize the economy. Low interest rates, balanced budget, and protectionist tariffs are the best remedies to restore economic health. Hoover also believed that the federal government involvement could be useful; however, the involvement should be based on persuasion rather than laws. His ideal was people ruling themselves, through voluntary cooperation, the theme he had developed at some length in his 1922 book *American Individualism*, and his approach to the economic recovery consisted in creating favorable conditions for the business community considering this as a warranty of success.

The US federal government had no experience in decisive involvement in the economy during economic crises. Immediately after the stock market crash, President Hoover urged state and local governments to start public work projects. He asked and received pledges from industry not to cut jobs or wages and from labor not to press for higher wages. He reduced all 1929 income taxes, for corporations and individuals, by 1% (owing to budget surplus); administration leaders and Federal Reserve officials agreed that a tax cut could promote growth by increasing private demand for goods and services. Hoover believed that this measure would increase people's confidence in the government's ability to fix economic problems. He said, "The action of the Federal Reserve Board in establishing credit stability, ample capital, the confidence of the administration in undertaking tax reduction, with the cooperation of both political parties, speaks a good deal stronger than any number of statements." Although Mellon, a well-known champion of tax cuts during his decade of service to the previous presidents (he proposed tax rate cuts, which Congress enacted in the Revenue Acts of 1921, 1924, and 1926), insisted that the tax cut was not a response to the market crash, he strongly supported this measure. Unfortunately, the psychological impact of these small tax cuts on the economy was minimal and the 1930 and 1931 deficits persuaded Hoover and Mellon that deficits were the most serious threat to business confidence and, hence, to the needed economic growth. This serious mistaken judgment resulted in taxes and tariffs increase—the measures focused to balance the budget.

Pursuing a conservative business-oriented approach to recovery, Hoover increased trade tariffs (United States Tariff Act of 1930). By raising the average tariff by some 20% (40% tariffs were imposed on imports), it also prompted retaliation from foreign governments, and many overseas banks began to fail. This contributed to the worsening worldwide depression, a steady decline in the world economy until 1933. American import declined from $5.2 billion in 1929 to $1.7 billion in 1933. Hoover is best remembered for the Revenue Act of 1932, the largest peacetime tax increase in American history. The top income taxes went from 25% to 63%. There is the consensus of opinion that it made the Depression worse.

That increase was justified on the grounds that the budget needed to be balanced to restore business confidence. However, despite the tax increase, the $462 million deficit of 1931 jumped to $2.7 billion by 1932. The major reason of the deficit rise was a sharp decline in income tax revenue, which fell from $1.15 billion in 1930 to $834 million in 1931, $427 million in 1932, and just $353 million in 1933. Moreover, the higher tax rates on the wealthy actually caused the tax burden to be shifted to the nonwealthy.

Economists belonging to different economics schools and/or having different political views give absolutely different analysis of the Great Depression. However, most of the economists agree that the main mistake of Hoover's administration was its inability to work efficiently with the Federal Reserve to inject money into the financial system, rather than allow the Federal Reserve to increase interest rates. Some Fed officials believed that a slower economic activity did not require any help from the Federal

Reserve. For example, the governor of the Federal Reserve Bank of Philadelphia stated: "We have been putting out credit in a period of depression when it was not wanted and could not be used, and we will have to withdraw credit when it is wanted and can be used." The governor of the Federal Reserve Bank of San Francisco argued that, "with credit cheap and redundant, we do not believe that business recovery will be accelerated by making credit cheaper and more redundant." (see Wheelock (2010) that includes the analysis of monitory policy during the Great Depression). By increasing interest rates, Hoover's administration only aggravated the situation. Some economist explain the Fed's policy failures by the United Kingdom's monetary policy: On September 21, 1931, England abandoned the gold standard and allowed the pound to float freely. Speculation that the United States would soon also leave the gold standard caused large withdrawals of gold and currency from US banks. In an attempt to halt and then reverse the gold outflow, and to demonstrate that the United States will maintain the gold standard, the Federal Reserve responded by increasing interest rates. Economists today recognize Hoover's tax increase as a huge mistake, which deepened and prolonged the depression.

However, it would be unfair not to indicate that Hoover understood the necessity of increasing government and private sector spending to reduce unemployment and improve the economy. Hoover's advisors drew up proposals to stimulate the economy with reductions in taxes, with loosening the Fed's credit policies and for more public work spending to combat unemployment. Some Republicans opposed high tariffs. Because the country suffered from unprecedented deflation, the appropriate measure was inflation. Some Republicans urged the government to abandon the gold standard and flood the economy with printed currency. Hoover rejected such demands arguing that a stable or *hard* currency system had always been a prerequisite for business investment. If the currency system was inflated by the government, businessmen would refuse to reinvest their funds in the economy.

The president's conservative beliefs hindered his actions. Hoover pressed Congress in 1930 to pass bills that would spur infrastructure construction, at the same time while reminding executive departments to hold the line on spending so as not to increase the federal budget deficit. He formed the President's Emergency Committee on Employment (PECE) in the fall of 1930 to coordinate private organizations' efforts to help the unemployed.

He believed that relief should be handled by the private sector or, if government help is needed, it should be state and local governments, where the programs would be cheaper and less bureaucratized.

In 1930, average annual unemployment rate was 8.9%, whereas in 1931, it was 15.9%. Only in late 1931, Hoover changed his approach to fight the depression. He understood that more drastic measures were needed. By 1932, unemployment had reached 24.9%. Hoover offered proposals that a historian David Kennedy called "the Hoover New Deal" (see Rothbard, 1963). They included direct loans to state governments for spending on relief for the unemployed; more aid to Federal Land Banks; the creation of the Federal Home Loan Bank Board to provide government help to the construction sector, to slow foreclosures and increase homeownership; the creation of the Reconstruction Finance Corporation to bring federal aid to banks, firms, and other institutions in need and local governments to continue relief programs; the creation of a Public Works Administration to coordinate Federal public works and expand them. In addition, Glass-Steagall Act of 1932 changed Federal Reserve and gold reserve policies as a means to loosen credit (the Federal Reserve rules regarding the acceptability of commercial paper for rediscount purposes were liberalized, and more than $750 million of the nation's gold reserve was made available for loans to credit-worthy businesses and industries).

During his battle with the Depression, Hoover had steadily increased federal spending. Over his 4 years, he increased federal spending by 48%. Taking into account deflation, the real size of government spending in 1933 was almost doubled that of 1929. The huge federal budget deficits of 1931 and 1932 were 52.5% and 43.3% of total federal spending, respectively.

However, the severe blunders mentioned earlier (protectionist trade policies and raising income taxes) erased the effect of the indicated positive measures. In the winter of 1932–1933, another wave of bank failures hit the country, creating a major banking crisis.

Being a slave of his conservative ideology, Hoover was stubborn in his actions and ignored opinions of professional economists. Even at the end of his presidency, he refused to begin federal relief or welfare programs because such a program would, he argued, be incredibly expensive, would unbalance the federal budget requiring deficit financing, and would cause businessmen to lose confidence, thus delaying reinvestment and the beginning of economic recovery. He relied only on business confidence, rather than on public confidence. He did not understand or did not want to understand that public confidence was the main factor in boosting business activity. As a leader, he failed because his decisions only aggravated the crisis situation.

Decision-making is the process of making choices by setting goals, gathering information, and assessing alternatives. President Hoover, for both ideological and financial reasons (the last one linked to his ideology), was unable to assess properly alternatives. As a result, he tried to test all approaches simultaneously, and such a policy did not work. It is quite possible that the analysis of his tests gave birth to Keynesian economics, which was realized in practice by President Roosevelt.

Franklin Roosevelt demonstrated better leadership skills. He surrounded himself with a huge group of advisors and created a "Brain Trust" including a group of Columbia University economists who helped develop policy recommendations leading to Roosevelt's New Deal. Adolf Berle, Rexford Tugwell, and John Galbraith became a part of President Roosevelt administration. Upon accepting the Democratic nomination, Roosevelt had promised a "New Deal" to help the country out of the Depression. He demonstrated leadership by reassuring the nation in his inaugural address that "the only thing we have to fear is fear itself." He stated that he would try something to end the depression and, if it failed, he would assess the failure and try something else.

His brain trust examined thoroughly "the Hoover New Deal," the potential effect of these measures. The trust economists were familiar with Keynes (1930, 1931, 1936) publications. Their recommendations brought to life Roosevelt's New Deal; much of what they created owed its origins, according to the Secretary of Commerce Rexford Tugwell, to Hoover's policies. Decade later, Tugwell said of Hoover: "We were too hard on a man who really invented most of devises we used." The First New Deal lasted from 1933 to 1935, and the Second New Deal continued from 1935 to 1938.

Executive Order 6102, issued by Roosevelt, on April 5, 1933, banning private gold ownership in the United States, forcing gold owners to take their bullion to a bank and exchange it for dollars at the prevailing rate of $20.67 per ounce, and raising in 1934 the official gold price to $35 per ounce increased significantly international gold inflow and became efficient measures to fight a monetary contraction. In addition, Banking Act of 1933 (sometimes called the *second* Glass-Steagall Act) prohibiting commercial banks from engaging in the investment business and the Banking Act of 1935 restructuring the Federal Reserve System to make it more independent of the Executive and Legislative Branches of the federal government, while consolidating the system power in Washington, focused to restore public confidence in the banking system. Many economists believe that the mentioned monetary policy was the main reason of recovery.

Under the New Deal, the government passed economic relief measures, relief for the unemployed, support for farmers, social security, laws helping unions, and other bills. The New Deal focused on improving living conditions of population. During the mentioned period, the following important acts were enacted: the National Housing Act of 1934 and the Housing Act of 1937 to make housing and home mortgages more affordable; the National Labor Relations Act of 1935, which guarantees basic rights of private sector employees to organize into trade unions and take collective action including strike if necessary; the Social Security Act of 1935, which created the Social Security system; and the Fair Labor Standards Act of 1938 that established the 40-h workweek and a national minimum wage, guaranteed overtime pay as one-and-a-half times regular pay, and prohibited minors to do certain dangerous jobs.

The New Deal programs made Democrats extremely popular and they kept majority in the House of Representative and in the Senate for a significant period of time. However, many of these useful programs required a huge government spending, and unfortunately, they were introduced in the unsuitable time—during the economic crisis. They increased significantly the role of the federal government in the economy, the size of the government, and the level of spending. Government debt started rocketing. If in 1930 the national debt was about $20 billion, in 1940 it became $50.7 billion.

President Roosevelt's liberal ideology and his desire to be reelected and strengthen the Democratic base resulted in the extensive government spending in 1935 ($ 8.81 billion) and in 1936 ($9.16 billion) (in 1932 it was only $4.26 billion). The high government spending led to the GDP growth (8.9% in 1935 and 12.9% in 1936) that ignited the stock market. However, the growing budget deficit (in 1936 it was $3.99 billion; in 1932 it was $1.63 billion) is always a warning factor. That is why when in 1937 Roosevelt decided to cut deficit spending (by increasing tax rates) and the Federal Reserve raised reserve ratio requirements for member banks, leading to a contraction of the monetary base, immediately the stock market reacted negatively (regime uncertainty led to its volatility, as investors moved to sell their shares), and the economy plunged back into recession in 1938 (the GDP rate was −3.3%, and unemployment, which had declined constantly after 1933, jumped to 20%). The recession ended when Federal Reserve and Treasury Department rolled back the indicated above contraction in the money supply and the government stopped its contractionary fiscal policies (see also Bordo and Haubrich, 2012; Romer, 1992, 2009; Rothbard, 1963). Political ideology of President Roosevelt did not allow him to get the United States out of the Great Depression. His policies were never aggressive enough to bring the economy completely out of recession. World War II helped to do that.

Similar to Franklin Roosevelt, President Ronald Reagan inherited the country with the economy in terrible shape: slow economic growth (it was negative −0.2% in 1980), high inflation (12.5%), and rising unemployment (about 7.5% in 1980).

Reagan, a former actor, a person with a certain managerial experience (as a governor of California from 1967 to 1975), demonstrated outstanding leadership skills. Having no serious knowledge in economics, he gathered a team of leading economists and followed their recommendations. Federal Reserve Chairman Paul Volcker played a decisive role in the economic policy of Reagan's administration. Donald Reagan, a former Chairman and CEO of Merrill Lynch, was chosen as the Secretary of Treasury. Beryl Sprinkel, the chief economist at Savings Bank of Chicago, became the Under Secretary of the Treasury for Monetary Affairs. Norman Ture, the chief tax policy officer of the Treasury in previous administrations, an advocate of tax cuts as an economic stimulus, became the Under Secretary of the Treasury for Tax Policy. Paul Roberts, a former associate editor of *The Wall Street Journal* editorial page, a fellow at the Georgetown Center for Strategic Studies, got a position of Assistant Secretary of the Treasury for International Economics. Myer Rashish, a Washington economic consultant, who served as the chairman of the Advisory Committee on Trade Negotiations, became the Under Secretary of State for Economic Affairs. Robert Hormats, who had high economic posts in both Republican and Democratic administrations, became an Assistant Secretary of State for Economic Affairs. The mentioned appointments indicated that the Reagan administration would focus on the tax cuts fiscal policy and the State Department would play a more assertive role in international economics. In addition, a famous economist Milton Friedman, who believed that the essence of the inflation problem was monetary policy and the discipline in the money supply was the main factor to deal with it effectively, was a member of the economic policy group.

Reagan promised Americans to restore prosperity by cutting taxes and slashing government spending and unnecessary extensive regulations. He abandoned long-fashionable Keynesian economic policies leading to increased spending and the incredible growth of the federal government. His fiscal policy focused on tax cuts accompanied by a smart Fed's monetary policy. To fight high inflation was the number one priority of his administration. Volcker sharply curtailed the growth of money supply, and as a result, the inflation rate fell from 13.5% in 1980 to 3.2% by 1983. However, monetary contraction produced a sharp decrease of interest rates causing the recession of 1981–1982 (unemployment jumped to 10.4%, the GDP growth rate became −1.9% in 1982, and the budget deficit reached $207 billion in 1983). In 1982, President Reagan's approval rating bottomed out at 35%. Being a strong leader, who had confidence in his economic team, Reagan continued the chosen economic course. In 1983, the economy began growing again (the GDP growth rate became 4.6%). That growth continued, unabated, through the rest of Reagan's presidency, marking a long peacetime period of unbroken economic expansion. The GDP growth rate was not less than 3.5% (in 1984, it was 7.3%), and unemployment was below 5.7% and 5.4% in 1988 and 1989, respectively. Despite Regan's conservative ideology, his belief in limited government, low taxes, and balanced budget, he and his economic team were unable to decrease the inherited budget deficit (in 1980 it was about $74 billion). Moreover, in 1989 it was more than doubled ($152.6 billion), and for the period of Reagan's presidency, the debt to GDP ratio jumped from 43.5% to 64.8%. The Cold War and the Reagan Doctrine to contain the Soviet Union, or the "evil empire" as he once referred to it, required government spending on defense. This explains the increased deficit, as well as a high GDP growth.

Many economists compare the 2008 economic crisis with the Great Depression. President Barak Obama (2009–2017), a person without any executive experience and knowledge in economics, inherited this crisis in its initial devastating stage: in 2009, unemployment reached about 10% and the GDP rate was −2.8%. Similar to President Reagan, he included in his economic team distinguished economists, many of them with a large practical experience. Chairman of the created Economic Recovery Advisory Board was Paul Volcker, who played an important role in the Reagan administration; Staff Director and Chief Economist of the Board was Austan Goolsbee, a professor of Economics, University of Chicago. The Board included professors of economics from the best American universities, as well as business leaders of various corporations. On his appointment, Volcker explained with a smile: "When the economy began going sour, then they decided I could be some kind of symbol of responsibility and prudence of their economic policy." Larry Summers was appointed to the post of Director of the National Economic Council. Timothy Geithner served as the Secretary of Treasury from 2009 to 2013, and Jack Lew took this position from 2013 to 2017. The Federal Reserve was led by Ben Bernanke and then after 2014 by Janet Yellen who continued his policy. All mentioned persons had deep and extensive knowledge of economic theory and an extensive practical experience. During the economic meltdown of 2008, Bernanke and Geithner worked to stabilize the banking industry and to restructure the regulation of the national financial system. Geithner was also involved in negotiations with foreign governments on global finance issues.

Summers emerged as a key economic decision-maker in the Obama administration. There had been friction between Summers and Volcker, as Volcker accused Summers of delaying the effort to organize a panel of outside economic advisers and Summers had cut Volcker out of White House meetings and had not shown interest in collaborating on policy solutions to the economic crisis.

Decision-making is the process of competition of ideas. When in the beginning of 2009 the Obama administration was going to pass an economic stimulus spending bill, Larry Summers was against extensive infrastructure spending. He supported tax cuts. Unfortunately, Obama decided that more of the stimulus should be spent on infrastructure. In 2010, Summers left the National Economic Council. Volcker believed that Summers had not gone far enough with financial reform, and the biggest banks that caused the financial crisis are allowed to resume their precrisis habits of behaving like hedge funds, trading recklessly with taxpayer-guaranteed money. He proposed rules (adopted as the Volcker Rule) that would prevent commercial banks from owning and investing in hedge funds and private equity and limit the trading they do for their own accounts. Volcker also believed that the United States should consider adding a national sales tax similar to the VAT imposed in European countries, stating "If, at the end of the day, we need to raise taxes, we should raise taxes."

President Obama had a brilliant economic team; most of his advisors analyzed in detail the Great Depression. However, his liberal ideology guided his actions—support Keynesian-type proposals with huge spending programs. Moreover, in a period of a severe crisis, using a political opportunity, he implemented the so-called Obamacare program that costed and would cost a lot of money. Instead of inducing investments, his administration produced numerous regulations on businesses that killed jobs. In addition, he significantly increased government. As a result, the federal government accumulated an enormous debt by borrowing and printing money. The Federal Reserve Chairman Bernanke (2002) was not shy saying: "The US government has a technology, called a printing press (or today, its electronic equivalent), that allows it to produce as many US dollars as it wishes at no cost...people know that inflation erodes the real value of the government debt and, therefore, that it is in the interest of the government to create some inflation."

He deserves credit for a smart monetary policy with a low interest rate. However, when questioned about taxation policy, he said that it was none of his business, his exclusive remit being monetary policy, and said that fiscal policy and wider society-related issues were what politicians were for and got elected for.

President Obama inherited a severe financial crisis—a result of the collapse of the American subprime real estate bubble setting off a chain of events, culminating in the failure of the fourth largest investment bank (Lehman Brothers Holdings Inc.) that triggered panic in international financial markets and caused the economy to fall into a deep recession. He deserved credit for several important measures to bring the US economy out of a recession, for the successful implementation of the Troubled Asset Relief Program (TARP). The TARP bailout programs (bank support and credit market programs focused on purchasing mortgage-related toxic assets) cleaned suffered banks' balance sheets and lessened economic uncertainty. The government's measures helped keep mortgage rates low so that Americans could continue to buy homes, refinance mortgages in the wake of the crisis, prevent avoidable foreclosures, and keep families in their homes. TARP helped the Federal Reserve and Treasury take action to stabilize American International Group (AIG) because its failure during the financial crisis would have had a devastating impact on American financial system and the economy. TARP helped stabilize America's banking system so that it could withstand the downturn and start lending again. TARP helped prevent the collapse of the American auto industry, saving more than a million American jobs.

However, President Obama cannot claim full credit for this outcome; he should share it with his predecessor, President George W. Bush, who signed this program into law in October of 2008.

Many economists and politicians are critical of the banks and auto bailouts. However, the government has returned the invested money, and this is the best evidence of the righteousness of its policy. To protect the country against such type of crises in the future, the administration implemented a number of measures: created and conducted a comprehensive stress test for the nation's largest banks to ensure they had sufficient capital to withstand deep recessions; limited the ability for commercial banks to engage in speculative trading; established higher capital and liquidity standards for financial institutions both domestically and internationally; and created the Consumer Financial Protection Bureau (CFPB) to hold financial institutions accountable and protect consumers from the types of abuses that preceded the crisis.

The Obama administration was able to stabilize the economy. However, it was unable to restore it to its precrisis level and move forward. Despite the effective monetary policy and actions of the Federal Reserve and US Department of the Treasury, the economy still remains timid. It may look strange that such a situation exists when the official unemployment rate is below 5%.

The 2008 economic crisis was accompanied with significant job losses: At the beginning of 2010, employment had declined by 8.8 million from its prerecession peak. Although President Obama claims that his administration created 14 million new private sector jobs, in reality during his term the United States added only about 5.6 million private sector jobs. All depends on the initial date to compare with—February 2010, when the job market hits bottom, or the previous jobs peak in January 2008. Most of jobs were created in the service sector—particularly health care (about 1.6 million), food service (about 1.6 million), and temporary help agencies (about 1.5 million). Government employment grew significantly; more than 1.4 million people received *government* salaries as new federal employees or contractors. Such a type of created jobs can partially explain the 2016 economic situation. The government fiscal policy during 2008—2016 does not look persuasive. Investment in infrastructure did not focus on important projects (bridges, airports, etc.). Tax cuts were insignificant, and their influence on the economy was minuscule. A lot of money flew away with useless grants. Obama's National Robotics Initiative was handled mostly by bureaucrats of the National Science Foundation who had no experience and knowledge in this area. Solar energy investment cannot be profitable now for such a country as the United States—the country rich of oil and coal resources. However, silly environmental laws kill the related industries in the United States in the period when sustainable economic growth is highly needed. Many manufacturing initiatives still have not produced real results.

Amid the 2008 financial crisis, Barack Obama ran for president promising to piece together the shattered US economy and reduce the national deficit. After 8 years in office, Obama's economic performance fell short of expectations and he left the country's economy still in a bad shape (the 2016 GDP growth rate is only 1.6% and although the official unemployment data around 5%, the actual unemployment rate (taking into account that the labor force participation rate is only around 63%; discouraged workers and the underemployed were not included in unemployment data) was above 10%). In such a situation, any small shock could roll back the economy into a recession.

A comparison of the 2016 economic indicators (unemployment, gross domestic product, the budget deficit, government debt, and interest rates) with the 2009 CBO's 10-year forecast for the US economy shows that either the economic policy failed or the economic forecasts were biased and too wrong, or, what looks more plausible, both. The labor force participation rate was near its 38-year low. Other economic indicators were significantly worse than CBO's 2009 forecast. The 2016 budget deficit, as a percentage of GDP, was more than twice larger, and the ratio of government public debt to GDP was about 1.7 larger than CBO's 2009 forecast, respectively. The 3-month treasury yield stagnated at near-zero percent, instead of recovering to the near 5% as the CBO forecasted.

That is why the United States chose as its new president a person who offered a drastically different economic policy—some aspects of which we will discuss later.

As mentioned earlier, monetary policy of central banks focuses to offset the deficiencies of fiscal policy. Economists involved in decision-making of central banks can be considered as independent decision-makers. The US Federal Reserve System (Fed) consists of 12 regional Reserve Banks, the Board of Governors, and the Federal Open Market Committee (FOMC). Its macroeconomic objectives are maximum employment and stable prices to promote sustainable growth and to help preserve the purchasing power of the dollar and moderate long-term interest rates. The Fed is an independent agency and it can make decisions without approval from any other branch of government. Economists of the Federal Reserve System conduct research on a broad range of topics in economics and finance and present their research to policymakers. FOMC reviews economic and financial conditions in the United States and abroad, determines the appropriate stance of monetary policy, and assesses the risks to its long-run goals of price stability and sustainable economic growth. It adjusts the short-term interest rates in response to changes in the economic outlook. During eight regularly scheduled yearly meetings, FOMC summarizes the Committee's economic outlook and the policy decision concerning key interest rates and whether to increase or decrease the money supply, which the Fed does by buying and selling government securities. FOMC's decisions are the result of a group decision-making process based on the voting system. This enables the group to present the opinion of the majority of high-level professionals. However, the Fed is only theoretically independent. In reality, it is not free from political pressure and its Board members are nominated by the President and must be approved by the Senate. Its chairman regularly testifies to both the Senate and the House. The roots of the 2008 financial crisis lie in the legislative branch of government, which, in turn, often blames the Fed for not warning about possible crises.

However, compared with the professional decision-making related to the monetary policy, in the decision-making process related to the fiscal policy, economists play mostly a modest advisory role. As indicated earlier, the main factors characterizing macroeconomic processes are market forces producing self-regulation through feedback human activated channels and government actions (its fiscal and monetary policies).

Classical theory denies any active role of government in macroeconomic policy. Its fundamental principle is that the economy is self-regulated; individuals and businesses are able to allocate resources in the most efficient manner to meet their needs. Self-regulated tools include flexible wages, prices, and interest rates. Government interference should be minimal because it can only increase economic instability. The US 1920–1921 economic crisis (in 1920, unemployment had jumped from 4% to nearly 12%, and GNP declined 17%) can serve as an example supporting this theory. President Harding cut the government budget nearly in half between 1920 and 1922, slashed tax rates for all income groups, reduced federal expenditures, and reduced, by one-third, the national debt. By the late summer of 1921, signs of recovery were already visible. The following year, unemployment was back down to 6.7% and it was only 2.4% by 1923. Not surprisingly, many modern economists who have studied the depression of 1920–1921 have been unable to explain how the recovery could have been so swift and sweeping even though the federal government and the Federal Reserve did not use any stimuli measures. There was no a stimulative policy; government interference to moderate the depression and speed recovery was minimal.

In contrast to classical theory, the main concept of Keynesian theory is the necessity of an active economic policy to stabilize the economy. Fiscal policy is considered as the most efficient means of macroeconomic stabilization because government spending influences directly consumption and consumer spending and, in turn, taxes influence the efficiency of consumption and investment. The Keynesian approach was used by many governments during the Great Depression. If the expenditure equation (see Eqs. (1.1)–(1.4)) is the basis for the Keynesian approach, classical theory considers as its base the Eq. (2.3), where the production output is determined by the supplies of labor and capital, and the equation of exchange establishing the relationship between money supply, velocity of money, an index of expenditures, and price level, that is between the quantity of money and nominal GDP (see, e.g., Mankiw, 2015). If at any moment labor or capital is not fully employed, their prices would drop, and this would generate movement in opposite direction. Traditional Keynesian fiscal policy focuses to direct money to the middle- and lower-class stimulating the *demand side* of the economy (as a result of government spending by investing in infrastructure or decreasing taxes for these groups of individuals). However, the so-called *supply-side* economists believe that better economic growth is achieved by cutting business and corporate taxes, as well as by reducing capital gain taxes and personal income taxes for wealthier taxpayers, because the money saved through these tax cuts will be reinvested in the economy and generate more jobs. This is not a new idea. We can trace parts of it back to the 18th century. French economist Jean-Baptiste Say indicated that the government should focus on helping the economy save and produce more, rather than consume more: "The encouragement of mere consumption is no benefit to commerce; for the difficulty lies in supplying the means, not in stimulating the desire of consumption; and we have seen that production alone furnishes those means. Thus, it is the aim of good government to stimulate production, of bad government to encourage consumption." One more direct channel to stimulate production is a proper monetary policy which would encourage investment. The magnitude of the combined fiscal/monetary stimulus should be set large enough to raise aggregate demand back to normal and should be gradually phased out as the economy recovers from recession. Some economists (e.g., Friedman, 2010; Buchanan, 1987) considered the Keynesian fiscal stimulus as the unnecessary and inefficient approach to cure a recession. They believed that the economy would recover on its own from a recession as long as the central bank kept the money supply from contracting. Hayek (2009), an opponent of Keynesian economics, was against massive monetary easing to prevent a recession. He believed that if unprofitable investments were made during a boom, it was better to shut those firms down and clear the way for new, more productive investment. Lucas (1981), Sargent (1987), Barro (1981), and Prescott (2002) warned that government fiscal stimulus would generate harmful government indebtedness.

Economic crises are testing grounds for existing theories. Financial crises of the previous century brought to life economic theories, which later were modified and improved. Although scientists belonging to different economic schools often try to empathize their rightness (e.g., the US 1920—1921 economic policy of President Harding is called Reaganomics; in turn, some economists consider Reagan's economic policy as Keynesian policy), it looks like now there is a growing consensus among leading economists that fiscal stimulus should be accompanied by a proper monetary policy. It is unwise to rely only on self-regulating process. Properly implemented fiscal and monetary policies can speed up this process. As we indicated earlier, monetary policy can increase the value of spending multipliers. A positive effect of fiscal and monetary policies can be expected only if government and central banks are well informed about shocks of aggregated supply and demand and use this information properly. The failure of shock therapy in postcommunist transitional economies demonstrates possible negative consequences of economic policies conducted by ignorant politicians trying in a hurry to copy economic measures of free-market economies.

The briefly described general approaches (without discussing differences between classical and neoclassical, Keynesian and neo-Keynesian models) that can potentially improve the economy are the tools economists operate with. Decisions how to improve the health of the economy can be compared with the treatment of a seriously sick patient. Self-regulation of macroeconomic processes is similar to a patient's immune system. Countries with a strong economic base are potentially more resistant to economic shocks. Similar to drugs strengthening the human immune system, a proper monetary policy can play the same role. The more channels are available to affect economic growth—the better, and all the aforementioned approaches should be taken into consideration. They all are prescriptions to cure the economy. The problem is how to use them properly. Sir William Osler, a Canadian physician, wrote many years ago: "the good physician treats the disease; the great physician treats the patient who has the disease." The great economist used in the decision-making process should not only know all possible measures to restore the health of the economy but also deeply understand the country and its specifics to apply them properly. The process of understanding is an imperative piece of the decision-making process.

The design of fiscal packages, both in terms of the composition of individual measures as well as their timing, is a result of a decision-making process. It looks like, during the 2008 global financial crisis, China designed and implemented stimulus packages, covering a variety of sectors, including transportation, infrastructure, environment, technological innovations, housing, and social programs such as health care and education, more efficiently and, as a result, restored the economy faster than the United States and many other European countries. However, this is a short-run success. It is difficult to estimate long-term consequences of stimulus measures.

The question is not whether a stimulus created jobs but whether the benefits of the stimulus will exceed its costs. Stimuli create budget deficits and debt, which hampers investment and growth and can become unsustainable for many countries. In Europe, a significant increase in public debt shifted the priority of stimulus policy to fiscal consolidation by cutting spending and/or raising taxes. Decision should be made when the mentioned measures should be applied. Economists should explain politicians that any time delay can significantly worsen a country's economy. As a part of austerity measures, Denmark, Estonia, and Greece increased excise taxes on goods such as tobacco, alcohol, and fuel; in the United Kingdom, Portugal, Latvia, and Estonia, politicians have chosen to increase VAT; and Hungary, Spain, and Latvia increased income taxes. Additionally, some countries were forced to freeze or cut programs and social benefits: Denmark froze unemployment aid, student financial aid, welfare, and foreign aid, as well as cut the duration of unemployment and the amount of family benefits; France, Italy, Latvia, Lithuania, Croatia, and Estonia introduced significant spending cuts in the health sector. However, austerity measures applied in big doses and/or too soon can produce dangerous contractionary effects on the economy.

As a rule, policymakers chose economists who share their political views. Although they are not decision-makers, they are a part of the decision-making process, and their recommendations, as well as the way they defend them and argue with opponents, have a crucial influence on the future economic policy. An efficient decision-making should include economists belonging to different economic schools. This will create alternative proposals. Participating economists should be able to communicate with policymakers explaining them advantages of their approaches. Being very simple and easy to understand, the above developed models can be applied for policy analysis. By using them, many rosy economic scenarios can be rejected immediately. More detailed models can be used later, if necessary. However, the existing complex models contain so many uncertain parameters that they allow one to justify almost any economic proposal.

The material of Chapter 2 and 3 can help pure economists to provide policymakers with information related to the results of considering spending and/or tax policy measures, which would allow them to cut off not perspective variants and focus only on several more realistic approaches. The usage of the models of Chapter 2 can persuade policymakers that spending, for example, on infrastructure above a certain level is inadmissible, and only several alternative scenarios for certain growth rates and multiplier values should be selected. Of course, some infrastructure projects can be needed under all conditions, and government money should be allocated for this. However, for a high debt level, any spending should be accompanied by austerity measures.

One of the most important decision-making problems concerning stimulus measures is to determine the composition, size, and the duration of the stimulus package. Economists still continue to argue whether stimulus spending is useful. Many of them believe that the policy success depends on the choice of proper projects. Other insist that government should not spare money and should not pull back too soon. The material of Chapter 2 enables one to evaluate whether the extra budget deficit caused by stimulus measures can be repaid in the near future. Although the examples of Chapter 2 assume that stimuli act 10 years, in reality the duration of these measures depends on the initial level of unemployment, the future GDP growth rate, which depends on the type and level of stimulus measures, and some other factors. The models of Chapter 2 enable one to analyze not only the dynamics of the debt to GDP ratio presented in the related tables but also all necessary parameters to evaluate deeply the effect of stimulus packages.

Curing the economy is a dynamic process. Previous assumptions embedded in the model parameters can be evaluated in 1−2 years and modified so that based on the new calculations the corrected decisions can be made related to the future economic policy.

Table 4.6 Evaluation of stimulus

Year	1	2	3	4	5	6	7	8	9	10
Debt/GDP	1.02	1.05	1.08	1.1	1.12	1.13	1.14	1.15	1.16	1.17
$l_G = 3.8$										
∇G	29	60	93	128	164	203	243	286	331	378
∇T	19.4	40	61	83	107	132	158	185	214	244

Although the generalized model (2.43) [(2.50)] is the best fit to this adaptive procedure, here, for simplicity, we analyze the additional data given in Table 2.2, which can be useful for decision-making.

In Table 4.6, ∇G and ∇T are the additional spending and tax revenues (in billion dollars), respectively, as a result of stimulus spending that changed the GDP rate from $g_0 = 0.022$ to $g_1 = 0.03$ (for the spending multiplier $l_G = 3.8$ and $d_0 = 0.99$; $D_0 = 16,051$; $\tau = 0.15$; $r = 0.026$; $l_2 = 0.13$; $l_3 = 0.194$).

If we assume that a low unemployment rate can be achieved in 4 years and stimulus spending can be ended, then, as it can be easily concluded from Table 4.6, we can expect that it would require about two more years to compensate the additional spending. However, for the spending multiplier $l_G = 1.59$, stimulus spending is significantly larger, and it is impossible to expect that they can be paid back in the near future.

As indicated in Chapter 1, the spending and tax multipliers represent a class of multipliers with different values for different types of spending and taxes. The problem of choosing a stimulus package can be formulated as the portfolio optimization problem. Its solution determines the components of the stimulus package, the amount of money associated with each component, and the multipliers value for the whole package. It can be formulated as a static or dynamic problem.

Infrequently, policymakers ask economists to evaluate the effect of their proposals, usually in 10–20 years. In contrast to such an approach, the considered models enable one to estimate the values of the chosen macroeconomic parameters (the debt, the debt to GDP ratio) as a result of spending and austerity measures in accordance with the chosen criteria (to grow the economy with the rate $g(t)$ (g_t), to decrease the debt or balance the budget in 10 years). The concrete measures should be detailed after the policy related to the chosen criterion is adopted.

As shown in Chapter 3, the 10 years' goal can be decomposed to yearly goals so that concrete economic measures can be considered for each consecutive year. A set of various projects should be considered, and the chosen projects can satisfy additional criteria, their prioritization can be determined, etc. Operations research methods are appropriate tools for solving such problems. The current level of software development allows scientists to create and test sophisticated models and analyze alternative decisions within a short period of time. During the 1929 and 1980 crises, economists had no such tools.

Realization of the established goals depends on one important factor—the GDP growth rate. This parameter is in all considered models and influences significantly the output values of the considered models. As mentioned earlier, according to Reinhart and Rogoff (2010), in countries with debt to GDP ratios above the threshold of 90%, the GDP growth is very small, less then considered in the examples of Chapter 2 and 3. However, for such a powerful country as the United States, it is still possible to expect the growth rates above 3%.

Based on Eq. (2.45) the GDP growth rate can be described by the following expression:

$$g_{t+1} = \frac{Y_{t+1} - Y_t}{Y_t} = \frac{\Delta C_{t+1}}{Y_t} + \frac{\Delta G_{t+1}}{Y_t} + \frac{\Delta I_{t+1}}{Y_t} + \frac{\Delta X_{N,t+1}}{Y_t} \qquad (4.8)$$

where the right part of Eq. (4.8) is written by using Eq. (1.2) and Δ is a symbol meaning the difference between $t+1$ and t values of the corresponding parameters.

The analysis of the US GDP components for the past 10 years shows large negative values of net exports X_N. A huge negative trade balance accounts about 3% of the GDP. Its decrease by half would add at least 1% to the GDP rate (of course, this measure can decrease slightly consumer spending because prices on foreign goods would jump up). A higher level of investment I (to restore a weak manufacturing base) can easily bring one more additional percent to the GDP growth rate. Any attempt to decrease the size of the overcrowded federal government and to fight the fraud inside the government system can decrease government spending G and contribute to the GDP growth. The below data show that an effective decision-making can restore the country's economic health.

4.5 HOW TO IMPROVE THE ECONOMY

A realistic approach to restoring the country's economic health starts with programs focused on balancing the budget. As shown in Chapter 3, to balance the US federal budget in 10 years, the government should be able to decrease its debt about $100 billion at least during initial several years.

To treat successfully a disease, doctors should make a proper diagnosis. The main economic reason of a slow recovery in the United States and many European countries is high unemployment. As mentioned earlier, the official 2016 about 5% unemployment rate in the United States is deceptive because the real labor force participation rate is only about 63%.

The US Bureau of Labor Statistics explains the low rate mostly by the retirement of baby boom generation and also by giving up job hunting of many Americans in favor of staying home or going back to school. To defend its economic policy, the government does not miss a chance to use fuzzy statistics and remind that the labor force participation rate in the United States averaged 63% from 1950 until 2016, reaching an all time high of 67.3% in January of 2000 and a record low of 58.1% in December 1954. Statistical averages are often misleading. However, the 2000 data show a hidden working force potential. That is why many economists believe that a more realistic unemployment estimate is above 10%. Higher employment translates to a higher GDP growth rate and higher government revenues.

As we indicated earlier, tax cuts, as well as spending stimuli, alone cannot serve as an appropriate medicine when the national debt and the debt to GDP ratio reached such a dangerous level. However, the results of Reinhart and Rogoff (2009, 2010) should not discourage. What happened in the past is the result of the past economic policies, which should be critically evaluated to find new ways to find better results.

4.5.1 Entitlement Programs

The so-called entitlement programs, government programs that provide individuals with personal financial benefits (or sometimes special government-provided goods or services), that started devouring more and more money from government budgets attracted attention of economists. The modification of these programs focused on decreasing the national debt is offered by some economists as the first medical aid and necessary cure for the economy.

In Europe, the entitlement programs include public pensions, public health-care and health insurance, unemployment insurance, and others— such as primarily child care, maternity benefits, family cash benefits, and means-tested social assistance, plus sickness benefits, long-term care insurance, and many smaller programs. Together, these entitlement programs represent between 20% and 30% of GDP in most European countries, with considerable variation especially in Eastern Europe (see, e.g., Börsch-Supan, 2013).

In the United States the most important examples of entitlement programs at the federal level include Social Security (the program that provides monthly benefits designed to replace, in part, the loss of income owing to retirement, disability, or death), Medicare (health insurance program for people aged 65 years or above), and Medicaid (a health-care program that pays for medical services for low-income and disabled people), most Veterans' Administration programs, federal employee and military retirement plans, unemployment compensation, food stamps, and agricultural price support programs.

Public pension expenditures are the single largest item in the social budget in almost all European countries. They alone represent a substantial share of GDP. In 2011, Italy and France were "leaders" with about 14% of GDP, and in Greece, Portugal, and Austria, this share was about 12%, roughly twice the share of GDP compared with the United States (6.7% of GDP). Health care, in turn, accounts for the largest share of entitlements in the United States and Canada with more than 40%, whereas it is only about 22% in Estonia and Finland (see Börsch-Supan, 2013).

In the United States, entitlement programs represent about 18.5% of GDP. Medicare has had a cash shortfall every year since its creation except two: 1966 and 1974. Medicare's annual cash shortfall in 2012 was $472 billion. In 2015, it reached $546 billion. Medicare now covers nearly 51 million people at a cost of $586 billion. The program is responsible for more than 25% of all federal debt since 2000. Medicaid provides health care for 62 million poorer Americans. Its cost was $308 billion in 2012. In 2015, it jumped to $446 billion. Social Security, Medicare, and Medicaid already cost now about $1.9 trillion per year. Social Security costs $887.8 billion per year. In 2010, estimated 49% of households received benefits from these three entitlement programs or other federal and state government assistance. Social Security and Medicare, as currently structured and financed, cannot come close to meeting the demand. Viewed from a GDP perspective, Social Security spending has been relatively stable. In 2005, spending was 4% of GDP. By 2015, it had increased to about 5% GDP. For 10 years, Medicare costs increased by about 80%. As to Medicaid, its costs—as a result of a huge influx of new beneficiaries owing to Obamacare—reached about 500 billion.

The mentioned millions of retiring baby boomers will increase significantly the cost of Social Security, Medicare, and Medicaid in the United States and pension plans in Europe. According to the US Chamber of Commerce, 36 million Americans are already retired. During this decade and the next, the number of Americans 65 or above will jump by 75%, whereas those of working age will increase by just 7%. During the next 17 years, 77 million workers will retire. The cost to make these programs financially solvent for the next 75 years is almost $40 trillion (see https://www.uschamber.com/report/10-truths-about-americas-entitlement-programs).

Many European countries have begun (or have announced) programs intended to reduce the growth of entitlement programs, in particular, of public pensions. As to the United States, this process is only in the embryo. Politicians who deal with entitlement programs are interested in expanding these programs, rather than in cutting them back. Most of them are under the influence of the organized special interest groups that support the programs because they benefit from them.

For politicians to speak about cutting the amount of money spent on entitlement programs is equivalent to political suicide. That is why they discuss only how to restrain the increases and make the program sustainable. The United States has not reached yet a boiling point when tough decisions must be made. However, the example of 2009 Greek government debt crisis demonstrated to many politicians that their political life can be very short. Hunting for votes and giving false promises, thinking about their career, rather than about the people they represent, passing not thoroughly thought-out laws—these features, unfortunately, characterize many current politicians.

In the current high technology era, a country with leaders whose knowledge is limited by the social science area has small chances to be prosperous. On the one hand, entitlement programs, not being adjusted properly to the requirements of the time, hurt the economic growth. On the other hand, an economic growth can help to improve these programs. A smart economic policy should work in both directions—create conditions for the GDP growth and, simultaneously, try to improve entitlement programs. As indicated earlier, the necessary condition for the economic growth is increased employment. The desire of many politicians (Democrats—in the United States) to save entitlement programs by increasing taxes, mostly on the rich (a popular method to demonstrate the care for poor people), only hurts the economy and aggravates the situation with entitlement programs because tax increase cannot create new jobs. The only way to move in the right direction is to cut taxes (at least for businesses to stimulate capital investment); however, even being dosed properly, this measure alone is not sufficient.

Practical measures to save entitlement programs include the increase of retirement age and/or establishing occupational and individual funded pensions by moving substantial parts of retirement income from public pensions to private savings. Various related proposals present the implementation of two obvious but unlikely popular strategies—work longer and save more.

Well-known drawbacks of governmental systems (sluggishness because of inefficient bureaucracy, corruption, overstaffing) present a real opportunity to save money needed to decrease a country's debt. Medicare and Medicaid fraud is the result of inefficient implementation of these programs. It is difficult to evaluate precisely the level of medical fraud. A special structure should be created. Only in 2011, the government recovered $4.1 billion from health-care providers billing for services that never being done and from suppliers billing for equipment that never being sent, as well as for services, supplies, and equipment obtained by stolen Medicare and Medicaid cards, for misleading diagnostics and unnecessary treatment, etc.

"Our estimate is that the federal government, in Medicare and Medicaid alone, loses between $70 billion and $120 billion a year to crooks. You ought to be able to identify those," said former House Speaker Newt Gingrich, who criticized the federal government inability to fight health-care fraud (see http://www.factcheck.org/2011/05/gingrich-overshoots-the-truth/0http://www.factcheck.org/2011/05/gingrich-overshoots-the-truth/). It is true that Medicare and Medicaid paid about $70 billion in "improper payments" in 2010, but not all of those payments were fraudulent. In 2012, Donald Berwick, a former head of the Centers for Medicare and Medicaid Services (CMS), and Andrew Hackbarth, of the RAND Corporation, estimated that fraud (and the extra rules and inspections required to fight it) added as much as $98 billion, or roughly 10%, to annual Medicare and Medicaid spending—and up to $272 billion across the entire health system. According to the Government Accountability Office, 10% of Medicaid payments (about $36 billion) were found to have been improper in 2016 alone.

Gingrich (2013) was more realistic: "What if new technology could save $160 billion in Medicare and Medicaid costs over 10 years?" A cautiously optimistic estimate is that with a help of current sophisticated technology, the efficiently managed antifraud system can save yearly on average $15—30 billion.

4.5.2 Trade Deficit

Being preoccupied with entitlement programs, such as Medicare and Social Security, and revenue increases through taxesAmerican politicians have paid no attention to one of the largest contributors to the national debt— America's failed trade policies. If in the early 1990s the US net exports were about −1% of GDP, they were −3.4% of GDP in 2016.

One can find the following definitions of the term *free trade*:

1. international trade free from protective duties and subject only to such tariffs as are needed for revenue;
2. the buying and selling of goods, without limits on the amount of goods that one country can sell to another, and without special taxes on the goods bought from a foreign country.
3. a system of trade between nations in which there are no special taxes placed on imports;
4. trade between countries, free from governmental restrictions or duties;
5. free trade is the unrestricted purchase and sale of goods and services between countries without the imposition of constraints such as tariffs, duties, and quotas.
6. free trade, also called laissez-faire, a policy by which a government does not discriminate against imports or interfere with exports by applying tariffs (to imports) or subsidies (to exports).

Some above definitions differ so that it is impossible to state that the term has a unique interpretation. The word *free* in the above term assumes that the trade is based on an agreement that is assumed to be mutually beneficial for all participants. A logical inference is that if this does not take place, a participant has the right to ask to reconsider the agreement or simply cancel it. Unfortunately, the existing trade agreements contain many gaps that are used by many governments to impose some protectionist policies that are intended to support local employment, such as applying tariffs to imports or subsidies to exports. Governments may also restrict free trade to limit exports of natural resources. Other barriers that may hinder trade include import quotas, taxes, and nontariff barriers, such as regulatory legislation.

During the 1960s, the United States exported more than we imported, but our total trade was less than 3% of GDP. Now trade is close to 25% of GDP, and over the past 40 years, trade has become a larger and larger portion of the US economy.

Since the beginning of the globalization era, America has consistently (excluding two times after 1970) imported more goods and services than it has exported, leading to larger and larger trade deficits over the years. In recent years, the trade deficit has regularly topped half a trillion dollars annually. According to the Census Bureau, Canada, China, Mexico, Japan, Germany, South Korea, and the United Kingdom are America's top trading partners. These seven countries represent more than 50% of the US total trade deficit. In 2015, the trade deficit with China was $367.2 billion, with Germany $74.8 billion, with Japan $68.9 billion, and with Mexico $60.7 billion.

As usual in economics, there are different views of trade deficits. Some economists see only positive in trade deficits and believe that they enable the United States to import capital to finance investment in productive capacity and boost employment. Another group of economists emphasize negative features of trade deficits—borrowing to finance current consumption rather than long-term investment that hurts employment. Each group supports their views by concrete historic examples. However, it looks like they do not want to see that the examples correspond to different periods of time and absolutely different economic conditions. In a period of economic booms, trade deficits are not dangerous. On the contrary, they can be useful to help financing long-term investment and target the most prospective projects. However, in the period of economic recessions accompanied by rising unemployment and lack of growth in consumer demand and business activity, trade deficits present an economic burden.

Using frivolously, without deep understanding, the term *free trade* American politicians signed trade agreements strongly believing that they were good for their counties in the globalization era. Signing in 1993 the North American Free Trade Agreement (NAFTA) Implementation Act, eliminating trade and investment barriers between the United States, Canada, and Mexico, President Clinton said: "NAFTA means jobs. American jobs, and good-paying American jobs. If I didn't believe that, I wouldn't support this agreement." The above data show that he was wrong. President Clinton opened the way for China to be a member of the World Trade Organization (WTA) and to use all advantages of its membership. Now China is the most important competitor for the US exporters in markets around the world. It is no coincidence that China is also the world's foremost currency manipulator that uses this strategy to raise its trade surplus at the expense of other countries.

The most recent trade agreement, the Korea U.S. Free Trade Agreement (KORUS FTA), which went into effect in March 2012, was also a mistake.

Nevertheless, President Obama asked Congress for fast-track trade authority to move forward on the two trade agreements that have been in negotiations behind closed doors for the past 4 years: the Trans-Pacific Partnership Agreement and the Trans-Atlantic Trade Agreement. It looks like the incompetence of current politicians has no limits. Failed free-trade agreements and lowered tariffs have added more than $10 trillion to the national debt. That means that the nation's cumulative trade deficit is directly responsible for a significant part of the national debt.

The failed trade policies open doors to cheap imports from around the world. As a result, millions of American jobs have been lost. Those jobs represent tax revenues that could be used to help cover annual budget gaps. In addition, the failed trade policies encouraged companies to outsource jobs. Once outside of America, those companies can hoard money overseas and avoid paying their tax obligations despite still being considered an American. Hence, the outsourced factories also contribute to the debt. The free-trade agreement destroyed the nation's very important manufacturing sector, which lost ground to competitors not only in China but also in Germany, Japan, and Korea that have pursued advanced industrial and trade policies. The jobs in manufacturing have been shipped to China, India, or Mexico. The offshoring of manufacturing of so many products has resulted in the loss of 5.8 million American manufacturing jobs, nearly a third (32%) of manufacturing employment, and the closure of over 57,000 manufacturing firms. As a result, the government created unemployment and lost tax-related revenues.

Economists usually disagree about whether or not the trade deficit constitutes a debt to be repaid. Without discussing whether this is right or wrong, we consider how a smart trade policy can decrease national debt.

According to Scott et al. (2013), "Global currency manipulation is one of the most important causes of growing U.S. trade deficits, and of unemployment and slow economic growth in the United States and Europe. Currency manipulation distorts international trade flows by artificially lowering the cost of U.S. imports and raising the cost of U.S. exports. This leads to goods trade deficits that displace U.S. jobs, particularly in the manufacturing sector." Currency manipulation involves artificially reducing the value of a country's own currency, in effect providing a subsidy for national exports. Currency manipulators often buy US treasury bonds to prevent their own currencies from strengthening. Eliminating currency manipulation would reduce the US trade goods deficit by at least $190 billion and as much as $400 billion over 3 years, allowing the United States to "reap enormous benefits" without any increase in federal spending or taxation; this would create 2.2—4.7 million jobs; 620,000—1.3 million of those jobs would be in manufacturing; in addition, the US GDP would increase by 1.4%—3.1% (see Scott et al., 2013).

President Trump deserves credit for attracting attention of a wide public to the US trade deficit with China, Mexico, South Korea, and Japan and the currency manipulation problem. However, his proposed solution to raise tariffs against foreign competitors up to 45% was labeled by many politicians as protectionism. Some ideas to decrease the trade deficit and recover manufacturing, which is one of the best generators of wealth for the economy, range from cutting regulations that kill businesses and raise the cost and effort of running a manufacturing operation to imposing a VAT on imports and even the broad-based VAT (see Senator Cruz's tax plan) that is used by more than 130 countries. Almost all countries with VATs waive them on exports but impose them on imports, at an average rate of about 17%. According to Harry Moser, president of the Reshoring Initiative (bringing manufacturing and services back to the United States from overseas), a 17% tax on $2 trillion a year of imports could generate more than $300 billion a year in revenue. In addition, a VAT would make imports more expensive, boosting the demand of US-made goods that would be more attractive to consumers if the mentioned initiative realization is accompanied with tax cuts.

A world-known investor Warren Buffet offered an alternative approach to tax imports. The companies that export goods from the United States would accumulate certificates equal to the value of their exports. However, companies that wanted to import goods would have to purchase certificates from exporters. As a result, US exporters, with the cash cushion from the sale of their certificates, could offer US-made goods to foreign customers at lower prices, making them more compatible and shrinking the trade deficit over time. At the same time, foreign-made items imported in the United States would be more expensive to reflect the cost of import certificates, making US-made goods more cost compatible with cheap imports. The market forces would regulate the price of the certificates, and the price could eventually tend to zero if the trade surplus was achieved. Buffet believes that his approach is a more efficient way to decrease significantly the trade deficit than waiting for the US export to become more attractive as a result of a weaker dollar. Unlike standard tariffs that usually penalize a specific product from a certain country, the certificates provide direct and immediate benefit to US exporting companies. However, this approach is based on the unrealistic assumption that the opposite side would not undertake at least similar countermeasures.

In addition to the aforementioned ways to reduce or eliminate currency manipulation, certain legal and regulatory tools can be used to reach this goal. The government can refuse to sell Treasury bills and other government assets to China and other countries that refuse to allow the United States to purchase their government assets (currency manipulators generally refuse to sell their government assets to the United States, effectively closing their capital markets). The United States and other countries may legally refuse to sell government assets to currency manipulators because the World Trade Organization and International Monetary Fund do not require the United States to maintain free markets in capital flows, only in goods and services. Refusing to sell assets to currency manipulators would eliminate the principal tool used by foreign central banks to manipulate their currencies: purchases of Treasury bills and other government securities (see Scott (2012) for a summary of research on trade, currency manipulation, and policy alternatives that could be used to address it).

Some economists believe that it is economically implausible to solve currency wars by tax policies. Floating currencies can be depreciated faster than import taxes can be adjusted. Rising impost taxes would intensify the very problem of protectionism. They believe that the currency problem, or a monetary problem, must be solved by the same kind of tools—by a currency and monetary solution, more precisely—by the currency that does not encourage predatory currency depreciation. In their opinion, floating exchange rates should be eliminated, and a system of stable exchange rates without official reserve currencies should be created. The offered solution is to establish a system of stable exchange rates among the nations of the G-20 or at least the G-7 to which other countries will conform. Such an international monetary system of stable exchange rates would eliminate the burden and privilege of the dollar role as a reserve currency.

Is this a realistic solution? Now the international monetary system consists of a disordered arrangement of floating currencies, and any country can depreciate its currency against the dollar. As an example, China's industrialization growth in the 1990s coincides with establishing interest rates to the dollar at an undervalue level. That is why some economists believe that the floating exchange rate system, combined with the official reserve currency role of the world dollar standard, hurts the American economy. However, it is naïve to expect that the G-7, with its member,

China, constantly manipulating its currency and imposing tariffs on American imports, can agree to create the proposed system. There is no need to fear currency wars and try to avoid them. Trade wars existed and will exist. In 2016, the United States slapped Chinese cold-rolled steel imports with 267% duties accusing China of selling products below cost.

Of course, the mentioned approaches to make the trade fair (there is no need to be afraid of using the word protectionism) can result in higher prices for imported consumer items. However, benefits from them overbalance the potential consumers' losses, especially if the chosen policies are combined with tax cuts. Without arguing whether the above indicated $300 billion estimate is accurate, based on the above material, it is possible to state that the successful implementation of the discussed measures will allow the US government to balance its budget in 10 years (maybe even earlier) and to produce a healthy economy. However, the average GDP growth rate should be at least 3% (see Chapter 3), and appropriate measures are needed to grow the economy with such a growth rate.

4.5.3 The Size of Government

The growth of government and its spending present one more channel of waste that should be thoroughly examined to improve the economy. The founders of the United States believed in limited government, especially limited central government whose rights should be limited by the people. However, these rights, and accordingly the size of government, were increased with the growth of the country (its economy and population), as well as during the economic crises and wars. Fiscal and monetary policies of the government affect the allocation of economic resources, the distribution of wealth, and the rate of economic growth. The growth of government can be judged by indexes of government taxing, spending, and employing.

In the early years of the 20th century, federal, state, and local governments took in revenues equal to 6%—7% of the gross domestic product. By 1950, revenues had risen to 24% of GDP. Over the past 40 years, the tax proportion has drifted irregularly upward and now stands at about 32% of GDP.

At the beginning of the 20th century, federal, state, and local governments spent an amount equal to 6%—7% of GDP. In 1913, for example, in a group of 17 economically advanced countries, government spending was higher and averaged about 13% of GDP. In Austria, France, and Italy, government spending came to 17%. By 1950, the US government expenditures, net of intergovernmental grants, had risen to 21% of GDP. Over the past 40 years, the spending proportion has drifted irregularly upward and now is about 34% of GDP. In contrast, by 1996, government expenditures in the same 17 countries had, on average, reached nearly 46% of GDP (Sweden's government expenditures were the highest, at more than 64%). Now it is about 47%.

In the early 20th century, federal, state, and local governments employed about 4% of the civilian labor force. By 1950, the US government employment had risen to about 10%. During the past 40 years, it rose and fell: it reached a peak in the mid-1970s at nearly 16% and then fell to its present level of roughly 14%; as a percent of GDP, it was 7.2% and 6.9%, respectively. (This figure does not include the 2 million members of the armed forces.) However, the latest figure is deceptive and explained by the increasing outsourcing of government functions to private contractors that began in the 1990s under President Clinton's "reinventing government" initiative. Many people who were classified as members of the private labor force actually worked for governments as contractors (or employees or subcontractors of contractors). Government has "privatized" more functions by contracting out the performance of tasks previously performed by workers on the regular government payroll.

In addition to the above factors showing the increased role and size of government, a bigger factor in determining the allocation of economic resources, the distribution of wealth, and the rate of economic growth became increased regulations: statutes, executive orders, and judicial decisions as well as the directives of regulatory agencies (e.g., the Environmental Protection Agency and the Securities and Exchange Commission). The regulatory state had continued to grow and impede growth in the economy. Over the past 10 years, nonindependent agencies added between $78–$115 billion in estimated annual costs through the finalization of new regulations. Because of high taxes, high regulations, and poor economic policies real private nonresidential fixed investment has grown by only 1.3% each year (on a fourth quarter-over-fourth quarter basis) since 2007, compared with 4.9% annually before the recession.

Organizations, once created during crises and wars, tried to survive later and were supported by many politicians because their existence would bring them votes of people who benefited from the related programs. The crises and wars contributed to shifting American views about the proper role of government in economic life, and this shift in the limited-government ideology of the 19th century was used by skillful politicians.

By the 1970s the entire economy had been thoroughly politicized. The Grace Commission, an investigation requested by President Reagan, focusing on waste and inefficiency in the US federal government, discovered that the federal government alone was conducting 963 separate social programs, many of them designated "entitlements." Its revenue-enhancing recommendations to save $424 billion of "waste" in the federal government over 3 years, which "can be achieved without raising taxes, without weakening America's needed defense build-up and without in any way harming necessary social welfare programs," remained unrealized.

In his inaugural address, Ronald Reagan announced a recipe to fix the nation's economic mess: "Our government has no power except that granted it by the people. It is time to check and reverse the growth of government, which shows signs of having grown beyond the consent of the governed. It is my intention to curb the size and influence of the federal establishment and to demand recognition of the distinction between the powers granted to the federal government and those reserved to the states or to the people."

In 1989 letter to the Speaker of the House and the President of the Senate, Ronal Reagan indicated, "The main role of government is to provide a stable economic environment that allows each individual to reach his or her full potential. Individuals and businesses must be able to make long-run plans confident that the government will not change the rules halfway through the game. Government's drain on the economy, both through its resources that could be used more productively by the private sector and through taxes that destroy individual incentives, must be minimized."

Reagan had a mandate to cut the federal government. However, he failed to radically reduce the size of the government. Under Reagan, the federal workforce increased by about 324,000 to almost 5.3 million people. His phrase "In this present crisis, government is not the solution to our problem; government is the problem." can be interpreted as an excuse for his inability to fulfill his promise—to decrease the size of the federal government. It is difficult and almost impossible to cut government workforce in the crises and postcrises periods because the crisis ideology supports the expansion of government programs focused to improve life of the most vulnerable part of population during the crises.

Policymakers are divided as to whether government expansion helps or impedes economic growth. Advocates of bigger government argue that additional government programs and increases in government spending can bolster economic growth by putting money into people's pockets. Proponents of smaller government have the opposite view. They explain that government is too big and that higher spending undermines economic growth. A government that grows larger than required to provide basic services may slow down economic growth in a number of ways. The larger the government, the greater its involvement in activities it does poorly. More government means higher taxes or borrowing. Taxes and borrowing drain money from the private sector. Compared with the private sector, government is less innovative and less responsive to change.

Today, 18 million Americans work in government—in health, education, the military, and local, state, and federal bureaucracies. The federal government employs 2.1 million civilian workers in hundreds of agencies at offices across the nation. The federal workforce imposes a substantial burden on America's taxpayers. In 2016, wages and benefits for executive branch civilian workers cost $267 billion.

Since the 1990s, federal workers have enjoyed faster compensation growth than private sector workers. In 2015, federal workers earned 76% more, on average, than private sector workers (US Bureau of Economic Analysis, GDP & Personal Income, www.bea.gov/iTable/index_nipa.cfm.)

In 2015, federal civilian workers had an average wage of $86,365, whereas the average wage for the nation's 112 million private sector workers was $58,726. According to the BEA data, when benefits such as health care and pensions are included, the federal compensation advantage over private workers is even larger. In 2015, total federal compensation averaged $123,160 or 76% more than the private sector average of $69,901. (In 1990, average federal compensation was 39% higher than the average private compensation.) In 2015, federal workers enjoyed average annual benefits of $36,795, which compared with average benefits in the private sector of just $11,175.

The 2012 CBO study concluded, "On average for workers at all levels of education, the cost of hourly benefits was 48 percent higher for federal civilian employees than for private sector employees with certain similar observable characteristics." Federal workers receive health insurance, retirement health benefits, a pension plan with inflation protection, and a retirement savings plan with a government match. They typically receive generous holiday and vacation schedules, flexible work hours, training options, incentive awards, and generous disability benefits.

Federal workers are almost never fired. Just 0.5% of federal civilian workers a year get fired for any reason, including poor performance and misconduct. For the senior executive service in the government, the firing rate is just 0.1%.

Although the persuasiveness of the above material is obvious, there are economists who, defending the size of the current federal government, assert that its size is relatively small when comparing with its history and with other developing countries if to exclude military and health care (see Kleinbard, 2015). No surprise. In social science, it is possible to justify almost everything.

4.5.4 Other Useful Measures

During 8 years after the severe financial crisis, the American economy performed poorly.

Between 1980 and 2007, the GDP growth rate averaged 3%. Since then it has averaged 1.2%. The US Congressional Budget Office thinks that the long-run potential growth is only around 2%. However, even getting these 2% will require a pickup in productivity growth from 0.5% in recent years, the worse in decades. The 2008 financial crisis and recession undermined the country's potential by driving workers out of the labor force and forcing businesses to slash their capital spending.

A favorable climate for capital investment is the most important necessary condition for the GDP growth. Unfortunately, a high unemployment and unwillingness of businesses to invest were accompanied with the so-called *offshoring*, the term that means registration of American companies as foreign companies and/or moving jobs of US companies overseas.

In recent years, about 60 American companies have relocated outside US borders, usually through mergers with or purchases of a foreign company to avoid US high corporate tax. Among them, world-known companies such as Halliburton (oil field technologies and services to upstream oil and gas customers worldwide), Cooper Industries (electrical products and tools), Noble Drilling Services (the fourth largest US offshore oil and natural gas driller), Global Crossing (telecommunications solutions over the world's first integrated global IP-based network), Seagate Technology (designer, manufacturer, and marketer of rigid disk drives), and Nabors Industries (the world's biggest onshore oil and gas drilling contractor). Since 2011,

22 companies changed their address to avoid high corporate tax. In 2012, Aon (the insurance broker and human resources firm) moved from Chicago to London. In 2015, Medtronic (a global leader in medical technology and services) moved its address from Minnesota to Ireland. Such giants as Monsanto (an American multinational agrochemical and agricultural biotechnology corporation), Walgreens (the nation's largest drug store chain), Burger King (a global chain of hamburger fast food restaurants), and Pfizer (one of the world's premier biopharmaceutical companies) incline to "immigrate" as well. Companies reincorporate in a place like Ireland, where the corporate tax rate is 12.5% compared with 35% in the United States.

American lawmakers, particularly Democrats, support punishment of companies that moved their headquarters abroad with punitive taxes and limits on government contracts. Politicians use words such as *economic patriotism* to label companies such as *corporate deserters*. Instead of using such unhealthy rhetoric, the government should cut corporate tax and create an appropriate climate for business operations. All Republican presidential candidates insisted on such measures. US companies would certainly continue to seek tax shelter if the US government does not cut corporate tax. (President Trump cut the corporate tax rate from 35% to 21%; see Tax Cuts and Jobs Act of 2017.)

The survey of Harvard Business School shows that although American companies successfully compete internationally, US workers are not able to do that. The questioned business executives believe that one of the reasons is the uncompetitive K-12 educational system and that is why US companies shift cautiously (fearing of a backlash) well-paid technology jobs to India, China, and other low-cost centers. It is impossible to ignore the fact that the US educational system is broken. On the one hand, many high school graduates and bachelor degree graduates do not have enough knowledge to work efficiently in high-tech companies. On the other hand, the inexplicable substantial raise of professors' salaries in state and many private universities resulted in an increasing payment for higher education, which many potential students cannot afford, so that US companies lose highly qualified workforce (professors' salaries are competitive now with companies' salaries and a "free regime" of universities is more attractive for many well-educated professionals) and potentially able young people who cannot afford paying for higher education.

Of course, jobs offshoring bring the companies an additional profit because they pay Chinese wages and sell at US prices. In addition, in

India and China, there are no so many regulations as in the United States that kill businesses. Small businesses in the United States are literally being suffocated by red tape. They are tightly constrained by thousands of rules and regulations. Many believe that in America today, it is rapidly getting to the point where it is nearly impossible to start or to operate a small business. In 2010, the Small Business Administration has conducted studies on how regulations affect small businesses. The produced report "The Impact of Regulatory Costs on Small Firms" explains how in 2008 compliance with federal regulations cost $1.78 trillion, that is, 14% of US national income. The per employee cost of federal regulatory compliance was $10,585 for businesses with 19 or less employees, compared with $7,755 for companies with 500 employees and more. Following 6 years added more and more unnecessary regulations. Toxic federal regulations and state licensing laws have poisoned the formation of new firms that drive growth. The 2% growth economy does not inspire confidence and desire to invest.

Abolishing unnecessary regulations would increase development of America's energy resources, create new jobs, and lower the price of electricity and transportation fuels, which, in turn, would drive down the cost of consumer goods.

As mentioned earlier, the findings of Reinhart and Rogoff (2009) concerning low growth rates of countries with the high debt to GDP ratio are suggestive, rather than conclusive, because they are based on historic data. The new technological era and global economy create opportunities for a vigorous economic growth, especially for such a country as the United States with a huge scientific and technological potential. The earlier discussed proposals of Republican presidential candidates present growth-oriented policies—tax cuts, reduction of the size of federal government, abolishment of numerous regulations that hurt businesses, and improvement the US educational system—which altogether with the above considered measures can restore the average 3% GDP growth rate, that is, at least bring the country to the level before the 2008 financial crisis.

4.5.5 Evaluating the 10-Year Balanced Budget Proposal

The White House 2018 proposed budget is based on President Tramp's campaign promises. It calls for the decrease of the size of the federal government—the elimination of about 3200 staff positions including over 20% of the Environmental Protection Agency (EPA) workforce. Its proposed $5.7 billion budget is $2.6 billion less than the 2017 budget (this is a 31% decrease).

As part of the plan to achieve a balanced budget by 2027, the budget reduces nondefense budget authority by 2% each year, to reach approximately $385 billion in 2027, or just over 1.2% of GDP.

In President Trump's proposal, the discretionary spending for the State Department and the Agency for International Development would be cut by 29% (from 38 billion in 2017 to 27.1 billion in 2018). The discretionary spending of the departments Agriculture and Labor would be cut by 21% (from 22.6 billion to 17.9 and from 12.2 billion to 9.6 billion, respectively). The discretionary spending of the Department of Justice would be decreased by 20% (from 20.3 billion to 16.2 billion). The discretionary spending cuts of other departments are below 16%: Health and Human Services—16% (from 77.7 to 65.1 billion), Commerce—16% (from 9.2 to 7.8 billion), Educations 14% (from 68.2 to 59 billion), Transportation—13% (from 9.2 to 7.8 billion), Housing and Urban Development—13% (from 36 to 31.7 billion), Interior—12% (from 13.2 to 11.6 billion), Energy—6% (from 29.7 to 28 billion), and Treasury—4% (from 11.7 to 11.2 billion).

The mentioned cuts are accompanied by the increased spending on Defense—10% (from 521.7 to 574 billion), Homeland Security—7% (from 41.3 to 44.1 billion), and Veterans Affairs—6% (from 74.5 to 78.9 billion).

The expected government reform focuses to eliminate unnecessary, overlapping, outdated, and ineffective programs as well as unnecessary and wasteful regulations. President Trump asked lawmakers to cut $3.6 trillion in government spending over the next decade, taking aim at such politically sensitive cuts as health-care and food assistance programs for the poor. The biggest savings would come from cuts to the Medicaid health-care program (at least $610 billion) embedded in a proposed Republican health care in the House of Representatives and from cuts to Supplemental Nutrition Assistance Program, better known as food stamps (more than $192 billion). The reform of the existing welfare system that discourages able-bodied adults from working would also decrease government spending. Federal aid to states would shrink by 3%. The proposal would also eliminate funding for nearly 20 smaller independent agencies, including the National Endowment for the Arts, the National Endowment for the Humanities, the Corporation for Public Broadcasting, and the Legal Services Corporation, which finances legal aid groups.

In parallel, the President's budget proposal includes $639 billion of discretionary budget authority for the Department of Defense. It includes $44.1 billion for the Department of Homeland Security (DHS), $27.7

billion for the Department of Justice (DOJ) for law enforcement, public safety, and immigration enforcement programs, and \$2.6 billion to invest in high-priority tactical infrastructure and border security technology. The budget includes also \$200 billion in spending related to the infrastructure initiative.

An important part of the proposal relates to the tax reform. The administration intends to cut taxes expecting to reach a 3% GDP growth rate and generate an additional \$2 trillion in revenue over 10 years. This growth would balance the budget over the decade. Lawrence Summers, a former economic adviser to Democratic President Barack Obama, said the Trump administration was double-counting that money by saying it would help close budget deficits while also offsetting the revenue lost by cutting tax rates. There were not any available related calculations with an expected tax multiplier values. The tax proposal in its current form lacks of specificity. It is assumed that the budget plan would boost economic growth by fostering capital investment and creating jobs for workers who gave up their job hunts during tough times (from World War II to 2007, the average growth rate was 3.5%; over the last 9 years, average growth has been 1.3%).

The proposed 10-year program to balance budget by 2027 is based on the eight pillars: health reform, tax reform, immigration reform, reductions in federal spending, regulatory rollback, American energy development, welfare reform, and education reform. For each pillar reform, experts in the corresponding field made their estimates and recommendations concerning the amount of spending cuts and their distribution during the projected period.

The above indicated financial data combined with a detail analysis of the government financial data for previous years were used to present the expected picture of the US recovering economy up to 2027.

Table 4.7 contains data of the president's proposed budget (see https://www.whitehouse.gov/sites/whitehouse.gov/files/omb/budget/fy2018/budget.pdf).

Here g and g_n are the real and nominal GDP growth rates, respectively; the lower index p relates to the public debt and GDP ratio; the lower index $\sum$ relates to total rather than prime spending G, which values are obtained by deducting the interest spending from $G_\sum$. The deficit $G_\sum$-T and its prime part G-T are calculated based on the G, T, and net interest data. Assuming that the revenue T levels indicated in the proposed budget can be reached, to evaluate the budget proposal we compare the expected G with the prime spending G_{opt} obtained from the solution of the optimal

Table 4.7 Budget totals (in billions of dollars)

	2017	2018	2019	2020	2021	2022	2023	2024	2025	2026	2027
Y	19,162	20,014	20,947	21,981	23,093	24,261	25,489	26,779	28,134	29,557	31,053
g	2.3	2.4	2.7	2.9	3.0	3.0	3.0	3.0	3.0	3.0	3.0
g_H	4.3	4.5	4.7	5.0	5.1	5.1	5.1	5.1	5.1	5.1	5.1
T	3460	3654	3814	3982	4161	4390	4615	4864	5130	5417	5724
$G\sum$	4062	4094	4340	4470	4617	4832	4933	5073	5306	5527	5708
Interest	276	316	372	431	487	542	592	634	670	706	741
G	3786	3778	3968	4039	4130	4390	4341	4439	4636	4821	4967
$G\sum-T$	602	440	526	488	456	442	318	209	176	110	-16
$G-T$	326	124	154	57	-31	-100	-274	-425	-494	-596	-757
$\tau\%$	18.1	18.3	18.2	18.1	18.0	18.1	18.1	18.2	18.2	18.3	18.4
$l_3\sum\%$	21.2	20.5	20.7	20.3	20.0	19.9	19.4	18.9	18.9	18.7	18.4
D	20,354	21,093	21,840	22,503	23,114	23,647	24,071	24,410	24,639	24,781	24,676
$D\%$	106.2	105.4	104.3	102.4	100.1	97.5	94.4	91.2	87.6	83.8	79.5
D_p	14,824	15,353	15,957	16,509	17,024	17,517	17,887	18,150	18,379	18,541	18,575
$d_p\%$	77.4	76.7	76.2	75.1	73.7	72.2	70.2	67.8	65.3	62.7	59.8

problem (3.29)−(3.31) [(3.11)−(3.13)]. The used earlier models (3.21) and (3.22) [(3.1)] do not fit the data in Table 4.7. The equalities are satisfied when the models would contain an additional term F, the so-called *other means of financing* is added. The additional term f will be in the debt to GDP ratio model (3.30) [(3.11)] (see Eqs. (D1.10) and (D1.11) in Appendix D). For positive F and f terms, the prime deficit values of the solution of the optimal problem (3.31) [(3.13)] will be negative and their absolute values will be more than for the more habitual models considered in the previous chapters; that is, in this case the values of G_{opt} will be less than for the described basic modes (the solution of the optimal problems with the additional terms is given in Appendix C). Because it is natural to expect that the optimal prime spending would be less than in the proposed budget, we choose the larger G_{opt} and consider the basic models (3.29)−(3.31) [(3.11)−(3.13)].

As seen in Table 4.7, the negative deficit values start only in 2021. That is why, assuming that the budget 2020 goals are achieved, we consider the optimal problem (3.29)−(3.31) to balance the budget by 2027 with the initial conditions in 2020: $Y = 21{,}984$; $D = 22{,}503$; $d = 1.024$.

Table 4.8 contains data of the projected optimal debt, the debt to GDP ratio, and spending corresponding to the expected GDP growth based on the economic data of 2020 (the optimal solution is obtained for the average GDP growth rate $g = 0.03$ and interest on debt $r = 0.019$; inflation rate $\pi = 0.02$).

The comparison of the debt changes in Tables 4.7 and 4.8 shows that the optimal solution $D = 23{,}431$ is less than in the proposed budget (24,676); the debt to GDP ratio is 75.5%, 4% less than it is projected in the budget. It is natural to expect that optimal spending is less than indicated in Table 4.7. The comparison of 2021−2027 spending data in Tables 4.7 and 4.8 enables us to evaluate the budget projections, which were obtained based on the expected results of the above described planned government actions.

Table 4.8 Optimal solution for the balanced budget in 2027 (in billions of dollars)

	2021	2022	2023	2024	2025	2026	2027
Y	23,096	24,265	25,493	26,783	28,138	29,562	31,057
g	3.0	3.0	3.0	3.0	3.0	3.0	3.0
d	0.985	0.947	0.908	0.87	0.831	0.793	0.755
D	22,751	22,963	23,141	23.281	23,380	23,431	23,431
$G_{opt} - T$	−628	−651	−691	−734	−779	−827	−878
G_{opt}	3539	3739	3924	4130	4351	4590	4846

The planned tax cuts and investment in infrastructure do not produce immediate results. That is why it would be plausible to expect an increase in the prime deficit in 2018—2020. However, government spending G in 2021—2025 is significantly higher than G_{opt}. The difference in spending is more than $2.5 trillion, the amount that is more than twice larger than the difference between the budget projected and optimal balanced debt values. In addition, in the 2021—2026 period the other means of financing (other borrowing) add to the debt about $600 billion. All this makes the budget projections questionable.

The considered optimal approach enables us to evaluate roughly the long-term budget proposals and indicate ways to reach the projected results. To reach the goals of the 2018—2027 budget proposal, additional measures to decrease government spending are needed.

By reaching in the second and third quarters of 2017, the 3% GDP growth rate level, beating economic forecasts of the 2.3% growth (see Table 4.7) and with the unemployment rate 4.1%, the Trump administration put the country on a sustainable path of the economic recovery. This is a result of starting the implementation of the above discussed measures (lifting counterproductive regulations, increasing the manufacturing base, etc.).

According to the preliminary deficit estimate of the 2017 US tax cuts bill, it would add about $1.5 trillion to the budget deficit over the coming 10 years. However, taking into account that during two sequential quarters of 2017 the GDP growth rate exceeded 3%, it is easy to estimate that the average GDP growth rate of 3.5% would correspond to the tax multiplier of about 1.5; for the rates 4% and 4.5%, the tax multipliers would be about 2.4 and 3.4, respectively. Using the 2017 data from Table 4.7, the estimates of the lower limit of the debt to GDP ratio in 2027 obtained based on the developed models (2.14) and (2.18) [(2.33)] show that the ratio would not increase significantly for the growth rates 3.5% and 4% and may even decrease it if 4.5% can be reached.

However, to balance the budget by 2027, the government should implement a smart austerity policy, without which its goals do not look realistic.

The austerity policy should not be interpreted as a significant change in public policy, although, in many macroeconomic models, austerity policies increase unemployment that requires additional government spending on welfare and other supporting programs. However, this is not the reason why politicians prefer to use the term *fiscal responsibility policy*. Austerity by word of politicians' mouth sounds as a warning of bad times ahead. Austerity does not necessarily require reducing public spending on social programs (e.g., health care, education). The main focus of public policy should be economic growth and jobs. A growing economy would enable government to spend on necessary public projects (e.g., investment in infrastructure). Austerity can and should accompany this growth. In the period of austerity, the structure or composition of budgets becomes a pivot of a successful fiscal policy. Government should try not to spend beyond its basic functions (i.e., national defense, police, courts) and align federal salaries and benefits with market rates. The elimination of the existing imbalance between wages in the public and private sectors and elimination of fraud and corruption in the public sector are two obvious avenues to follow for decreasing budget deficits.

4.6 EXTENDING MACROECONOMIC TOOLS

The term *macroeconomic policy* relates to the policy concerned with the operation of the economy as a whole that focuses on achieving certain macroeconomic goals and uses policy instruments to achieve those objectives. The most important aspect of macroeconomic policy, as an important part of public policy, is the government's growth policy aiming for the long-run economic growth that would improve, on average, the standards of living or the quality of life of people. The second major branch of macroeconomic policy is the government's stabilization policy. There exist no stable smooth upward economic trends characterized by higher production and employment. History shows that economic trajectories fluctuate above and below long-run trends. Economists call such ups and downs in the economic performance *business cycles*. In the short run, such fluctuations may exhibit decline (recession) or prosperity (boom). Above we analyzed the US government economic policies (fiscal, monetary, and exchange rate) during several 20th-century recessions, as well as the policy of Trump administration, consistent with the established macroeconomic goals (i.e., growth, employment, inflation, external debt).

The macroeconomic tools became more sophisticated, and each new recession provided new information how to improve them. Advances in computer science and information technology have enabled economists and policymakers to collate and monitor extensive statistical information; mountains of data at their disposal can be used to develop and test new models and policy scenarios.

Now the state of the economy is evaluated mostly by the following indicators: the real GDP, the unemployment rate, the inflation rate, the interest rate, the exchange rate, and the level of the stock market. The first two are the most important: They are directly connected to people's current material well-being. The other four influence the economic trend.

Politicians in the developed economies have learned that, if they fail to preside over low and stable inflation rates, then they are likely to lose the next election. Interest rates, as discussed earlier, are an efficient tool in monetary policy. Exchange rates (the price of one currency in terms of another) are determined by national authorities or in the legally sanctioned exchange markets. Some countries prefer to use the nominal exchange rate as their instrument of monetary policy and commit to keep it fixed to either specific or all currencies. The exchange rate governs the terms on which international trade and investment take place. In contrast to the above indicators, the level of the stock market is the key economic indicator that appears in everyday news but is not discussed in traditional macroeconomic books.

Variations in macroeconomic indicators affect the performance of the stock markets. It is intuitively clear that the macroeconomic parameters defining changes in economic policy (monetary and/or fiscal) influence the stock market behavior, which is very sensitive to any events directly or indirectly linked with a country's economic policy. This topic was discussed in many publications (see, e.g., Fischer and Merton, 1984; Pilinkus, 2010). Research results indicate that there is a causal relationship between market index and GDP, unemployment, foreign direct investment, trade balance, debt, consumer price index, exchange rate, money supply, and interest rate.

A more interesting and important question is whether the stock market behavior can provide information of the future of a country's economy. The reciprocal relation between the stock market development and changes in the country's economy was noticed long ago. When the economic situation in a country improves, its stock market performs more actively. However, it is also valid that the stock market performance characterizes the expected economic trend: if stock prices start to fall, economic downturn is likely to take place and, conversely, rising stock prices show possible economic growth. The forward-looking property of stock prices makes it possible to consider the stock market as a possible predictor of the business cycle.

Many macroeconomists believed that stock prices fluctuate far too much to be justified by rational economic assessment and that the stock market is a poor predictor of GDP and its components. Keynes (1936) described the stock market as a casino—dominated by psychological games—playing with only a modest relation to rational phenomena. In his lecture "The Pretence of Knowledge," the economist Hayek, who won the 1974 Nobel Prize said, "in the study of such complex phenomena as the market, which depend on the actions of many individuals, all the circumstances which will determine the outcome of a process ... will hardly ever be fully known or measurable."

Nowadays, stock market is the pulse of current economic activity. It facilitates investment decisions and plays pivotal role in the growth of sectors of the economy. Many developed countries have well-functioning stock markets with open-up trade channels that allow foreign investment inflow. Companies get the opportunity to list their shares, which help raise capital for investment and expenditure. The market enables investors to earn profit from trading and government to get revenues from stock market operations. Despite its volatility, the level of the stock market can be considered as an index of expectations for the future. There is a definite relationship between stock market development and economic growth or economic downturn. Corporate profits are an important part of GDP, and changes in stock prices reflect revised expectations about future corporate earnings. Changes in stock prices reflect both revised expectations about future corporate earnings and changes in the discount rate at which these expected earnings are capitalized. That is why the analysis of stock prices justifies to consider the stock market as an accurate predictor of the business cycle.

Now the stock market prices are formed as a result of decisions of not only separate investors but also mutual and hedge fund managers who use experts specializing in different economic sectors and providing detail information about companies and their potential.

On the one hand, the established relationship between macroeconomic variables and the movement of stock prices, well documented in the literature over the past several decades, shows that stock prices are determined by some fundamental macroeconomic variables; hence, macroeconomic variables can influence investment decisions. On the other hand, a detailed analysis an industry, including a comparative analysis of companies in the same industry, provides mutual and hedge fund managers with valuable information concerning their investment decisions. Now, developed countries have well-functioning investment industries, and the stock market prices have a significant role in investment decisions.

Regression models used by Fama (1981) established positive relationship between stock return and the subsequent GDP growth rate (by analyzing real returns on the NYSE value-weighted portfolio on quarterly production growth rates). Doan et al. (1983) believe that stock prices are the best predictor of the business fixed component of investment and consumption and a poor predictor of government expenditures and residential housing investment. Analyzing monthly averages of the Standard and Poor's Index of 500 securities' (the S&P 500 index) prices, the autoregressive model of Doan et al. (1983) showed that the stock market information could be well used for GDP forecasts.

The S&P 500 composite index is one of the leading indicators of the stock market performance as a whole. Tracking a selection of large-cap stocks listed on US exchanges across 11 sectors, it is better structured (a market-weighted average) than the world's most famous Dow Jones index (price-based) and provides a more accurate measure of the overall stock market movements. In addition to the Dow and the S&P indexes, there are hundreds of other indexes providing information about the stock market and considered as market-tracking tools. The most popular after the top two are Nasdaq indexes, American Stock Exchange Composite Index, Russell Indexes, NYSE Composite Index, 30-year Treasury Bond Index.

Stock market indices are the statistic indicators, which enable to show the state of the stock market and its dynamic tendencies. In unison with a sarcastic statement of one of the most well-respected economists in modern history, Paul Samuelson, "Wall Street indexes predicted nine out of the last five recessions," the S&P 500 index shows 8 out of the 14 recessions based on its data during recessions and predicts only 5 recessions based on its data a half a year before recessions start (see Table 4.9).

Macroeconomists are blamed that their models had not predicted the last economic crisis. However, as we indicated earlier, the existing macroeconomic theory and its tools do not allow macroeconomists to predict crises, which we compared with unknown diseases. The reasons of many crises lie in the financial sphere. Macroeconomics analyzes the behavior of the entire economy and, hence, by definition formally includes the field of finance. However, traditionally (this is also explained by the existing narrow specialization) the important financial field in macroeconomics is the money and debt. In contract to finance, where the stock market information plays a decisive role in corporate investment decisions, the stock market characteristics play a minor role in macroeconomic models and policy analysis. With the progress in information technology, investment decisions became more rational. More available information and more sophisticated analytical tools result in more investment decisions with heads rather than with hearts. Maybe this fact explains that the S&P 500 forecasted properly the 2007 recession and the 2009 recovery.

Table 4.9 Economic indicators before and during recession

Recession period	S&P 500 index performance during recession %	S&P 500 index performance six months before recession %	Total corporate defaults	Net debt to EBITDA ratio (mean all S&P 500 firms)
08/1929–03/1933	−74.5	14	8–15	
05/1937–06/1938	−24.2	−2.4	22–21	
02/1945–10/1945	27.7	8.6	3–2	
11/1948–10/1949	4.1	9.8	1–0	
07/1951–05/1954	27.6	−6.5	0–1	
08/1957–04/1958	−6.5	9.3	0–1	
04/1960–02/1961	18.4	−1.0	0–2	
12/1969–11/1970	−3.5	−7.8	1–0	
11/1973–03/1975	−17.9	2.9	5–5	
01/1980–07/1980	16.1	7.7	1–4	1.0
07/1981–11/1982	14.7	−1.0	2–18	1.2
07/1990–03/1991	7.6	3.1	69–93	1.8
03/2001–11/2001	−7.2	−14.6	136–229	1.6
12/2007–06/2009	−35.5	11.3	24–127	1.4

It is logical to expect the improvement of the quality of predictions by combining several forecasts from a variety of independent sources and methodologies. To increase predictive power of S&P 500 index, several additional financial indicators were added in the recession predictor models: the Leading Economic Index (see, e.g., Levanon et al., 2012) and various employment and interest rate measures (see, e.g., Estrella and Mishkin, 1998; Berge and Jordà, 2011).

However, it is difficult to agree with those who believe that the inclusion of more variables in the predictor model would decrease the prediction error because the prediction errors for its components tend to compensate each other. This is more a wish rather than a rigorous proof. All depends on the model specifics and its structure.

A recession is often associated with at least two consecutive quarters of declining GDP. However, because there is little agreement on this definition and it is blurry, the recession forecasting model should be thought as a warning signal for policymakers about a possible economic decline. Forecasting a downturn is a more precise formulating problem than predicting a recession. Moreover, this is also a more important problem. The duration of downturns depends on the efficiency of government economic policy and other factors, which is impossible to predict. Taking into account a limited economic forecasting ability, the developed model should include the forecast of several parameters and a threshold for each of them. Among chosen variables should be only those that can serve as a possible warning of an economic downturn. There is no assurance that the forecast is correct. However, for policymakers a false alarm is better than to miss an economic decline and it is of importance not to miss deep recessions. The S&P 500 provides analysts with daily information, which allow them to obtain more reliable forecasts than that based on traditional forecasting macroeconomic models.

Although now, as never before, a country's debt becomes an important economic parameter, it is worthwhile to indicate, especially to Keynesians, that Keynes, whose name is associated mostly with spending, understood its danger for economic health.

In the elegantly written Keynes's biography, Davenport-Hines (2015) states: "He lived long enough to see the emergence of a school of economists known as Keynesian, and to joke in his intimate circle that Maynard Keynes was not a Keynesian. Already the adjective 'Keynesian' was being applied to describe policies that had been implemented in European industrialized democracies and by Roosevelt administration without any debt in ideas to him or to his *General Theory*. Although Keynes is nowadays identified with deficit finance, as a wartime Treasury official he opposed its government going into debt in order to maintain individual levels of consumption: 'the ordinary Budget should be balanced at all times,' in his own words. 'If serious unemployment does develop, deficit financing is absolutely certain to happen, and I should like to keep free to object hereafter to the more objectionable forms of it,' he warned Treasury colleges in 1943. He proposed the use of countercyclical demand management policies during periods of economic depression and higher unemployment but affirmed that in ordinary times the budget should always be balanced". According to Davenport-Hines (2015), although Keynes is portrayed as a deficit-loving interventionist, in reality he was not. What is left out of the description of his theory in regard to countercyclical fiscal policy is that Keynes also believed that, in times of relative prosperity, sovereigns should create budget surpluses.

In macroeconomics, the debt to GDP ratio is similar to the financial term *debt ratio* that compares a company's total debt with its total assets. A debt ratio is a measure of how risky it would be for a bank to extend a loan to a company, with a higher ratio indicating great risk. The term *debt to equity ratio* (the ratio of a company's debt to the value of its common stock (equity)) is also used that evaluates a company's *leverage* and the more informative term *net leverage*—the net debt to EBITDA ratio (or how many years it would take to pay off debt; the net debt means the difference between the total value of a company's cash, cash equivalents, and other liquid assets and the total value of its liabilities and debts; EBITDA means earnings before interest, depreciation, and amortization).

For S&P 500 companies the mean of the net debt to EBITDA ratios, as it is seen from the data in the report (IMF, 2017), can be used as one of predictors of downturns; for the last five recessions, its values increased at least for half a year before recessions and were above a 100% threshold (see Table 4.9). However, it is not clear what threshold value should be considered as dangerous. Dealing with dynamic processes, it is important to operate with the rate of change of their parameters; more informative is a threshold related to such variables.

The Leading Economic Index (LEI), used to predict future economic activity, a measurement of 10 indicators rolled into one, is based on monthly changes computed for each component. In addition to the S&P 500 stock index, it includes indices related jobless benefits, factory orders among manufacturers, consumer sentiment, vendor performance, the inflation-adjusted monetary supply, and the spread between long and short interest rates. During its existence, there were some changes in its composition and methodology. Typically, three consecutive monthly LEI changes in the same direction suggest a turning point in the economy; consecutive negative readings would indicate a possible recession.

The LEI components characterize the main factors accompanying downturns (higher unemployment, falling rate of economic growth, lower investment, lower consumer spending).

Formally, the LEI is a vector criterion, and mathematical problems with many criteria are not rigorously formulated. To obtain a practical solution, the compromised criterion as the monthly change in the sum of the contributions from each LEI component is considered. The contributions of the individual components vary over time, and in the case of linear indices convolution, the LEI estimate depends on weights of its components. The justification of the chosen weights presents a separate mathematical problem that was not discussed. Some components of the LEI have their own trends. Others are either stationary or have no definite trends. In the case of the unweighted components, the LEI lacks of a meaningful trend. Despite the mentioned problematic aspects of the LEI, some economists prefer it to the models based on likelihood concepts.

The likelihood of a default (the failure to pay interest or principal on a loan or security when due) over a particular time horizon is described by a financial term *probability of default* (PD) and is used in a variety of credit analyses. It provides an estimate of the likelihood that a borrower will be unable to meet its debt obligations. A high level of debt ratio and default, the failure to make payments in time, characterizes an organization's creditworthiness, its ability to function productively in the future. The major external rating agencies Standard and Poor's and Moody's Financial Services created extensive databases with information concerning creditworthiness of consumers, public and private firms, commercial real estate, financial institutions, and other asset classes. They developed models and methodologies to determine default probability rates (describing the likelihood of a default over a particular time horizon), which can serve as an indicator of the economic climate in a country.

The 2008 global financial crisis led to a record of default volume with the failure of a number of large financial institutions. Table 4.9 contains the S&P data concerning the US corporate default (1 year before and at the beginning of a recession). However, the mentioned agencies did not warn about the coming crisis. Their failure can be explained by the high ratings they gave to risky securities before the 2008 financial meltdown. These agencies were criticized for benefiting by not pointing out deficiencies of the structured debt products; they were paid by the companies that issued debt. The accuracy of the existing PD models can be improved. Yanushevsky (2018) used the Standard & Poor's PD model to evaluate the 2017 tax reform impact on the various sectors of the US economy. The PD changes of a country's economy (or only for the S&P 500 companies) can be considered as a useful economic health indicator. The combination of the stock market and creditworthiness data enables to improve macroeconomic tools and makes them more efficient.

It is doubtful that the generalized index (for example, the LEI) is more informative than its separate components. Several properly chosen economic indicators enable decision-makers easier to determine the economic disease and the way how to treat it. It is of importance to determine the alarm zone for each indicator; this presents a separate problem.

The more the useful macroeconomic instruments are available, the higher the probability that policymakers would make proper decisions. The combination of traditional monetary policy that was used successfully in the United States during the last economic crisis with better tools for fiscal policy that would determine the optimal composition of fiscal packages and estimate the effect of spending increases or/and tax cuts, as well as measures to decrease debt, would prepare better the country to counteract efficiently future economic downturns.

REFERENCES

Barro, R., 1981. Money, Expectations, and Business Cycles. Academic Press, New York.

Berge, T., Jordà, A., 2011. Evaluating the classification of economic activity into recessions and expansions. American Economic Journal: Macroeconomics 3 (2), 246–277.

Bernanke, B., November 21, 2002. Deflation, Before the National Economists Club. Washington, D.C. http://www.federalreserve.gov/boardDocs/speeches/2002/200211 21/default.htm.

Bordo, M., Haubrich, J., June 2012. Deep Recessions, Fast Recoveries, and Financial Crises: Evidence from the American Record. NBER Working Paper 18194. National Bureau of Economic Research, Cambridge, MA.

Börsch-Supan, A., 2013. Entitlement reforms in Europe: policy mixes in the current pension reform process. In: Alesina, A., Giavazzi, F. (Eds.), Fiscal Policy After the Financial Crisis. The University of Chicago Press, Chicago.

Buchanan, J., 1987. Towards the simple economics of natural liberty: an exploratory analysis. Kyklos 40 (1), 3–20.

Cole, A., 2015a. Details and Analysis of Senator Rick Santorum's Tax Plan. http:// taxfoundation.org/article/details-and-analysis-senator-rick-santorum-s-tax-plan.

Cole, A., 2015b. Details and Analysis of Donald Trump's Tax Plan. http://taxfoundation. org/article/details-and-analysis-donald-trump-s-tax-plan.

Davenport-Hines, R., 2015. Universal Man. The Lives of John Maynard Keynes. Basic Books, New York.

Doan, T., Litterman, R., Sims, C., 1983. Forecasting and Conditional Projection Using Realistic Prior Distributions. NBER Working Paper No. 1202.

Estrella, A., Mishkin, F., 1998. Predicting U.S. recessions: financial variables as leading indicators. The Review of Economics and Statistics 80 (1), 45−61.

Fama, E., 1981. Stock returns, real activity, inflation, and money. The American Economic Review 71 (4), 545−565.

Fischer, S., Merton, R., 1984. Macroeconomics and Finance: The Role of the Stock Market. NBER Working Paper No. 1291.

Friedman, M., 2010. Price Theory: A Provisional Text. Martino Publishing, Mansfield Centre.

Gingrich, N., 2013. Breakout in Healthcare. https://www.gingrichproductions.com/2013/10/breakout-in-healthcare/.

Hayek, F., 2009. A Tiger by the Tail. The Institute of Economic Affairs, London.

International Monetary Fund, 2017. World Economic and Financial Surveys. Global Financial Stability Report: Getting the Policy Mix Right. IMF, Washington, DC. https://www.imf.org/en/Publications/.../global-financial-stability-report-april-2017.

Keynes, J.M., 1930. A Treatise on Money. Macmillan, London.

Keynes, J.M., 1931. Essays in Persuasion. Macmillan, London [includes "The Economic Consequences of Mr. Churchill" (1925), and "Proposals for a Revenue Tariff" (1931)].

Keynes, J.M., 1936. The General Theory of Employment, Interest, and Money. Macmillan, London.

Kleinbard, E., 2015. We Are Better than This: How Government Should Spend Our Money. Oxford University Press, New York.

Kotlikoff, L., Smetters, K., Walliser, J., 1999. Privatizing social security in the U.S.: comparing the options. Review of Economic Dynamics 2 (3), 532−574.

Kotlikoff, L., Smetters, K., Walliser, J., 2001. Finding a Way Out of America's Demographic Dilemma. NBER Working Paper No. 8258. National Bureau of Economic Research, Cambridge, MA.

Kotlikoff, L., Smetters, K., Walliser, J., 2002. Distributional effects in a general equilibrium analysis of social security. In: Feldstein, M.S., Liebman, J.B. (Eds.), The Distributional Aspects of Social Security and Social Security Reform. University of Chicago Press, Chicago, pp. 327−361.

Lee, M., Rubio, M., 2015. Economic Growth and Family Fairness Tax Reform Plan, Office of Senator Mike Lee and Office of Senator Marco Rubio. http://www.rubio.senate.gov/public/index.cfm/files/serve/?File_id=2d839ff1-f995-427a-86e9-267365609942.

Levanon, G., Manini, J., Ozyildirim, A., Schaitkin, B., Tanchua, J., 2012. Using a Leading Credit Index to Predict Turning Points in the U.S. Business Cycle. Economics Program Working Papers 11−05.

Lucas Jr., R., 1981. Studies in Business-cycle Theory. MIT Press, Cambridge.

Lundeen, A., Schuyler, M., 2015. The Economic Effects of Rand Paul's Tax Reform Plan. http://taxfoundation.org/blog/economic-effects-rand-paul-s-tax-reform-plan.

Mankiw, G., 2015. Principles of Macroeconomics. Cengage Learning, Stamford.

McBride, W., 2015. Critics of Rubio-Lee Tax Reform Are Way off the Mark, Real Clear Markets. http://www.realclearmarkets.com/articles/2015/03/12/critics-of-rubio-lee-tax-reform-are-wayoff-the-mark-101575.html.

Pareto, V., 1935. The Mind and Society, Vol. IV. Harcourt, Brace and Company, New York.

Pilinkus, D., 2010. Macroeconomic indicators and their impact on stock market performance in the short and long run: the case of the baltic states. Ukio Technologinis ir Ekonominis Vystymas 16 (2), 291−304.

Pomerleau, K., 2015. No, Senator Paul's Plan Will Not Blow a $15 Trillion Hole in the Federal Budget. Tax Foundation. http://taxfoundation.org/blog/no-senator-paul-s-plan-will-not-blow-15-trillion-hole-federal-budget.

Pomerleau, K., 2015a. Details and Analysis of Governor Jeb Bush's Tax Plan. Tax Foundation. http://taxfoundation.org/article/details-and-analysis-governor-jeb-bush-s-tax-plan.

Pomerleau, K., Schuyler, M., 2015. Details and Analysis of Senator Ted Cruz's Tax Plan. Tax Foundation. http://taxfoundation.org/article/details-and-analysis-senator-ted-cruz-s-tax-plan#_ftn1.

Prescott, E., 2002. Prosperity and depressions. The American Economic Review 92 (2), 1—15.

Reinhart, C.M., Rogoff, K.S., 2009. This Time Is Different: Eight Centuries of Financial Folly. University Press, Princeton, NJ.

Reinhart, C.M., Rogoff, K.S., 2010. Growth in a time of debt. The American Economic Review: Papers and Proceedings 100 (2), 573—578.

Romer, C., 1992. What ended the great depression? The Journal of Economic History 52, 757—784.

Romer, C., June 18, 2009. The lessons of 1937. The Economist.

Romer, C., Romer, D., 2010. The macroeconomic effects of tax changes: estimates based on a new measure of fiscal shocks. The American Economic Review 100, 763—801.

Rothbard, M., 1963. America's Great Depression. Ludwig von Mises Institute, Auburn, AL, 2008.

Santorum, R., October 11, 2015. A flat tax is the best path to prosperity. The Wall Street Journal. http://www.wsj.com/articles/a-flat-tax-is-the-best-path-to-prosperity-14446 00639.

Sargent, T., 1987. Dynamic Macroeconomic Theory. Harvard University Press, Cambridge.

Schuyler, M., McBride, W., 2015. The Economic Effects of the Rubio-Lee Tax Reform Plan. Tax Foundation Fiscal Fact No. 457. http://taxfoundation.org/article/economic-effects-rubio-lee-tax-reform-plan#_ftnref10.

Scott, R., 2012. The China Toll: Growing U.S. Trade Deficit with China Cost More than 2.7 Million Jobs between 2001 and 2011, with Job Losses in Every State. Economic Policy Institute, Briefing Paper 345. http://www.epi.org/publication/bp345-china-growing-trade-deficit-cost/.

Scott, R., Jorgensen, H., Hall, D., 2013. Ending Currency Manipulation by China and Others Is the Place to Start. Economic Policy Institute, Briefing Paper 351. http://www.epi.org/publication/bp351-trade-deficit-currency-manipulation/.

Solow, R., 1956. A contribution to the theory of economic growth. Quarterly Journal of Economics 70 (1), 65—94.

Solow, R., 1957. Technical change and the aggregate production function. The Review of Economics and Statistics 39 (3), 312—320.

Trump, D., September 28, 2015. Tax Reform that Will Make America Great Again. https://www.donaldjtrump.com/positions/tax-reform.

Wheelock, D., 2010 March/April. Lessons Learned? Comparing the federal reserve's responses to the crises of 1929—1933 and 2007—2009. Federal Reserve Bank of St. Louis Review 92 (2), 89—107.

Yanushevsky, C., February 21, 2018. Looking for winners and losers of tax reform amid earnings beat. S&P Global Market Intelligence. https://marketintelligence.spglobal.com/blog/looking-for-winners-and-losers-of-tax-reform-amid-earnings-beat.

CHAPTER FIVE

Debt-Related Models Software

Contents

Software is a great combination between artistry and engineering.

Bill Gates

5.1 INTRODUCTION

A well-structured and efficient program gives the programmer the same sort of pleasure that an artist feels when he/she creates a new work or a mathematician gets after elegantly proving a theorem. Although the programs presented in this chapter cannot be considered as highly sophisticated, they can be used to analyze the previously considered models and will help readers to develop their own programs. The programs presented are written using MATLAB® (see, e.g., Higham and Higham, 2000).

It is obvious that programming languages oriented on special classes of problems are more efficient than general-purpose languages. MATLAB® is one of such specialized languages, which is very useful for scientific programming. The very first version of MATLAB® was written in the late 1970s for use in courses in matrix theory, linear algebra, and numerical analysis. MATLAB® is a high-performance language for technical computing. MATLAB® is fundamentally built upon a foundation of sophisticated matrix software, in which the basic data element is a matrix that does not require dimensioning. This allows users to solve many technical computing problems, especially those with matrix formulations, spending a fraction of time it would take to write programs in a scalar noninteractive language such as C or FORTRAN. MATLAB® allows easy matrix manipulation, plotting of functions and data, implementation

Applied Macroeconomics for Public Policy
ISBN: 978-0-12-815632-2
https://doi.org/10.1016/B978-0-12-815632-2.00005-5

of algorithms, creation of user interfaces, and interfacing with programs in other languages. Focused on various industry applications, MATLAB® developed the so-called toolboxes, comprehensive collections of M-files, functions that extend the MATLAB® environment to solve particular classes of problems in areas such as dynamic systems, control systems, neural networks, and fuzzy logic. The MATLAB® mathematical function library includes a vast collection of computational algorithms. Software packages for modeling, simulating, and analyzing specific problems are called toolboxes. Toolboxes are comprehensive collections of MATLAB® functions (M-files) to solve particular classes of problems. Areas in which toolboxes are available include control systems, neural networks, fuzzy logic, simulation, and many others. Toolboxes of functions useful in signal processing, optimization, statistics, finance, and a host of other areas are available from the MathWorks as add-ons to the standard MATLAB® software distribution. The CompEcon toolbox is a set of MATLAB® functions for solving a variety of problems in economics and finance (see Miranda and Fackler, 2002). The library functions include root finding and optimization solvers, a integrated set of routines for function approximation using polynomial, splines and other functional families, a set of numerical integration routines for general functions and for common probability distributions, general solvers for ordinary differential equations (both initial and boundary value problems), routines for solving discrete- and continuous-time dynamic programming problems, and a general solver for financial derivatives (bonds, futures, options).

The programs for models written in MATLAB® can be written in other languages such as FORTRAN, BASIC, Pascal, and C. However, for the considered economic models, MATLAB® is preferable.

5.2 SOFTWARE FOR THE DEBT TO GDP RATIO MODELS

We considered two types of the debt to GDP ratio models—continuous described by the first-order differential equation and discrete described by the first-order difference equation. The discrete models reflect better the existing procedure of gathering data and reporting information (by quarters or years). That is why here we present programs developed for the discrete models (see also Appendix C).

Matrix representation, an initial core of MATLAB®, explains its specifics applied to dynamic systems described by difference equations. Its *for* loops do not start from "0", so that the initial conditions are presented, for example, as $d(1,1)$ and the examined value at time t will be $d(t+1,1)$.

The *for* loop in the below programs executes a statement or a group of statements a predetermined number of times. Its syntax is

```
for  index =start:injcrement:end
    statements
end
```

The default increment is 1.

Listing 5.1 presents the MATLAB® program to determine the lower limit of the debt to GDP ratio. The program corresponds to the example for 2015 data considered in Chapter 2 (see Table 2.9; in the MATLAB® programs, we use symbols T and b instead of symbols τ and β in the equations of Chapter 2).

LISTING 5.1

MATLAB® Program for the Lower Limit of the Debt to GDP Ratio

```
function discretedebt1
    r = 0.0222; g0 = 0.021; g1 = 0.04; T = 0.174; c = 1; b = 0.69;
    13 = 0.205; 11 = 3.8; 12 = 0.1;

for  t = 1:11
    d(t,1) = 0.;
end
    d(1,1) = 1.01;

for  t = 1:10
    d(t+1,1)= (1+(r-g1)/(1+g1))*d(t,1)+ (1+g1)ʳ(-t)*(13-12*13*
        (exp ((g1-g0)/b*t)-1)+11ʳ(-1)*((1+g1)ʳt-(1+g0)ʳt)) - T
end
```

In the case of the government stimulus policy accompanied with decreased spending (see Table 2.12; $h = 0.02$), the modification of the above program is presented in Listing 5.2.

LISTING 5.2

MATLAB® Program for the Lower Limit of the Debt to GDP Ratio

Stimulus and Spending cuts

```
function discretedebt2
    r = 0.0222; g0 = 0.021; g1 = 0.04; T = 0.174; c=1; b=0.69; h = 0.02;
    13 = 0.205; 11 = 3.8; 12 = 0.1;
```

```
for t = 1:11
    d(t,1) = 0.;
end
    d(1,1) = 1.01;
for t =1:10
    d(t+1,1)=(1+(r-g1)/(1+g1))*d(t,1)+(1+g1)'(-t)*((1-h)'t*13 -
             12*13*(exp((g1-g0)/0.69*t)-1)+11'(-1)*((1+g1)'t -
             (1+g0)'t)) - T
end
```

The above programs allow one to analyze various scenarios: higher and lower future growth rates, interest rates on debt, and tax rates, as well as various stimulus policies characterized by the related multipliers, as it has been done in Chapter 2.

Listing 5.3 presents the generalized model for the debt to GDP ratio (see Eqs. (2.41, 2.42, 2.48, and 2.49), Tables 2.16 and 2.17).

LISTING 5.3

MATLAB® Program for the Debt to GDP Ratio. Generalized Model

```
function discretedebtgeneral
    g0 = - 0.01; c = 1; b = 0.69; 12 = 0.12; 130=0.2;
%   h=0.02;
    g(1,1) = - 0.035; g(2,1) = 0.027; g(3,1) = 0.019; g(4,1) = 0.026;
    g(5,1) = 0.017; g(6,1) = 0.023;
    g(7,1) = 0.0215; g(8,1) = 0.025; g(9,1) = 0.028; g(10,1) = 0.08;
    T(1,1) = 0.15; T(2,1) = 0.14; T(3,1) = 0.15; T(4,1) = 0.15;
    T(5,1) = 0.17; T(6,1) = 0.17;
    T(7,1) = 0.18; T(8,1) = 0.18; T(9,1) = 0.18; T(10,1) = 0.18;
    r(1,1) = 0.0321; r(2,1) = 0.0307; r(2,1) = 0.0305; r(3,1) = 0.0224;
    r(4,1) = 0.0248; r(5,1) = 0.0242;
    r(6,1) = 0.0222; r(7,1) = 0.0222; r(8,1) = 0.022; r(9,1) = 0.022;
    r(10,1) = 0.022;
    11(1,1) = 3.8; 11(2,1) = 3.8; 11(3,1) = 3.8; 11(4,1) = 3.8;
    11(5,1) = 3.8; 11(6,1) = 3.8;
    11(7,1) = 3.8; 11(8,1)=2.5;11(9,1)=1.5; 11(10,1)=1.;
    13(1,1)=0.24; 13(2,1)=0.23; 13(3,1)=0.23; 13(4,1)=0.22;
    13(5,1)=0.21
    13(6,1)=0.2; 13(7,1)=0.21; 13(8,1)=0.21; 13(9,1)=0.2;
    13(10,1)=0.2;
for t = 1:11
    d(t,1) = 0; g1(t,1) = 0;
end
```

```
d(1,1) = 0.624; g1(1,1)=1+g(1,1);
for t = 1:9
  g1(t+1,1) = g1(t,1)*(1+g(t+1,1));
end
for t = 1:10
  d(t+1,1) = (r(t,1)+1)/(1+g(t,1))*d(t,1)+ g1(t,1)^(-1)*
  (13(t,1)-130*c*12*((g1(t,1)/(1+g0)^t)^(1/b) -1)
  + 11(t,1)^(-1)*(g1(t,1) - (1+g0)^t)) - T(t,1)
% decreased spending;
%   d(t+1,1) = (r(t,1)+1)/(1+g(t,1))*d(t,1)+ g1(t,1)^(-1)*(130*
            (1-h)^t - 130*c*12*
%           ((g1(t,1)/(1+g0)^t)^(1/b) - 1))+ 11(i,1)^(-1)*(g1(t,1)-
            (1+g0)^t)) - T(t,1)
end
```

Here two cases covered by Listing 5.1 and Listing 5.2 are combined in one program. For the case when the stimuli are accompanied with the government spending cuts, the symbol "%" that excludes a certain line from the program should be deleted from the line $h = 0.02$ and the last several lines of the last *for* loop. The *for* loop for g1(t,1) determines $\prod_{i=0}^{t+1} (g_i + 1)$. To simplify the above programs for the case of a conditionally balanced budget does not present any difficulties.

5.3 SOFTWARE FOR OPTIMAL PROBLEMS

Although MATLAB® developed several toolboxes related to various control problems, including optimal control theory applications (Symbolic Math Toolbox can be used to solve optimal problems; RIOTS_95, a group of programs and utilities, written mostly in C, Fortran, and M-file scripts, is designed as a toolbox for MATLAB®), in the below programs we present in detail all procedures of solving the considered optimal control problems.

The optimal problems of Chapter 3 deal with the debt D and the debt to GDP ratio optimizing the chosen performance index. Their specifics are that the coefficient c of the optimized function should be chosen to satisfy a certain terminal condition. Because the debt and debt to GDP ratio dynamics are described by different equations, the Riccati equations W are different.

Listing 5.4 and Listing 5.5 present the optimal solution for the debt D and the debt to GDP ratio d, respectively (see Eqs. (3.25–3.27 and 3.31–3.33)).

LISTING 5.4

MATLAB® Optimal Debt Reduction Strategy

```
function debt_optimal;
    c = 14.5; r = 0.0224; g = 0.03;
for q = 1:10
    D(q,1) = 0;
    W(q,1) = 0;
end
for m = 1:9
    i = 10 - m;
    W(10,1) = 1;
    W(i,1) = (1+r)^2*W(i+1,1)*(1+1/c * W(i+1,1))^(-1);
end
    D0 = 16.6; d0 = 0.99;
    D(1,1) = [(1+r)-(c+W(1,1))^(-1)*(r+1)*W(1,1)]*D0
    d(1,1) = (1+g)^(-1)*(1+r)*[1-(c+W(1,1))^(-1)*W(1,1)]*d0
for t = 1:9
    D(t+1,1) = [(1+r)-(c+W(t+1,1))^(-1)*(r+1)*W(t+1,1)]*D(t,1)
    d(t+1,1) = (1+g)^(-1)*(1+r)*[1- (c+W(t+1,1))^(-1)*W(t+1,1)]*
    d(t,1)
end
```

The above program uses the 2012 data. In contrast to Listings 5.1–5.3, here the *for* loops index t = 1:9 because we determined separately D(1,1) and d(1,1) based on the initial conditions D0 and d0.

The expressions for the debt to GDP ratio are included in the program because in Chapter 3 we calculated also the value d(10,1)—the debt to GDP ratio under the optimal debt reduction law.

The indicated c value corresponds to the $4 trillion debt reduction condition in 10 years (see Table 3.1). For the 2014 and 2015 debt data, the coefficient c is different. Simulation results are given in Tables 3.2 and 3.3. It was found by iterations that are not included in the program. The program can be easily enhanced to automatize this search (e.g., by using Fibonacci search or Gauss–Seidel method).

LISTING 5.5

MATLAB® Optimal Debt to GDP Ratio

```
function debtratio_optimal;
    r = 0.0224; g = 0.03;
    c = r(-1) ;
for q =1:10
    d(q,1) = 0;
    W(q,1) = 0;
end
for m = 1:9
    i = 10 - m;
    W(10,1)=1;
    W(i,1) = (1+g)(-2)*(1+r)2*W(i+1,1)*(1+1/c* W(i+1,1))(-1);
end
    d0 = 0.99;
    d(1,1) = (1+g)(-1)*(1+r)*[1-(c+W(1,1))(-1)*W(1,1)]*d0
for t = 1:9
    d(t+1,1)=(1+g)(-1)*(1+r)*[1-(c+W(t+1,1))(-1)*W(t+1,1)]*
    d(t,1)
end
```

Listing 5.5 repeats the procedures of Listing 5.4. However, the coefficient c corresponding to the balanced budget condition is determined directly based on the interest rate on debt. Simulations results for the 2012, 2014, and 2015 data are given in Tables 3.4—3.6.

LISTING 5.6

MATLAB® Optimal Debt to GDP Ratio for Time-varying GDP Growth Rate

```
function debtratio1_optimal;
    r = 0.0224; g = 0.03
    c=r(-1);
    g(1,1) = 0.019; g(2,1) = 0.022; g(3,1) = 0.025; g(4,1) = 0.03;
    g(5,1) = 0.031;
    g(6,1) = 0.033; g(7,1) = 0.035; g(8,1) = 0.035; g(9,1) = 0.035;
    g(10,1) = 0.035;
for q =1:10
    d(q,1) = 0;
    W(q,1) = 0;
end
```

```
for m = 1:9
    i = 10 - m;
    W(10,1)=1;
    W(i,1)=(1+g)^(-2)*(1+r)^2*W(i+1,1)*(1+1/c* W(i+1,1))^(-1);
end
    d0 = 0.99;
    d(1,1) = (1+r)*[(1+g(1.1))^(-1) - (1+g)^(-1)*(c+W(1,1))^(-1)*
    W(1,1)]*d0
for t = 1:9
    d(t+1,1) = (1+r)*[(1+g(t+1,1))^(-1) - (1+g)^(-1)*(c+W(t+1,1))^
    (-1)*W(t+1,1)]*d(t,1)
end
```

Listing 5.6 corresponds to the case when the optimal control (Riccati equation) is the same as in Listing 5.5 for the GDP growth rate g = 0.03. However, the growth rates are assumed time-varying with the average 0.03 and presented by g(i,1) (i = 1, 2,..., 10). That is why d(t,1) in this program are different from d(t,1) (t = 1,2,..., 9) in the previous program (see Table 3.8).

LISTING 5.7

MATLAB® Optimal Estimate of the Ten Years Balanced Budget Proposal

```
function balanced budget_optimal;
    r=0.019;
    N=7;        % time period;
    g1=0.0491;  % average nominal rate;
    g=0.03;     % average real rate;
    h=0.02;     % inflation rate;
    c=(r+h*(1+r))^(-1); % balanced budget condition for inflation h;
    Yp=21.984;  % initial value of GDP in nominal prices:
for q=1:N
    D(q,1)=0;
    W(q,1)=0;
    Z(q,1)=0;   % Z= G-T;
    Y(q,1)=Yp*((1+g)* (1+h))^q; % GDP in nominal prices;
end

for m = 1:N-1
    i = N-m;
    W(N,1)=1;
    W(i,1)=(1+g)^(-2)*(1+r)^2*W(i+1,1)*(1+1/c*W(i+1,1))^(-1);
end
```

```
dp=1.024; % initial value of debt to GDP ratio;
Dp= 22,503 % initial value of debt;
d(1,1)=[(1+g)^(-1)*(1+r)*[1-(c+W(1,1))^(-1)*W(1,1)]]*dp
for t=1:N-1
    d(t+1,1) = (1+g)^(-1)*(1+r)*[1-(c+W(t+1,1))^(-1)*W(t+1,1)]*
    d(t,1);
end
    D(1,1) = d(1,1)*Y(1,1);
    Z(1,1)=dp*(c+W(1,1))^(-1)*(r+1)/(1+g)*W(1,1)*Dp
for t=1:N-1
    D(t+1,1) = d(t+1,1)*Y(t+1,1)
    Z(t+1,1)= - (c+W(t+1,1))^(-1)*(r+1)/(g+1)*W(t+1,1)*d(t,1)*
    Y(t,1)
    Y(t,1)=Y(t,1)
    d(t,1)=d(t,1)
    W(t,1)=W(t,1)
end
end
```

Listing 5.7 relates to the optimal problem, considered in Chapter 4, to balance the US budget in 10 years. Earlier we explained why the 7-year period, starting from 2021, is chosen to evaluate the government 2018−27 proposal. Specifics of the above program are that it takes into account the projected 2% inflation. The balanced budget condition for this case is written based on Eq. (3.43); the obvious expressions in the program for nominal rates and GDP values are accompanied with notes (see also Appendix D). The related expressions for the GDP Y_t, debt D_t, coefficient c, and the difference Z_t between prime spending and revenues ($t = 1,2,...7$) are obtained based on Eq. (D1.4). The program uses average interest, inflation, and GDP growth rates. It is not difficult to modify the program to use different projected rates for each year (see Listing 5.6).

REFERENCES

Higham, D.J., Higham, N.J., 2000. MATLAB Guide. SIAM, Philadelphia.
Miranda, M., Fackler, P., 2002. Applied Computational Economics and Finance. MIT Press, Cambridge, MA.

Afterword

Economic crises are laboratories for testing various economic theories. Unfortunately, the policies recommended by economists are "corrected" by politicians who treat *economy* as *political economy*. As a result, the distorted policies allow economists of opposite camps to reaffirm the correctness of their theories and accuse politicians of inability to properly implement them. In the United States, Republicans are blamed for impeding the implementation of stimulus policy. Krugman and his advocates believe that the insufficient stimulus stalled the economic recovery that began in June 2009. Krugman states that the actual policy in the United States and European Union is misguided. In turn, Democrats are blamed for their unwillingness to cut taxes for businesses, which would stimulate the economic growth, to reduce the budget deficit, and to choose a balanced budget path.

In times of economic crises, economists should play a role of experienced physicians—find a proper medicine and prescribe its proper dosage to restore a country's economic health. Unfortunately, economists cannot agree what medicine to use—which economic policy a country should follow. As to the question of a proper dosage—the size of stimulus or spending cuts—it still remains open. It is not clear why stimulus and austerity measures cannot coexist and be combined in one hybrid policy—cuts in some sectors of economy can be used as stimulus in other sectors.

President Harry Truman said: "Give me a one-handed economist." All my economists say, "on the one hand…on the other." The current crisis provides economists with extensive experimental data—the results of governments' policies—which can help economists to test the existing theories and to develop reliable approaches to cure the economy and to consign to the oblivion the above quote.

More than two centuries ago Thomas Jefferson said: "I wish it were possible to obtain a single amendment to our constitution; I would be willing to depend on that alone for the reduction of the administration of our government to the genuine principles of its constitution. I mean an additional article taking from the federal government the power of borrowing."

Many current politicians ignore this statement. Knowing little about the economy they operate by slogans, that help them to keep their positions, rather than based upon a solid knowledge of facts and science. Decisions must be based on solid knowledge about the subject rather than on desire to follow the beliefs or standards established by the political elite. This relates to both - politicians and economists.

The old joke that economists were invented to make weathermen look good lost its attractiveness.

Recent advances in satellite and computer technology have led to significant progress in meteorology, especially in weather forecasting, so that it is now time for economists to find efficient approaches for economic forecasting. The authors hope that the models considered in the book are a step in the right direction.

Appendix A

A1. PARAMETERS OF THE COBB–DOUGLAS FUNCTION

Solow (1957) formulated properly the main approach to building economic models: "As long as we insist on practicing macroeconomics we shall need aggregate relationships." The Cobb–Douglas production function presents the aggregate relationship between the output Y, i.e., GDP, and inputs, i.e., capital K and labor L. In the form (2.3) $Y(t) = AK^{\alpha}(t)L^{\beta}(t)$, it is widely used in practice. However, usually, macroeconomic models consider the case $\alpha + \beta = 1$. Although this result was obtained by Cobb and Douglas based on modeling the growth of the American economy during the period 1899–1922, it was accepted by many economists and applied to analysis of many complex macroeconomic models.

Formally, the Cobb–Douglas production function is written in the form $\beta = 1 - \alpha$. Solow (1957) considered the time-varying coefficient $A(t)$ reflecting "technical change." However, Cobb and Douglas did not provide any theoretical reason why the coefficients α and β should be constant. The mentioned production function has no macro foundation. The output is influenced by many other than capital and labor factors. As to the time-varying coefficient $A(t)$, Solow's (1957) results of modeling the US economy during the period 1909–1949 show that its derivative does not reflect realistically the rate of technical progress. As Simon and Levy (1963) pointed out, the good fits to the Cobb–Douglas production function "cannot be taken as strong evidence for the classical theory, for the identical results can readily be produced by mistakenly fitting a Cobb–Douglas function to data that were in fact generated by a linear accounting identity (value of output equals labor cost plus capital cost)". Samuelson (1979) believed that "this is an operationally meaningful law, since it can be empirically refuted."

The condition $\alpha + \beta = 1$ allows to simplify the analysis by introducing $y = Y/L$ and $k = K/L$, so that the production function becomes a function of only one variable $y = Ak^{\alpha}$. The form per capita or *per hour* looks very attractive, and maybe this fact explains the popularity of the Cobb–Douglas production function written in the form $\beta = 1 - \alpha$.

It looks like to justify the *constant return to scale* the indexing approach was offered (see, e.g., Bureau of Labor Statistics, 2016). For a chosen basic year, all variables have indexes equal 100; in other years, indexes reflect the change of real Y, K, and L values with respect to the basic year. For the basic year, we automatically have $A = 1$ and $\alpha + \beta = 1$. However, the mentioned approach assumes in advance the *constant return to scale*, the assumption that does not correspond to reality. In the current economy, a proportional change in labor and capital (taken from various industries) cannot produce the same proportional change of the GDP. To justify the mentioned assumption, the BLS methodology uses the term "Labor input," the number of working hours, which is different from the nominal total working hours, and takes into account workers' qualifications and their professions. The hours of all persons (classified by age, education, and gender) are aggregated by using their hourly compensation to determine weights (see Harper et al., 2008).

Building the regression model under the mentioned assumption decreases significantly the accuracy of the model. Regression models cannot be interpreted as laws. They reflect the input—output relationships between the chosen variables and should be built based on carefully chosen data. It is obvious that the values of A, α, and β parameters of the Cobb—Douglas model depend on the considered time period. Below we use the following data presented by the US. Bureau of Labor Statistics (see Table A1) based on the BLS and the Bureau of Economic Analysis (BEA) methodology (see Harper et al., 2008) focused "to expand and improve the integration of the national income and product accounts and productivity statistics."

The standard procedure of determining A, α, and β follows from the equation

$$\log Y = \log A + \alpha \log K + \beta \log L \qquad (A1.1)$$

and (see, e.g., Albert, 1972)

$$\left\| \begin{array}{c} \log A \\ \alpha \\ \beta \end{array} \right\| = \left(H^T H \right)^{-1} H^T z \qquad (A1.2)$$

where

$$z = \begin{Vmatrix} \log Y_1 \\ \dots \\ \log Y_n \end{Vmatrix}; \quad H = \begin{bmatrix} 1 & \log K_1 & \log L_1 \\ \vdots & \ddots & \vdots \\ 1 & \log K_n & \log L_n \end{bmatrix} \quad \text{(A1.3)}$$

However, formally the output Y is a function of labor L and capital K, rather than A. In Eq. (A1.1), $\log A$ can be interpreted as the approximation error. If it equals zero, then $A = 1$. In Solow (1957), $1 \leq A < 2$. However, the A-values obtained based on Eqs. (A1.2) and (A1.3) are significantly larger, and the result of such an approximation cannot be considered as satisfactory.

Because in the developed model the GDP growth rate g is a function of α and β, below the alternative procedure is used

$$\frac{\dot{Y}}{Y} = \alpha \frac{\dot{K}}{K} + \beta \frac{\dot{L}}{L} \quad \text{(A1.4)}$$

for which

$$\begin{Vmatrix} \alpha \\ \beta \end{Vmatrix} = \left(H^T H \right)^{-1} H^T z_1 \quad \text{(A1.5)}$$

where (see columns 3, 5, 7, and 9 of Table A1)

$$z_1 = \begin{Vmatrix} \dfrac{Y_2 - Y_1}{Y_1} \\ \dots \\ \dfrac{Y_n - Y_{n-1}}{Y_{n-1}} \end{Vmatrix}, \quad [H] = \begin{bmatrix} \dfrac{K_2 - K_1}{K_1} & \dfrac{L_2 - L_1}{L_1} \\ \dots & \dots \\ \dfrac{K_n - K_{n-1}}{K_{n-1}} & \dfrac{L_n - L_{n-1}}{L_{n-1}} \end{bmatrix} \quad \text{(A1.6)}$$

The following parameters of the regression model, which are substantial to determine the GDP growth (see Eqs. (2.5) and (2.6)), are obtained.

Based on 1987–2014 data:

with Labor input based on the adjusted hours at work of all persons in billions:

$$\alpha = 0.2779, \quad \beta = 0.7245;$$

with the real L-hours at work of all persons in billions:
$$\alpha = 0.3051, \quad \beta = 0.6916.$$

Based on 1994—2014 data:
with Labor input based on the adjusted hours at work of all persons in billions:
$$\alpha = 0.2566, \quad \beta = 0.7797;$$

with the real L-hours at work of all persons in billions:
$$\alpha = 0.2996, \quad \beta = 0.7040.$$

The examined period of time includes the financial crises of 2008—2014. This period is less than 35% of the considered total period starting in 1987 and 1994. The effect of the 2008—2014 economic slump is smoothed, and the examined parameters for 1987—2014 and 1994—2014 are close and $\alpha + \beta \approx 1$.

In contrast to Solow (1957), we do not assume that $\alpha + \beta = 1$ and A is a time-varying coefficient. The parameters $\alpha = 0.3051$ and $\beta = 0.6916$ obtained for real labor hours are used in Chapter 4 because the average corresponding growth rate based on Eq. (4.3) [(4.6)] for 2007—2014 is very close to the presented in Table A1 (see column 3).

Unrobustness of the output elasticities of capital α and labor β supports the above-indicated Samuelson's (1979) opinion concerning the Cobb—Douglas production function. It should be used cautiously in the developing models, and its parameters should be determined thoroughly. In dynamic models, when the growth rate of the Cobb—Douglas function is an important parameter that influences significantly simulation results, the regression based on Eqs. (A1.4)—(A1.6) is preferable.

Table A1 The BLS data to determine parameters of the Cobb–Douglas function

Year	Real value-added output in billions of dollars	Change a year ago in %	Labor input in billions of hours	Change a year ago in %	Capital income in billions of dollars	Change a year ago in %	Hours at work of all persons in billions	Change a year ago in %
1987	8,561.291		186.576		1,785.419		84.018	3.0
1988	8,955.861	4.6	192.722	3.3	1,905.270	6.7	86.527	3.0
1989	9,880.818	10.3	198.962	3.2	2,419.161	27.0	88.922	2.8
1990	9,579.680	−3.0	199.611	0.3	2,212.370	−8.5	89.074	0.2
1991	9,469.992	−1.1	198.649	−0.5	2,261.157	2.2	87.826	−1.4
1992	9,713.885	2.6	199.356	0.4	2,327.190	2.9	87.901	0.1
1993	9,972.746	2.7	205.412	3.0	2,508.974	7.8	89.977	2.4
1994	10,400.790	4.3	213.733	4.1	2,631.805	4.9	92.815	3.2
1995	10,838.938	4.2	220.447	3.1	2,894.592	10.0	95.098	2.5
1996	11,192.251	3.3	223.766	1.5	3,051.980	5.4	96.291	1.3
1997	11,687.081	4.4	230.585	3.0	3,279.079	7.4	99.137	3.0
1998	12,212.218	4.5	237.612	3.0	3,404.776	3.8	101.300	2.2
1999	12,724.693	4.2	242.508	2.1	3,570.374	4.9	103.296	2.0
2000	13,193.005	3.7	245.890	1.4	3,645.095	2.1	104.686	1.3
2001	13,414.716	1.7	244.109	−0.7	3,776.464	3.6	103.382	−1.2
2002	13,706.755	2.2	242.363	−0.7	4,075.186	7.9	102.079	−1.3
2003	14,218.310	3.7	243.070	0.3	4,486.541	10.1	101.586	−0.5

(Continued)

Table A1 The BLS data to determine parameters of the Cobb–Douglas function—cont'd

Year	Real value-added output in billions of dollars	Change a year ago in %	Labor input in billions of hours	Change a year ago in %	Capital income in billions of dollars	Change a year ago in %	Hours at work of all persons in billions	Change a year ago in %
2004	14,814.789	4.2	246.780	1.5	4,950.928	10.4	102.725	1.1
2005	15,574.201	5.1	250.311	1.4	5,782.281	16.8	104.251	1.5
2006	16,030.800	2.9	255.505	2.1	6,195.300	7.1	106.140	1.8
2007	16,222.156	1.2	258.631	1.2	6,825.062	10.2	106.912	0.7
2008	16,058.336	−1.0	257.633	−0.4	7,011.038	2.7	105.805	−1.0
2009	15,502.535	−3.5	245.779	−4.6	6,814.315	−2.8	100.000	−5.5
2010	15,919.450	2.7	246.326	0.2	7,059.966	3.6	99.980	0.0
2011	16,220.094	1.9	250.985	1.9	7,225.056	2.3	101.514	1.5
2012	16,648.294	2.6	256.077	2.0	7,519.270	4.1	103.283	1.7
2013	16,935.243	1.7	259.669	1.4	7,818.531	4.0	104.605	1.3
2014	17,323.703	2.3	264.943	2.0	7,880.619	0.8	106.619	1.9

REFERENCES

Albert, A., 1972. Regression and the Moor-Penrose Pseudo inverse. Academic Press, New York and London.

Bureau of Labor Statistics, 2016. Multifactor Productivity. http://www.bls.gov/mfp/.

Harper, M., Moulton, B., Rosenthal, S., Wasshausen, D., 2008. Integrated GDP-Productivity Accounts. http://www.bls.gov/mfp/integrated_prod_accounts.pdf.

Samuelson, P.A., 1979. Paul Douglas's measurement of production functions and marginal productivities. Journal of Political Economy 87, 923—939.

Solow, R., 1957. Technical change and the aggregate production function. The Review of Economics and Statistics 39 (3), 312—320.

Simon, H.A., Levy, F.K., 1963. A note on the Cobb-Douglas function. Review of Economic Studies 30, 93—94.

Appendix B

B1. EVALUATION OF THE MULTIPLE VALUES FOR A STIMULUS PACKAGE

As indicated earlier, financial multiples have an important role in the analysis of economic models. Their values have a significant influence on the results produced by using these models and on the related decision-making.

As indicated in Chapter 1, the spending and tax multipliers present families of submultipliers, and in any concrete situation, the considering multiplier contains a different combination of submultipliers.

To determine the value of the spending multiplier l_G, we should know the values of all submultipliers l_{Gi} and the amount of money P_{Gi} ($i = 1, 2, \ldots, n$) related to each multiplier. Then

$$l_G = \frac{\sum_{i=1}^{n} l_{Gi} P_{Gi}}{\sum_{i=1}^{n} P_{Gi}} \tag{B1.1}$$

Analogously for the tax multiplier l_T, we have

$$l_T = \frac{\sum_{i=1}^{n} l_{Ti} P_{Ti}}{\sum_{i=1}^{n} P_{Ti}} \tag{B1.2}$$

where l_{Ti} is the tax multiplier corresponding to a specific tax cut and P_{Ti} ($i = 1, 2, \ldots, n$) is the related change in tax revenue.

If the above-indicated parameters are known, the determination of l_G and l_T does not present any difficulty. However, in the case of spending multipliers, the total amount of money P_0 allocated for stimulus programs can be determined in advance before concrete projects are chosen. Then from considered m projects a certain number n of projects should be chosen that would satisfy to the limit P_0 on spending and an additional criterion or criteria based on which the decision is made.

It looks logical at the initial stage of crises, when unemployment is high, to choose such projects that involve maximal additional workforce L_{Gi} ($i = 1, 2, ..., m$). In this case the optimal problem can be presented in the following form: choose such projects that

$$\max_{z_i} \sum_{i=1}^{m} z_i L_{Gi} \qquad (B1.3)$$

subject to

$$\sum_{i=1}^{m} z_i P_{Gi} \leq P_0 \qquad (B1.4)$$

$$z_i \in \{0, 1\}, \quad i = 1, 2, ..., m \qquad (B1.5)$$

This is an integer programming problem; methods of solving this class of problem and related computational algorithms can be found, for example, in Karlof (2006). The number of non-zero z_i determines n and i-es that can be used in Eq. (B1.1) to find the spending multiplier.

In the case when the main concern is economic growth, the following integer programming problem can be considered:

$$\max_{z_i} \sum_{i=1}^{m} z_i l_{Gi} P_{Gi} \qquad (B1.6)$$

$$s.t. \ \sum_{i=1}^{m} z_i P_{Gi} \leq P_0, \quad z_i \in \{0, 1\}, \quad i = 1, 2, ..., m \qquad (B1.7)$$

Finally, it is possible to consider the multicriteria problem—maximization of both criteria (B1.3) and (B1.6).

Because for a nontrivial multicriteria optimization problem there is no a single solution that simultaneously optimizes each objective, the so-called Pareto optimal solutions are considered. Without additional subjective preference information, all Pareto optimal solutions are considered equally good. One of the approaches to solve such a problem is to consider a compromised criterion

$$\max_{z_i} \sum_{i=1}^{m} z_i l_{Gi} P_{Gi} + \lambda z_i L_{Gi} \qquad (B1.8)$$

$$s.t. \sum_{i=1}^{m} z_i P_{Gi} \le P_0, \quad z_i \in \{0, 1\}, \quad i = 1, 2, ..., m$$

where λ depends on the workforce constraints.

The considered decision problem can be objectively solved although its construction contains both subjective and objective components. The compromised criterion allows decision-makers to determine what must be done dealing with a set of subjective values of λ. To determine an appropriate set of λ, it is worthwhile to consider first two criteria (B1.3) and (B1.6) separately (it corresponds to $\lambda = 0$ and $\lambda \to \infty$) to find the optimal solution and the values of all two performance indices, respectively. The obtained 2×2 matrix enables us to determine the most perspective set of parameters λ for the compromised criterion (see, e.g., Yanushevsky and Yanushevsky, 2015).

As indicated earlier, a more detailed analysis of financial multipliers shows that they change in time; that is, in discrete time the spending multiplier can be presented as $l_{Gt_i} \left(t_i = t_{i0}^1, ..., t_{if}^1, \quad i = 1, 2, ..., m \right)$, where t_{i0}^1 and t_{if}^1 characterize the time interval related to the implementation of the ith project. In contrast to the model (B1.8), the below model reflects dynamics of the stimulus process. Separate projects, as well as the related resources P_{Gt_i}, L_{Gt_i}, and P_{0t_i} ($t_i = t_{i0}$, ..., t_{if}, $i = 1, 2, ..., m$; t_{i0} and t_{if} are times of the beginning and ending of the ith project), are distributed in time. Usually, the stimulus effect acts with a delay so that $t_{i0}^1 > t_{i0}$ ($i = 1, 2, ..., m$) and these values should be evaluated.

Instead of (B1.8), we have

$$\max_{z_i, \, t_{i0}} \sum_{i=1}^{m} \sum_{t} z_i l_{Gt_i} P_{Gt_i} + \lambda z_i L_{Gt_i} \tag{B1.9}$$

$$s.t. \sum_{i=1}^{m} z_i P_{Gt_i} \le P_{0t_i}, \quad z_i \in \{0, 1\}, \quad i = 1, 2, ..., m$$

If for the stimulus projects the time schedule (t_{i0}, $i = 1, ..., m$) for a chosen period t is known, the problem (B1.9) is similar to the problem (B1.8). However, if the sequence of the chosen projects should be ordered in time, the solution of the above-formulated problem becomes more complicated and requires knowledge of scheduling theory (see, e.g., Conway et al., 2003).

In reality, many projects have a high priority, so that they and the related allocated resources should be excluded from the considered model, and the number of unknown remained variables will be small. This will significantly simplify the computational procedure.

B2. GENERALIZED MODEL. INVERSE PROBLEM AS AN APPROACH TO EVALUATE MULTIPLIER VALUE

Various mathematical models to evaluate the effect of spending or tax cuts consider the influence of these factors separately, as parts of fiscal policy, and ignore the fact that usually financial measures are accompanied by changes in monetary policy. That is why the spending multiplier values obtained by Christiano et al. (2011), who first examined the influence of monetary policy on fiscal multipliers, differ significantly from the values indicated by many other authors (see, e.g., Auerbach and Gorodnichenko, 2012; Blanchard and Perotti, 2002; Heim, 2012; Ilzetzki et al., 2013; Mankiw, 2008). Below we will use the modified model (2.50)

$$d_{t+1} = \frac{1 + r_{t+1}}{1 + g_{t+1}} d_t + l^0_{3,t+1} - \tau_{t+1} + l^{-1}_{G,t+1} \frac{\left[\prod_{i=1}^{t+1} (g_i + 1) - \prod_{i=1}^{t+1} (g_{0i} + 1) \right]}{\prod_{i=1}^{t+1} (g_i + 1)}$$

$$t = 0, 1, 2, \dots$$

(B2.1)

to evaluate the spending multiplier $l_{G,t+1}$ using the US 2009—2015 economic data.

Because the tax cuts effect is excluded from the consideration, τ_{t+1} ($t = 0,1,2,\dots$) characterize the government revenues and $l^0_{3,t+1}$ ($t = 0, 1, 2, \dots$) characterize the government spending not related to the stimulus programs (not including interest payment on the debt) but take into account the welfare spending during the 2008 crises (this is more accurate than using the $\Delta G_{1,t+1}$ term (see Eq. (2.48) in Eq. (2.50)). We chose the initial moment corresponding to the third quarter of 2009 ($d_0 = 0.8236$; $g_0 = 0.0034$) to reflect the delayed effect of stimuli programs. The American Recovery and Reinvestment Act was enacted in February 2009, but its real effect started showing up only in 2010.

It follows from Eq. (B2.1) that

$$
l_{G,t+1} = \frac{\left[\prod_{i=1}^{t+1} (g_i + 1) - \prod_{i=1}^{t+1} (g_{0i} + 1) \right]}{\prod_{i=1}^{t+1} (g_i + 1)} \Bigg/
$$ (B2.2)

$$
\left(d_{t+1} - \frac{1 + r_{t+1}}{1 + g_{t+1}} d_t - l^0_{3,t+1} + \tau_{t+1} \right), \quad t = 0, 1, 2, \ldots
$$

Table B2 contains the results of calculations and the related data that show that, when fiscal policy has a proper balance with monetary policy, the spending multiplier values can be significantly higher than those obtained from the models ignoring the impact of monetary policy. It also shows a delayed effect of the spending stimulus.

Some too big fluctuations of l_G values can be explained by the input errors. The result is very sensitive to changes of the model parameters. This is very typical for many economic models, especially for the considered inverse problem. The insufficient amount of information available about the input parameters is the factor that can make the solution unrobust. In a case of several suspicious $l_{G,t}$ values (e.g., for $t = t_k$), the minimization problem indicated in Section 2.6 can be used. Usually, regularization refers to a process of introducing additional information to solve an ill-posed problem. Instead of the discrete model with yearly steps, a modified model with quarterly steps should be used if the quarterly data are available.

Table B2 Spending multipliers for properly balanced fiscal and monetary policies

Year	2010	2011	2012	2013	2014	2015
$g_{t+1}\%$	2.532	1.6	2.223	1.678	2.37	2.6
τ_{t+1}	0.1445	0.1484	0.1516	0.1665	0.1741	0.1805
$l^0_{3,t+1}$	0.177	0.18	0.18	0.165	0.16	0.158
$r\%$	3.05	2.89	2.588	2.43	2.4	2.35
$l_{G,t+1}$	0.444	2.881	2.426	3.925	1.521	3.823
Debt/GDP ratio d	0.904	0.9515	0.9935	1.003	1.03	1.01

REFERENCES

Auerbach, A.J., Gorodnichenko, Y., 2012. Fiscal multipliers in recession and expansion. In: Alesina, A., Giavazzi, F. (Eds.), Fiscal Policy after the Financial Crisis. University of Chicago Press, Chicago.

Blanchard, O., Perotti, R., 2002. An empirical characterization of the dynamic effects of changes in government spending and taxes on output. Quarterly Journal of Economics 117 (4), 1329–1368.

Christiano, L., Eichenbaum, M., Rebelo, S., 2011. When is the government spending multiplier large. Journal of Political Economy 119 (1), 78–121.

Conway, R., Maxwell, W., Miller, L., 2003. Theory of Scheduling. Dover Publications, Inc., New York.

Heim, J., 2012. Does crowd out Hamper government stimulus programs in recessions? Journal of Applied Business and Economics 13 (2), 11–27.

Ilzetzki, E., Mendoza, E.G., Végh, C.A., 2013. How big (small?) are fiscal multipliers? Journal of Monetary Economics 60 (2), 239–254.

Karlof, J., 2006. Integer Programming: Theory and Practice. CRC Press, New York.

Mankiw, G., 2008. Spending and Tax Multipliers, Greg Mankiw's Blog. http://www.aei.org/publication/spending-and-tax-multipliers.

Yanushevsky, R., Yanushevsky, D., 2015. An approach to improve mean-variance portfolio optimization model. Journal of Asset Management 16, 209–219.

Appendix C

C.1. BELLMAN APPROACH

C.1.1 Linear Continuous Models

Let us consider a dynamic system described by the following equation:

$$\dot{x} = Ax + Bu, \quad x(t_0) = x(0) \tag{C1.1}$$

where x is an m-dimensional state vector, u is an n-dimensional control vector, and A and B are matrices of appropriate dimensions.

We will determine the control law u that minimizes the cost functional

$$I = \frac{1}{2}\left(x^T(t_f)C_0 x(t_f) + \int_{t_0}^{t_f} \left(x^T(t)Rx(t) + c\|u(t)\|^2 \right) dt \right) \tag{C1.2}$$

where C_0 and R are symmetric positive semidefinite matrices.

To find the optimal control, we will use the dynamic programming approach (see, e.g., Bellman, 1957; Kwakernaak and Sivan, 1972; Yanushevsky, 2011). The derivation of the Bellman functional equation is given according to the optimality principle: Every tail of the optimal trajectory is the optimal trajectory.

Let the optimal functional value be

$$\varphi(x(t_0), t_0) = \min_{u(t)} I \tag{C1.3}$$

Then in accordance with the optimality principle, it can be written

$$\varphi(\pmb{x}(t_0), t_0) = \min_{u(t)} \frac{1}{2} \left\{ \pmb{x}^T(t_f) C_0 \pmb{x}(t_f) + \int_{t_0}^{t_0+\delta} \left(\pmb{x}^T(t) R\pmb{x}(t) + c\|\pmb{u}(t)\|^2 \right) dt \right.$$

$$+ \left. \int_{t+\delta}^{t_F} \left(\pmb{x}^T(t) R\pmb{x}(t) + c\|\pmb{u}(t)\|^2 \right) dt \right\}$$

$$= \min_{u(t)} \left\{ \frac{1}{2} \left[\pmb{x}^T(t_f) C_0 \pmb{x}(t_f) + \int_{t_0}^{t_0+\delta} \left(\pmb{x}^T(t) R\pmb{x}(t) + c\|\pmb{u}(t)\|^2 \right) dt \right] \right.$$

$$+ \left. \varphi(\pmb{x}(t_0 + \delta), t_0 + \delta) \right\}$$

$$\text{(C1.4)}$$

Suppose that δ is small enough and that there exist partial derivatives of $\varphi(\pmb{x})$ for $x \in [\pmb{x}(t_0),\ \pmb{x}(t_0+\delta)]$. Then expanding $\varphi(\pmb{x}(t_0+\delta),\ (t_0+\delta))$ into the Taylor series in the vicinity of $\pmb{x}(t_0)$, after appropriate transformations we obtain

$$\varphi(\pmb{x}(t_0), t_0) = \min_{u(t)} \left\{ \frac{1}{2} \left(\pmb{x}^T(t_0) R\pmb{x}(t_0) + c\|\pmb{u}(t_0)\|^2 \right) \delta + \varphi(\pmb{x}(t_0), t_0) + \frac{\partial \varphi}{\partial t} \delta \right.$$

$$+ \left. \frac{\partial \varphi}{\partial x}^T (A\pmb{x}(t) + B\pmb{u}(t)) \Big|_{\substack{x = x_0 \\ u = u_0}} \delta + O(\delta) \right\}$$

$$\text{(C1.5)}$$

where $\frac{\partial \varphi}{\partial x}^T = \left(\frac{\partial \varphi}{\partial x_1}, \ldots, \frac{\partial \varphi}{\partial x_m} \right)$ is a row vector, and it is assumed that $\lim_{\delta \to 0} O(\delta)/\delta = 0$.

Tending δ to zero and taking into account that, in accordance with the optimality principle, the strategy must be optimal regardless of the state in which the system is at the actual instant (i.e., $\pmb{x}(t_0)$ and $\pmb{u}(t_0)$ can be treated as the current values of the vectors $x(t)$ and $u(t)$), we obtain the required functional equation (the Bellman equation) as follows:

$$\min_{u(t)} \left\{ \frac{1}{2} \left(x^T(t)Rx(t) + c\|u(t)\|^2 \right) + \frac{\partial \varphi}{\partial t} + \frac{\partial \varphi^T}{\partial x} \left(Ax(t) + Bu(t) \right) \right\} = 0$$

(C1.6)

For the existence of minimum of the expression in brace brackets, its derivative with respect to $u(t)$ $\left(\frac{d}{du}\{\} \right)$ must be equal zero, i.e.,

$$u(t) = -\frac{1}{c}B^T\frac{\partial \varphi}{\partial x}$$

(C1.7)

Substituting Eq. (C1.7) in Eq. (C1.6), we obtain

$$\frac{1}{2} x^T(t)Rx(t) + \frac{\partial \varphi}{\partial t} + \frac{\partial \varphi^T}{\partial x}Ax(t) - \frac{1}{2c}\frac{\partial \varphi^T}{\partial x}BB^T\frac{\partial \varphi}{\partial x}u(t) = 0$$

(C1.8)

The solution of the considered problem reduces to finding the function $\varphi(x)$ satisfying the Bellman functional Eq. (C1.8) (or the equivalent Eq. (C1.6)).

The solution will be sought in the form

$$\varphi(x) = \frac{1}{2} x^T(t)W(t)x(t)$$

(C1.9)

where $W(t)$ is a vector function.

Its substitution in Eqs. (C1.7) and (C1.8) gives

$$u(t) = -\frac{1}{c} B^T W(t)x(t)$$

(C1.10)

$$\dot{W}(t) + A^T W(t) + W(t)A - \frac{1}{c} W(t)BB^T W(t) + R = 0$$

(C1.11)

This is the so-called Riccati differential equation. Comparing Eqs. (C1.2) and (C1.9) for $t = t_f$, we conclude that $W(t_f) = C_0$.

In the case of the criteria (3.4) and (3.13) $A = r$ (see Eq. (3.3)) and $A = r - g$ (see Eq. (3.12)), respectively; $B = 1$, $R = 0$, and $C_0 = 1$ so that Eqs. (3.7) and (3.15) follow immediately from Eq. (C1.11).

In the case of disturbances $f(t)$, instead of Eq. (C1.1) we have

$$\dot{x} = Ax + Bu + f(t), \quad x(t_0) = x(0)$$

(C1.12)

For the functional (C1.2) the functional Bellman equation can be presented as

$$\min_{u(t)} \left\{ \frac{1}{2} \left(x^T(t) R x(t) + c\|u(t)\|^2 \right) + \frac{\partial \varphi}{\partial t} + \frac{\partial \varphi^T}{\partial x} \left(A x(t) + B u(t) + f(t) \right) \right\} = 0$$

(C1.13)

and the optimal solution will be sought in the form

$$\varphi(x) = \frac{1}{2} x^T(t) W(t) x(t) + L_1(t) x(t) + L_0(t)$$ (C1.14)

where the functions $L_1(t)$ and $L_0(t)$ should satisfy (C1.13).

The optimal law

$$u(t) = -\frac{1}{c} B^T W(t) x(t) - \frac{1}{c} B^T L_1(t)$$ (C1.15)

where $L_1(t)$ is the solution of

$$\dot{L}_1(t) + A^T L_1(t) - \frac{1}{c} W(t) B B^T L_1(t) + W(t) f(t) = 0, \quad L_1(t_f) = 0$$

(C1.16)

(the terms of Eq. (C1.13) containing $x(t)$ were grouped to obtain Eq. (C1.16); the expression of $L_0(t)$ is not given because $L_0(t)$ is not present in Eq. (C1.16)).

C.1.2 Linear Discrete Models

Let us consider a discrete-time dynamic system described by the following equation:

$$x_{k+1} = A x_k + B u_k, \quad k = 0, 1, 2, \ldots, N - 1; \quad x(t_0) = x_0 \quad \text{(C1.17)}$$

where x_k is an m-dimensional state vector, u_k is an n-dimensional control vector, and A and B are matrices of appropriate dimensions.

We will determine the control law u_k ($k = 0, 1, 2, \ldots, N - 1$) that minimizes the cost functional

$$I = \frac{1}{2} \left(x_N^T C_0 x_N + \sum_{k=0}^{N-1} x_k^T R x_k + c\|u_k\|^2 \right)$$ (C1.18)

where C_0 and R are symmetric positive semidefinite matrices.

In the continuous case the interval δ is assumed to be small enough, so that we can approximate $\varphi(x(t_0 + \delta), (t_0 + \delta))$ by using only first two terms of the Taylor series in the vicinity of $x(t_0)$ (see the expressions (C1.4) and (C1.5)). In the discrete case, δ is equal to the discrete-time interval "1." That is why instead of Eq. (C1.4) we have

$$\varphi(x_0, 0) = \min_{u_k} \frac{1}{2} \left\{ x_N^T C_0 x_N + \sum_{k=1}^{N-1} x_k^T R x_k + c\|u_k\|^2 + x_0^T R x_0 \right.$$

$$\left. + c\|u_0\|^2 \right\}$$

$$= \min_{u_0} \left\{ \frac{1}{2} \left(x_0^T R x_0 + c\|u_0\|^2 \right) + \varphi(x_1, 1) \right\}$$

$$\text{(C1.19)}$$

In this case, the relationship between $\varphi(x_0,0)$ and $\varphi(x_1,1)$ cannot be presented similar to the continuous case. However, as it is seen from Eq. (C1.19) as well as from the considered continuous model, $\varphi(x_0,0)$ is a quadratic function of the initial state x_0, and the solution of Eq. (C1.19) can be sought in the form

$$\varphi(x_k, k) = \frac{1}{2} x_k^T W_k x_k, \quad k = 0, 1, ..., N \qquad \text{(C1.20)}$$

where W_k ($k = 0$, $1,...,$ N) is a discrete function that should satisfy the Bellman equation.

In contrast to the continuous case, here it is more convenient to move back from the end of the optimal trajectory.

Since for $k = N$

$$\varphi(x_N, N) = \frac{1}{2} x_N^T C_0 x_N \qquad \text{(C1.21)}$$

we have $W_N = C_0$.

For $k = N - 1$ (see Eq. (C1.19))

$$\varphi(x_{N-1}, N - 1) = \min_{u_{N-1}} \left\{ \frac{1}{2} \left(x_{N-1}^T R x_{N-1} + c\|u_{N-1}\|^2 \right) + \varphi(x_N, N) \right\}$$

$$\text{(C1.22)}$$

or by using Eqs. (C1.17) and (C1.20)

$$\frac{1}{2}x_{N-1}^{T}W_{N-1}x_{N-1} = \min_{u_{N-1}}\left\{\frac{1}{2}\left(x_{N-1}^{T}Rx_{N-1} + c\|u_{N-1}\|^{2}\right) + \frac{1}{2}x_{N}^{T}W_{N}x_{N}\right\}$$

$$= \min_{u_{N-1}}\frac{1}{2}\left\{\left(x_{N-1}^{T}Rx_{N-1} + c\|u_{N-1}\|^{2}\right)\right.$$

$$\left. + \left(x_{N-1}^{T}A^{T} + u_{N-1}^{T}B^{T}\right)W_{N}(Ax_{N-1} + Bu_{N-1})\right\}$$
(C1.23)

Taking u_{N-1} derivative from both parts of Eq. (C1.23), we determine the optimal value of u_{N-1} and the substitution of this value in Eq. (C1.23) gives the expression for W_{N-1}

$$u_{N-1} = -\left(cI + B^{T}W_{N}B\right)^{-1}B^{T}W_{N}Ax_{N-1}$$
(C1.24)

$$W_{N-1} = A^{T}W_{N}A - A^{T}W_{N}B\left(cI + B^{T}W_{N}B\right)^{-1}B^{T}W_{N}A + R$$
(C1.25)

where I is the identity matrix.

Repeating the above-described steps for $k = N - 2$, $N - 3$, etc. by induction, we conclude that for all k

$$u_{k} = -\left(cI + B^{T}W_{k+1}B\right)^{-1}B^{T}W_{k+1}Ax_{k}$$
(C1.26)

$$W_{k} = A^{T}W_{k+1}A - A^{T}W_{k+1}B\left(cI + B^{T}W_{k+1}B\right)^{-1}B^{T}W_{k+1}A + R$$
(C1.27)

For $A = r+1$ (see Eq. (3.22)) and $A = (r + 1)/(1 + g)$ (see Eq. (3.30)), $B = 1$, $R = 0$, and $C_0 = 1$, Eqs. (3.24), (3.32) and (3.26), (3.33) follow immediately from Eqs. (C1.26) and (C1.27).

In the case of disturbances f_k, instead of Eq. (C1.12) we have

$$x_{k+1} = Ax_{k} + Bu_{k} + f_{k}, \quad k = 0, 1, 2, \ldots, N - 1; \quad x(t_0) = x_0$$
(C1.28)

In contrast to the continuous case, here we indicate another approach to solving the optimal problem.

By introducing a new variable $y_k = f_k$, the sequence f_k is presented in the form

$$y_{k+1} = \Phi_k y_k, \quad k = 0, 1, 2, \ldots, N-1; \quad y_0 = f_{k0} \tag{C1.29}$$

where Φ_k is a time-varying term (for simplicity, we considered the constant matrices A and B, but all above equations are valid for time-varying matrices).

Then the optimal problem (C1.18) and (C1.28) reduces to the optimal problem (C1.17) and (C1.18)

$$x_{\Sigma,k+1} = A_\Sigma x_{\Sigma,k} + B_\Sigma u_k, \quad k = 0, 1, 2, \ldots, N-1; \quad x_\Sigma(t_0) = x_{\Sigma,0} \tag{C1.30}$$

$$I = \frac{1}{2}\left(x_{\Sigma,N}^T C_{\Sigma 0} x_{\Sigma,N} + \sum_{k=0}^{N-1} x_{\Sigma,k}^T R_\Sigma x_{\Sigma,k} + c\|u_k\|^2 \right) \tag{C1.31}$$

where $x_{\Sigma,k} = (x_k, y_k)$ is a new state vector, A_Σ, B_Σ, $C_{\Sigma 0}$, and R_Σ are matrices of appropriate dimensions.

For Eq. (3.40) and criterion (3.31), we have $f_{t+1} = \frac{F_{t+1}}{Y_{t+1}}$ (see Eqs. (3.41) and (3.42)) and

$$d_{t+1} = \frac{1+r}{1+g}d_t + \frac{G_{t+1} - T_{t+1}}{Y_{t+1}} + f_{t+1} = \frac{1+r}{1+g}d_t + f_{t+1} + v_t$$

so that

$$x_{\Sigma,t} = \begin{bmatrix} d_t \\ y_t \end{bmatrix}, \quad A_{\Sigma,t} = \begin{bmatrix} \dfrac{1+r}{1+g} & \Phi_t \\ \Phi_t & 0 \end{bmatrix}, \quad B_{\Sigma,t} = \begin{bmatrix} 1 \\ 0 \end{bmatrix}; \quad R_\Sigma = 0,$$

$$C_{\Sigma 0} = \begin{bmatrix} 1 & 0 \\ 0 & 0 \end{bmatrix}$$

Because the above optimal solutions are presented for time-varying matrices of Eqs. (C1.1), (C1.12), (C1.17), and (C1.28), the optimal problems in Chapter 3 and the related equations are valid for time-varying parameters of the considered models.

REFERENCES

Bellman, R., 1957. Dynamic Programming. Princeton University Press, NJ.
Kwakernaak, H., Sivan, R., 1972. Linear Optimal Control Systems, first ed. Wiley-Interscience, Hoboken, NJ.
Yanushevsky, R., 2011. Guidance of Unmanned Aerial Vehicles. Taylor & Francis, New York.

Appendix D

D1. HOW TO CHOOSE PROPER DATA

Interest rates are a common feature in economics, but there is a difference between real rates and nominal rates. The main difference between nominal and real values is that real values are adjusted for factors such as inflation, whereas nominal values (or current prices) are not. As we did not touch this topic in the main part of the book, here we explain it in detail because it is important to make calculations dealing with proper data.

We will rewrite the expression (2.20)

$$D_{t+1} = (1 + i_{t+1})D_t + G_{t+1} - T_{t+1} \tag{D1.1}$$

where i_{t+1} is the nominal interest rate at time $t+1$, the interest paid in $t+1$ over the preexisting debt D_t. (It is largely predetermined as the nominal interest on Treasury bills and bonds determined at the time of issuance. This interest is sometimes indexed to inflation but usually is not affected by changes in interest rates on new issuance of debt during $t+1$.)

The debt to GDP ratio in prices P_{t+1} at time $t+1$ has the form

$$
\begin{aligned}
d_{t+1} &= \frac{D_{t+1}}{P_{t+1}Y_{t+1}} = \frac{(1+i_{t+1})D_t}{P_{t+1}Y_{t+1}} + \frac{G_{t+1}}{P_{t+1}Y_{t+1}} - \frac{T_{t+1}}{P_{t+1}Y_{t+1}} \\
&= (1+i_{t+1})\frac{P_t Y_t}{P_{t+1}Y_{t+1}}\frac{D_t}{P_t Y_t} + \frac{G_{t+1}}{P_{t+1}Y_{t+1}} - \frac{T_{t+1}}{P_{t+1}Y_{t+1}} \\
&= \frac{(1+i_{t+1})}{(1+g_{t+1})(1+\pi_{t+1})}d_t + l_{3,t+1} - \tau_{t+1}
\end{aligned} \tag{D1.2}
$$

where π_{t+1} and g_{t+1} are a growth rate of the price component (inflation) and a real GDP growth rate, respectively, so that the nominal GDP growth rate φ_{t+1} is equal to

$$1 + \varphi_{t+1} = (1 + g_{t+1})(1 + \pi_{t+1}) \tag{D1.3}$$

Similarly, the nominal interest rate can be decomposed into a real component r_{t+1} and inflation

$$(1 + r_{t+1})(1 + \pi_{t+1}) = (1 + i_{t+1}) \tag{D1.4}$$

and based on Eq. (D1.4) the expression (D1.2) becomes

$$d_{t+1} = \frac{1 + r_{t+1}}{1 + g_{t+1}} d_t + l_{3,t+1} - \tau_{t+1} \tag{D1.5}$$

As seen in Eq. (D1.5), to stabilize the debt to GDP ratio ($d_{t+1} = d_t$), the primary balance (government net borrowing or net lending, excluding interest payments on consolidated government liabilities: $l_{3,t+1} - \tau_{t+1}$) should be $b_{t+1} = \frac{g_{t+1} - r_{t+1}}{1 + g_{t+1}} d_t$. Any primary balance lower than b_{t+1} will reduce the debt to GDP ratio. The ease with which a government can reduce the debt to GDP ratio depends on $g_{t+1} - r_{t+1}$. The larger the $g_{t+1} - r_{t+1}$ spread, the more difficult it is to reduce debt. If interest rates and growth rates are approximately the same, then a small primary balance is sufficient to keep the debt stable.

Based on Eq. (D1.3) the relationship between the nominal and real rates can be presented as

$$\frac{r_{t+1}}{1 + g_{t+1}} = \frac{i_{t+1} - \pi_{t+1}}{1 + \varphi_{t+1}} \tag{D1.6}$$

and Eq. (D1.5) can be transformed into

$$d_{t+1} = d_t + \frac{i_{t+1}}{1 + \varphi_{t+1}} d_t - \frac{\pi_{t+1}}{1 + \varphi_{t+1}} d_t - \frac{g_{t+1}}{1 + \varphi_{t+1}} d_t + l_{3,t+1} - \tau_{t+1} \tag{D1.7}$$

The right part of Eq. (D1.7) can be interpreted as the impact on changes in the debt to GDP ratio from interest costs, inflation, real growth, and fiscal adjustment through changes in the primary balance (variations in revenues and noninterest spending). It shows that inflation has an impact on the debt ratio only to the extent that it lowers the real interest rate paid by the government; two exceptions occur when past debt is indexed to inflation (or denominated in foreign currency) and future higher inflation is not anticipated. For the part of the debt that is indexed to inflation, changes in actual inflation translate one to one in changes in the nominal interest rate paid by individual governments.

Eq. (D1.1) (as well as other debt expressions in the book) assumes that total government expenditures $G_{t+1} + i_{t+1}D_t$ are funded by taxes T_{t+1} and new borrowing from the private sector $D_{t+1} - D_t$. The positive difference $G_{t+1} - T_{t+1}$ identifies a *primary deficit* (or a *primary negative surplus*). If total government expenditures are considered, the term *deficit* (or *negative surplus*) is used. The term *primary* usually refers to the current flow of taxes and government spending.

However, there exists one more channel of funding—changes in the stock of money $M_{t+1} - M_t$, so that the generalized form of the debt equation has the form

$$D_{t+1} = (1 + i_{t+1})D_t + G_{t+1} - T_{t+1} - (M_{t+1} - M_t) \qquad (D1.8)$$

showing that the change in nominal government debt is the sum of three factors: the interest paid on debt, the primary deficit, and changes in the money supply, so that instead of Eq. (D1.5) we have

$$d_{t+1} = \frac{1 + r_{t+1}}{1 + g_{t+1}} d_t + l_{3,t+1} - \tau_{t+1} - s_{t+1} \qquad (D1.9)$$

where $s_{t+1} = (M_{t+1} - M_t)/P_{t+1}Y_{t+1}$ denotes seigniorage in real terms.

The term *seigniorage* refers to the revenue a government generates by printing money. Seigniorage may serve as a means of paying part of a government expenses because the new currency can be used to purchase goods and services. Seigniorage adds to the money supply and can cause inflation, so it is sometimes calculated as *inflation tax*.

As mentioned earlier, there exist the *other means of financing*: ways in which a budget deficit is financed or a budget surplus is used. They are not included in the budget totals. In general, the cumulative borrowed amount (debt held by the public, gross national debt) will increase if there is a deficit and decrease if there is a surplus; however, other factors can affect the amount that the government must borrow. Those factors, known as *other means of financing*, include reductions (or increases) in the government cash balances, seigniorage, changes in accrued interest costs included in the budget but not yet paid, and cash flows reflected in credit financing accounts.

To reflect this fact, Eqs. (D1.8) and (D1.9) can be written in a more general form

$$D_{t+1} = (1+ i_{t+1})D_t + G_{t+1} - T_{t+1} + F_{t+1} \tag{D1.10}$$

$$d_{t+1} = \frac{1 + r_{t+1}}{1 + g_{t+1}} d_t + l_{3,t+1} - \tau_{t+1} + f_{t+1} \tag{D1.11}$$

where F_{t+1} and f_{t+1} characterize the other means of financing.

These terms reflect factors that affect the government's need to borrow but are not included in various budget categories.

Glossary

Aggregate production function The aggregate production function describes how total real gross domestic product (*real GDP*) depends on available inputs. This is the function that shows how productivity (*real GDP* per worker) depends on the quantities of *physical capital* per worker and *human capital* per worker as well as the state of technology.

Asset Anything of value owned by an individual, institution, or economic agent.

Bond A debt instrument issued for a period of more than 1 year with the purpose of raising capital by borrowing. It enables an investor to loan money to an entity (typically corporate or governmental), which borrows the funds for a defined period of time at a variable or fixed interest rate.

Budget deficit The difference between tax revenue and government spending when government spending exceeds tax revenue.

Business cycle An economic contraction (recession) followed by an expansion.

Capital gain A positive difference between the sale price of an asset and its purchase price.

Central bank An institution that oversees and regulates the banking system and controls the *monetary base*.

Constant returns to scale (CRS) A long-run production concept where a doubling of all factor inputs exactly doubles the amount of output.

Consumer An economic agent that desires to purchase goods and services with the goal of maximizing the satisfaction (utility) from consumption of those goods and services.

Consumer spending *Household* spending on goods and services from domestic and foreign firms.

Consumption function An equation showing how an individual *household's consumer spending* varies with the household's current *disposable income*.

Crowding-out The negative effect of *budget deficits* on private investment, which occurs because government borrowing drives up *interest rates*.

Debt to GDP ratio A *ratio* that expresses the *national debt* of a country as a percentage of GDP.

Deflation A decline in the aggregate price level over some defined time period.

Demand A relationship between market price and quantities of goods and services purchased in a given period of time.

Diminishing marginal productivity (DMP) A short-run production concept where increases in the variable factor of production lead to less and less additional output.

Disposable income Personal income less taxes paid.

Economic expansion Growth in real GDP for one fiscal quarter or more.

Economics The study of how a given society allocates scarce resources to meet (or satisfy) the unlimited wants and needs of its members.

Employment A measure of those individuals in the labor force working, at least 1 h per week, for pay.

Equilibrium A situation where there is no tendency for change.

Exchange rate The value of a domestic currency expressed in terms of a foreign currency or basket of foreign currencies.

Exports Goods and services sold to other countries.

Final goods and services Goods and services that are purchased for direct consumption.

Fiscal policy The use of government spending and taxation to influence the economy.

Free trade Trade that is unregulated by government *tariffs* or other artificial barriers; the levels of *exports* and *imports* occur naturally, as a result of supply and demand.

GDP: gross domestic product The market value of all final goods and services produced in a given time period.

Household A person or a group of people who share income.

Imports Foreign goods and services that residents of a country (businesses and the government) buy.

Income taxes Taxes that are based on and vary with personal or corporate income.

Inflation An increase in the price level over some defined time period.

Inflation rate The annual percent change in a price index—typically the *consumer price index*. The inflation rate is positive when the *aggregate price level* is rising (*inflation*) and negative when the aggregate price level is falling (*deflation*).

Infrastructure The basic physical and organizational structures and facilities (e.g., buildings, roads, power supplies) needed for the operation of a society or enterprise.

Interest rate The annualized cost of credit or debt capital computed as the percentage ratio of interest to the principal.

Investment The action or process of investing money for profit or material result.

Investment spending Spending on capital goods or goods used in the production of capital, goods, or services. May include purchases such as machinery, land, production inputs, or infrastructure.

Keynesian A school of thought emerging out of the works of John Keynes.

Labor force The sum of *employment* and *unemployment*, that is, the number of people who are currently working plus the number of people who are currently looking for work.

Labor force participation rate The ratio of those in the labor force (the employed and unemployed) and those that are available for work.

Liquidity A measure of the ease by which a financial asset can be converted into a form readily accepted as payment for goods and services.

Macroeconomic shock An event that produces a significant change within an economy, despite occurring outside of it. Macroeconomic shocks are unpredictable and typically impact supply or demand throughout the markets.

Macroeconomics The branch of *economics* that studies the behavior of the aggregate *economy*.

Marginal propensity to consume The fraction of each additional dollar of income devoted to consumption expenditure.

Marginal propensity to spend The fraction of each additional dollar of income devoted to any type of spending (i.e., consumption, investment, government, or net exports).

Market A place or institution where buyers and sellers come together and exchange factor inputs or final goods and services. A market is one of several types of economic rationing systems.

Monetarism A school of economic thought that the chief determinant of economic growth is the supply of money. In contrast to Keynesian economics, monetarism maintains that changes in money supply greatly influence aggregate demand. Monetary base. Also known as *high-powered money*. Reserves + currency in the monetary system—the main liabilities of the central bank.

Monetary policy Changes in the quantity of money in circulation designed to alter *interest rates* and affect the level of overall spending.

Money Any asset that can easily be used to purchase goods and services.

National income The sum of all types of income (wages, net interest, profits, and net rental income) earned in a given time period by any type of economic agent (individuals or corporation).

Net exports The difference between the value of *exports* and the value of *imports*. A positive value for net exports indicates that a country is a net exporter of goods and services; a negative value indicates that a country is a net importer of goods and services.

Net investment Investment exclusive of replacement of depreciated capital.

Nominal GDP GDP measured at current prices.

Nominal interest rate The interest rate published as part of a debt contract.

North American Free Trade Agreement (NAFTA) A *trade* agreement among the United States, Canada, and Mexico.

Personal income The income earned by individual households in a given time period.

Physical capital Manufactured resources, such as buildings and machines.

Price index A measure of the cost of purchasing a given *market basket* in a given year, where that cost is normalized so that is equal to 100 in the selected base year; a measure of overall price level.

Producer An economic agent that converts inputs (factors of production) into output (goods and services) with the goal of maximizing profits from production and sale of those goods and services.

Productivity Output per worker; a shortened form of the term *labor productivity*.

Profit The difference between sales revenue and the costs of production.

Public debt Government debt held by individuals and institutions outside the government.

Real GDP GDP measured at constant (some base period) prices.

Real interest rate An interest rate that has been adjusted for changes in the price level or changes in purchasing power over some time period; the *nominal interest rate* minus the *inflation rate*.

Recession Negative growth in real GDP for two or more fiscal quarters.

Risk A measure of uncertainty about the value of an asset or the benefits of some economic activity.

Savings The difference between income and expenditure in the current time period.

Self-regulating economy An *economy* in which problems such as *unemployment* are resolved without government intervention and in which government attempts to improve the economy's performance would be ineffective at best and would probably make things worse.

Spending multiplier The ratio of total change in *real GDP* caused by an *autonomous change in aggregate spending* to the size of that autonomous change.

Stabilization policy The use of government policy to reduce the severity of *recessions* and to rein in excessively strong *expansions*. There are two main tools of stabilization policy: *monetary policy* and *fiscal policy*.

Stagflation Stagnation accompanied by inflation; an inflationary period accompanied by rising unemployment and lack of growth in consumer demand and business activity.

Stagnation A prolonged period of little or no growth in the economy.

Standard of living The ratio of the output of an economy and population. Also known as per-capita output.

Supply A relationship between market price and quantities of goods and services made available for sale in a given period of time.

Surplus A market condition where the quantity supplied exceeds the quantity demanded.

Technology The technical means for the production of goods and services.

Trade deficit An economic measure of a negative balance of trade in which a country's imports exceed its exports. A trade deficit represents an outflow of domestic currency to foreign markets.

Unemployment The difference between the number of people in the labor force and those working for pay.

Unemployment rate The percentage of the total number of people in the *labor force* who are unemployed, calculated as *unemployment/(unemployment + employment)*.

Utility A measure of the satisfaction received from some type of economic activity (i.e., consumption of goods and services or the sale of factor services).

Velocity The number of times a given quantity (stock) of money changes hands in a given time period (the ratio of expenditure in that time period to a given measure of the money supply).

Velocity of money The ratio of *nominal GDP* to the *money supply*.

INDEX

Printed in the United States
By Bookmasters